Pirates

The Hunt for
Shamus's Booty

Tarrin P. Lupo

&

Ruby N. Hilliard

Porcupine Publications

DEDICATION FROM TARRIN P. LUPO

I dedicate this book to my best friend, Linus. I miss you every day and I hope, in the next life, I am lucky enough to come back as your dog.

DEDICATION FROM RUBY N. HILLIARD

I dedicate this book to my favorite cousin and one of my best friends, Mark Morris and my Grandma Ruby. Both avid readers and great people, I know you two would have been my biggest fans. Our love transcends all space and time and you live forever in my heart.

ACKNOWLEDGMENTS

Editors:
Chief Editor: Sandie Britt
Secondary, Layout and Creative Editor: Ruby N. Hilliard

Illustrators and Cover Art:
Scott A. Motley
Ruby Nicole Hilliard

Consultants:
Reagen Dandridge Desilets
Davi Barker

PREFACE

After the success I had with *Pirates of Savannah: The Birth of Freedom in the Lowcountry,* I really wanted to make a novel that was appropriate for all ages to read. This book is a modern day spin-off of that novel and packed full of real historical information. Although it is a stand-alone novel, readers who have already read *Pirates of Savannah: The Birth of Freedom in the Lowcountry*, will recognize some familiar names and places.

Some of the language in the book is southern slang, so it will not be spelled correctly. You will even see Gullah dialect in the book, so please do not write me and tell me I constantly misspelled Hurricane. Hurricane in Gullah is Harricane.

On a side note, *Pirates of Savannah: The Birth of Freedom in the Lowcountry* has been rewritten for a young-adult audience. Please be sure to put that on your reading list.

I hope this novel is as fun for you to read as it was for me to write.

Good Hunting,

Tarrin P. Lupo

CONTENTS

BLACK CATS
&
THREE CIRCLES

"**...**

One ninety-eight, one ninety-nine, two hundred!" Odessa counted off and commanded the other three teenagers to examine the old bricks. The group of students slowly inspected the sides of the tunnel wall.

"We need more light; do yuh have another flashlight in dat poke of yours?" Krystal twanged in her thick, Effingham County accent.

Leo's crooked smile could barely be seen in the reflections off the damp, slimy walls. "Of course! My Zombie Bug-Out Bag has everything!" The tall boy searched through the old canvas messenger bag until a cheap plastic flashlight appeared in his hand. "You can use this one," he said as he handed the LED light to the small girl with the braids.

"Thanks, Leo. I am not real fond of the dark and being underground and such."

Mohamed spoke up using his thick Ugandan accent. "What are we looking for, Wiki?"

Odessa responded, "Well, the map just shows three circles and a black cat at this point in the tunnel then another passage leading to a huge room. I don't see another passageway; I guess it was walled off years ago. I assume we are trying to find something on the walls that will give us a hint to where the old hallway was."

"Well, we ain't gonna see nothin' with all this slime on the walls!" The tomboy dug her small hands into the green ooze and threw a handful of it on the floor. Odessa winced at the sound of the green sludge as it made a splattering sound on the floor. The musty smell of the exposed goo was overpowering as Odessa, nicknamed Wiki, spoke up. "Owweee, that is so nasty! How can you touch it with your hands like that?"

"This is nothin'; yuh should come clean the pig pens with me if yuh want to smell somethin' real nasty," the country girl grinned. Her tiny hands continued to scrape the scum from the passageway walls.

A faint clanging could be heard farther down the passage from the direction they had just come. Mohamed interrupted their clumsy search. "I am telling you, Leo, there is that noise again; we are not alone down here."

The punk-rock-looking teen shined his light down the long passage and scanned the area. Leo finally concluded, "Dude, we are under all of Savannah; I am sure you can hear all kinds of noises from the surface. Don't worry about it. Just keep looking for clues."

Krystal shouted out, "Y'all come see this! I think I found somethin'!" The tiny, slime-covered girl dug frantically at a stone trying to clear off all of the ancient gunk. "Look! I think this is a carvin' of a cat on this brick here."

The group of four fell over each other trying to get a closer look. Odessa reasoned, "This has got to be it. Alright everyone, try to find the three circles." The party of four illuminated the wall and concentrated their light.

"Look at that block over there; it looks like something round is etched into it," said Mohamed. Fearing the filth, he pleaded, "Since you're already dirty, would you mind cleaning that section off, Krystal?"

She shot the pack a look of disgust. "Y'all a bunch of princesses, yuh know that?" The small girl swept the slime away until they were staring at three circles in a triangle formation. In the center of the triangles was a small hole bubbling with frothy slime.

Wiki made an observation saying, "Do you guys see how that spot in the middle is gurgling? That means air is blowing through it. There is air on the other side of this wall; it must be a secret door or something."

Clang! A noise from down the passage reverberated again. Leo looked at Mohamed and stated, "Okay, now I heard it, too. Maybe something is down here with us. Let's just open this door and keep moving faster." He turned his flashlight on Odessa. "So, Wiki, what does your gigantic Wikipedia of a brain know about old locks?"

"Well, they were not too complicated back then, but the keyhole was usually hidden. I think it might be as simple as jabbing a stick deep into this hole until it hits a plate, unlocking everything," the Greek girl explained.

Mohamed inquired, "Well, where do we find a stick fifty feet underground?"

Leo dug through his precious antique satchel. "Will this work, Wiki?" He held up a wire coat hanger.

"Yes, that should be small enough to fit into that little hole. Just unwind it into one long wire. I really want to ask you why on earth you have a coat hanger in your apocalypse bag, but I am going to let you work instead."

Splash! Splash! Splash! Echoed from down the hall. Mohamed frantically pointed his torch down the long tunnel. "That sounded like footsteps, Leo, but I still don't see anyone."

The punk kid became very serious and dropped his voice down. "Did you hear any moaning? Anything like "Brainsssss, Brainsssss, Brainsssss?""

The Ugandan teen thought about it for a minute and said, "Nope, all I heard was footsteps in the water."

"Whew, we are good then." He wiped his brow saying, "At least it is not zombies. You probably just heard a ghost."

Leo's attempt at humor did nothing to calm Mohamed's fears.

"Here, Wiki, try this," Leo said as he handed her a long, stiff wire.

The younger girl slowly fed the straightened coat hanger down into the bubbling gap. The group held their breath while Odessa/Wiki fed the wire two feet into the hidden keyhole. *Thump! Click!* "I think I got it. Okay, everyone push on the circle markings." The four students combined their strength and pushed as a scraping noise resonated from the wall. With a screech of protest, the secret door soon became visible and arose out of the slime.

A blast of musty-smelling wind blew in from the gap, causing the teens to choke on the smell. Odessa started coughing. "Oh man, that is horrible! My cat got sick once and puked in my shoes and it didn't even smell that foul."

Leo cut her off, "I don't think we can get this old door to move any further; there should be enough room for all of us to slip in if we suck in our guts."

The Greek girl shot daggers out of her eyes at Leo. Odessa, of course, took his comment the wrong way and thought he was making a joke about her weight. "Don't worry, we can all fit," she bit back.

The four squeezed past the clandestine opening and gathered on the other side to regroup. A flashing could be seen as Krystal's cheap flashlight flickered off. "I think it died already, Leo. Well, thanks for a little light anyway." The tall boy took the dead flashlight from her and dropped it back into is bag of holding. The remaining glow illuminated the new crude passageway.

Odessa was the only one of the four that had the good sense to ask, "Does this look safe? This tunnel is just cut right out of the dirt and those wooden planks holding it open look rotten. Heck, it looks like most of the supports have fallen down." Her light revealed a very rough opening dug into the earth. Stones, roots, and water rolled down the sides of the walls.

Leo shook it off without a thought. "Yep, I am sure it is safe. My grandfather said they really knew how to build stuff back then. Come on; treasure awaits."

"Um, this would be like two hundred years older than your granddaddy's time. I don't think he was talking about the 1700s," the Greek girl warned.

"You think too much girl, come on!" Leo grabbed her hand and led her into the dark, muddy passage.

The party pushed forward and Mohamed immediately slipped and fell into a giant puddle. His light flicked off as it became submerged in the mucky, tepid water. He stood up and knocked the gunky mud off his face. He checked his head to make sure he had not lost his Muslim hat in the fall. "Sorry you guys; I think I killed another torch. You know, this country makes the cheapest stuff."

Leo helped knock the mud off of his foreign friend. "Well, technically, China made all this cheap stuff; this country just buys it. Come on buddy, we still got two lights."

Krystal rarely feared anything, but this whole experience was really starting to get to her nerves. Her hands started shaking and Odessa noticed.

The Greek-looking Wiki spoke up to help ease her friend's fear. "Okay, until we figure a way out of here, we should keep talking. I don't care about what, but I don't like this pitch black darkness."

Krystal's anxiety was already taking hold. "Yes, yes, yes, I agree with Wiki. Let's all jabber about somethin'! Anythin'!"

"Okay, I will pick a topic and you guys have to each talk about it until we come up with an idea," Odessa offered.

The other three in the group halfheartedly mumbled, "Okay, whatever, sure."

The round girl with the curly black hair continued, "Okay, I am picking a topic and each of you HAVE to talk about it. The first topic is; what was your last day of school like before this summer? Leo you go first!"

Silence overcame the group as they waited for the punk rock kid's tale to distract them from their situation. Even though he could not see his friend's faces, he still felt the other three's eyes on him, all waiting for an answer. Leo Stedman bent to the peer pressure and finally groaned, "Fine, I will tell you my story about what happened on my last day, but it was completely unfair. I really hated that school."

LEO'S LAST DAY OF MIDDLE SCHOOL

"*BEEP! BEEP! BEEP!*" an annoying noise echoed loudly in the hallway. The crowds in the passageway turned their heads toward the flashing red lights and high-pitched squealing.

"Stop!" a balding, overweight security guard commanded the young man. "Step back through the metal detector and then come on back through."

The tall boy shot an irritated look at the man in the tight, sloppy uniform and let out an annoyed sigh. He slowly walked back through to the front of the gate as the entire hallway watched to see if he was going to make trouble again. The fourteen-year-old strutted back through the open gate. *"BEEP! BEEP! BEEP!"*

The greasy goliath guard smiled. "Step over here and empty your pockets onto the table."

The exasperated boy groaned out loud, "Not again; come on y'all! I can't be late to class again."

This response delighted the officer and he started his search in slow motion. "I'm gonna need some help to do a proper search." The sentry grabbed the walkie-talkie off his belt and pressed the large button on the side. "Ms. Gambit, I am going to need some back up at door five."

A hiss and crackle came over the handset and a cold, emotionless, low-pitched voice mumbled out, "I will be there in one minute; don't start the fun without me." The obese guard stood silently and stared at the boy. Leo could hear the man's loud mouth breathing over the busy hallway. The eighth grader watched sweat roll down the forehead of the large, bald man.

The perspiration dripped onto his nametag that read "Officer Bines."

Other students were now quickly passing through the security checkpoint, as the time for first period to start was rapidly approaching. The metal detector would go off every so often as a student passed under the plastic doorway. Mr. Bines would simply ignore them or wave them on through.

"Dude, that is not fair! Why are you stopping me and letting everyone else just pass on by? That is so not cool. You're being so lame! It would make your momma cry if she knew you acted like this to me," the boy sarcastically bit.

This struck a nerve with the guard. "My mother is an angel and you best not talk about her again if you ever want to get to class. Now take off your leather jacket and your belt and put them on the table to be searched."

Mr.Bines and Ms. Gambit search Leo Stedman at school.

The tall boy with the jet-black hair took off his jacket revealing a black tee shirt that read "Zombie Apocalypse Response Team" and a picture of a cricket bat. A gray, silk ribbon was pinned to his faded shirt and a thick, black, fancy pen was clipped to his collar. Although Savannah, Georgia, was entirely too hot to wear a leather jacket in May, the young skater accepted the discomfort for fashion. A tall, skinny, pale woman arrived and Mr. Bines handed her Leo's jacket.

She leered at the boy as she slowly and meticulously searched every zipper and all the lining of the worn-out motorcycle jacket. She grabbed the pen off Leo's collar, held it up to her face to study it, and then set it on the table with the rest of the contents from his jacket. The round man snatched the backpack off the punk rock kid's back and started using his greasy, grimy fingers to search it. Leo cringed a little when he saw the guard use his dirt-filled claws to open his lunch box. "Well, look here, Ms. Gambit. We have an illegal lunch." The sweaty man held up his vintage lunch box with a faded '80s punk band logo of Black Flag.

A crooked and unnerving smile forced its way onto her leathery, wrinkled, and sun damaged face. "It is a good thing we found this when we did. Now, young man, you know outside food isn't allowed in this school anymore. This change has been in effect all year long and I know that you know this. You could get in very big trouble if we reported this infraction."

The young man knew the extortion was coming and sighed again. "What do you want to take from me this time?"

The woman put her long, thin, tobacco-stained fingers to her lips and pretended to think hard. "Well, I guess if we confiscated your lunch box we could just let you off with a warning."

Knowing he was beat and had no time to argue, Leo agreed to the deal with the crooked officers. He sadly surrendered his favorite, rare, steel lunch pail.

The boy wanted to get away from this situation fast so he could still make it to class on time, and knew he really had to hustle. He stuffed his belt and everything else back into his pockets and grabbed his beat-up leather jacket. Leo started to jog away when the scary woman's voice commanded him to stop.

"You think just because we don't enforce school uniforms on the last day of school that you can wear whatever you like? Young man, you must turn your jacket inside out. Names of old punk rock bands and a large, yellow anarchy symbol are completely inappropriate at public school."

The young man gave her a very irritated look and quickly reversed his jacket. He then burst into a full sprint down the empty hall.

Ms. Gambit opened the vintage lunch box and dumped the food out on the table. "It's all yours! Eat up, Mr. Bines." The fat man dove into the food with delight as she held up the old lunch box and examined it closer. "How about that! And on the last day of school, too. The boss man should be happy we confiscated one more item to help fund the search. I bet this classic lunch box will fetch a great price from some little punk on eBay. We didn't do too bad for the year selling all of this confiscated stuff. Couple thousand, you think?" Ms. Gambit pondered aloud.

Leo ran down the hall as fast as he could, his loose backpack swinging side to side, slapping his flanks. A buzzer rang as he swung open the classroom door.

"You're late again, Mr. Stedman."

"No, I am not. I was in the classroom when the buzzer stopped."

"You know the rules; you must be in your seat when the buzzer sounds or it counts as a tardy. This was your last strike; I can't believe you are tardy on the very last day of school. This puts you over the limit and automatically fails you for this class," she explained in a nagging nanny tone.

"Really? I ace all your tests and I have some of the highest grades in class. How can you fail me for not being in my chair when the buzzer beeped?" he challenged.

She coldly continued, "School is not all about grades, young man; it is also about doing what you're told. Compliance with the system is just as important as knowledge of a subject. I am sorry, but I have to follow the rules. Looks like I will be seeing you again this summer"

KRYSTAL'S LAST DAY OF MIDDLE SCHOOL

The tomboy lost her footing on the loose rocks and slippery mud. Leo tugged her back up and gave the tiny girl's hand a squeeze. "Okay, you heard my last day. Now I want to hear yours."

"Well, my last day was not so great either. In fact, it was an awful day." Krystal scraped the slime off her boots and recounted her last day of school.

The lunch lady stared at Krystal while she asked for an extra serving of the meat-like substance. She scratched her hair net and wondered how such a small girl always ate so much.

"Thank yuh, Ma'am. Can I have double cobbler, too? I have been savin' up all week for seconds. I can't wait."

The lunch lady was always impressed with the young girl's country manners; it was a high point in her day. All day long she dealt with angry and moody kids who were rude to her. The well-mannered and grateful little girl was a welcomed relief.

She leaned over and dropped a cookie on the plate. "That is because you're always such a polite little lady; it is my treat!"

Krystal's face lit up. "Wow, thanks so much! Have a great summer, Ma'am."

She made her way to the cashier and dug handfuls of dimes, nickels, and pennies out of her dirty overalls. The freckled young lady made stacks of coins as she counted out the exact amount. "Here yuh go. I should have just enough to cover seconds."

The cashier checked her tray over and noticed the extra cookie. "I see you forgot to pay for that cookie and you are also three cents short for the rest of the meal." The lunch lady with the hair net walked over to the cashier and whispered into her ear. The cafeteria ladies nodded in agreement and then the cashier spoke up saying, "Um, Krystal, don't worry about the cookie or the three cents. Have a wonderful summer, baby."

With her sun-kissed faced, Krystal flashed the ladies a smile through her stray strands of hair. The farm girl with strawberry-blonde braids picked up her heavy lunch tray. As usual, she surveyed the lunchroom for an open seat, but only felt uninviting eyes looking back at her.

The tomboy heard the words "this seat is taken" at every empty chair she approached. The country girl finally headed to an empty table at the very corner of the large cafeteria. She kept her head down and did not try to make eye contact with anyone while she shoveled the large amount of food in her mouth. She watched as all the other empty tables in the lunchroom completely filled up while chowing down on her large helping of mystery government meat. A group of fashion-conscious girls approached Krystal's open table. "Um, redneck! We need this table; you need to go find a seat somewhere else," one of the better-dressed girls commanded rudely.

Krystal pretended not to hear her and kept eating. The same girl who was wearing fashionably extra-large, hoop earrings spoke up, "Cowgirl, ride your goat out of here. We need this table, now."

The small girl in the manure-stained overalls and ratty tee shirt kept eating and ignored the annoying cackle of commands.

Gloria, the girl with the hoops, grew angry and snatched the cookie from Krystal's tray. She threw the tasty dessert like she was skipping a rock across a pond. The group of fashion harpies laughed is it bounced across the filthy floor and broke into tiny pieces. "Now go fetch your cookie! Surely you understand fetch since you look and smell like a dog," Gloria taunted.

The tomboy shook with anger at the site of her gift smashed all over the dirty floor.

"You need to go now, or we are going put the rest of your tray on the floor, too," the teen with huge earrings threatened.

Consumed with anger and humiliation, the freckle-faced girl finally stood up and grabbed her lunch tray. She picked up her meal and angrily stormed away.

Gloria continued to threaten, "Smart move redneck! You just saved yourself an embarrassing beat down. Is it true you failed sixth grade and had to be held back because you were so retarded? Aren't you like, fourteen already? Sorry, we can't tell because you look like you're ten!"

The country girl was used to being made fun of because of her small stature, but teasing her about repeating the sixth grade lit a fire in her. To the group's amazement, her pig-tail-braided head whipped back around. Krystal's body followed her head and she charged straight for the group of socialites. Krystal tossed her tray on the table and stomped over to the bully.

"You need to get out of my face, redneck! You are making me sick because you smell like a horse!" Gloria threatened.

Krystal stood tall without fear and spoke in a low-pitched tone. "You girls have been givin' me grief all year. Yur mean when we see each other in skoo and y'all are rude to me at the stables because I can outride any of yuhs spoiled princesses. Then yuh start it with me now on the last day for no good reason. It seems I can never escape yuh mean and nasty, plastic girls. Y'all are only tough because yuh are never alone. Yuh always stay in a herd so yuh can safely act like jerks. Yuh know darn well, Gloria, if yuh were alone yuh would never have the guts to speak to me like this."

Gloria yelled, "Shut up trailer trash! I am not scared of you and I don't need a group to beat you down."

The small country girl laughed out loud as the eyes of the cafeteria were drawn to the commotion. "Gloria, I been ridin' horses since I could walk. I been bucked off into 'lectric fences and rocky ditches. Yuh think for a minute I am scared to get girly punched by yuh? Barbie doll, yuh better done git now before yuh get really hurt! See, I'm used to fightin' boys," her tone turned cocky but fearful, "and when I fight boys, I win! Barbie, yuh'd receive less pain cuddling with a bobcat than messin' with me."

Krystal Confronts Gloria in the cafeteria.

A wave of fear rushed over Gloria as Krystal's words of warning set in. Unfortunately, now that all of her followers were watching, it was too late. The bully could not back down without doing severe damage to her social standing. She shoved the tomboy, angrily shouting, "Shut up, I am not afraid of you."

Krystal's insides ignited with rage; she could no longer take the public humiliation. She drew back her fist to prepare a strike, only to feel someone grab it. The irate girl spun around and saw it was the lunch lady with the hair net holding her striking hand back.

The cafeteria worker said in a calming voice to the mad, tiny girl, "Don't do it. These girls are not worth getting thrown out of school. It's your last day; let it go." The lunch lady turned to the fashionably decked group of girls and ordered, "You girls best be on your way before I call security."

Gloria put on a show for all those in the lunchroom now watching. "You're so lucky she saved you from me! This is not over; we will see you this summer at the stables! We will finish this when the lunch lady can't save you!" Her group of mindless devotees dragged Gloria away, but she managed to shout one last insult at the cafeteria worker saying, "Oh and nice hair net, lady!" The gang of adolescent minions busted out laughing at the joke as they turned out the door and left. As Gloria departed, she knew deep down inside how lucky she was that the lunch lady had saved her from the fury that Krystal was about to deliver to her.

The lunch lady put a caring hand on the small, enraged girl. "Look here, darling. Why do you make it so easy for them? You get one day a year to dress however you want and this is what you choose to wear?" She then pointed at the other teens in the lunchroom. "The rest of these girls in school are wearing their best outfits and accessories. Now, look at you. You have on dirty overalls, a ripped-up, stained tee shirt and you kind of stink, honey. "

"I'm sorry, ma'am, but Gloria makes me blow up like a jackass in a tin barn." Krystal exhaled a frustrated breath and calmed down. "Well, I guess I am use to the smell. Once yuh shovel so much manure yuh can never really wash the stink out of your clothes completely. And honestly, I don't own any good clothes; this is it. The minute I am free from this awful place today I am goin' over to volunteer again at that charity

Horsin' Around. I figures I would save some time and come dressed to be ready to work in the stalls."

The kind woman gave the stinky little fourteen-year-old a hug and said, "Come on, let me get you another cookie!"

4 CHAPTER

ODESSA'S LAST DAY OF MIDDLE SCHOOL

Krystal swung her free hand out in the dark until it got stuck in a nest of curly hair. The tomboy smiled as she heard Odessa jump up and swat at her hair. "Relax, Wiki. It's just me. I think it is time yuh told your story, darlin'."

Odessa regained her composure. Although the others could not see, she still felt the need to straighten up. "Fair is fair. I will share my first day, too, but it doesn't sound as rough as yours were." She cleared her throat like she was about to make an important presentation for a class and recounted.

"Hey, Wiki, did you get our final project done last night?" Stacy inquired.

"Well, I emailed you, texted you, and even called you all week to get together to work on it. You never responded to any of it," the dark haired girl said as she called her class partner out on her lack of work.

"Umm, yeah, my phone and computer have not been working right. Anyway, did you get OUR project done in time? I really hope you did because if I don't get a good grade on this, my mom is canceling my birthday party," Stacy pleaded.

"I remember. You have only talked about this party for the entire last month in lab. It sounds like it is going to be so awesome. I will tell the teacher to share credit for the report with you if you tell me why everyone keeps calling me Wiki. I don't get it," Odessa said, completely confused.

Stacy explained, "Really girl? You don't know? It is because you are like Wikipedia; you seem to know the answer to everything! You're a walking encyclopedia. Everyone knows to come to you when they need help with class work and tests."

Odessa was not sure how to take that comment. Was that a compliment, or were people only being nice to use her when they needed a good grade? She chose to believe it was a compliment and smiled. "Oh that's cool. Okay, you can call me Wiki! I did get the report all finished last night, but ten minutes is way too short. To do this presentation right I need at least thirty minutes; there is a ton of information on pirates of the Lowcountry. I have no idea how to cut all this knowledge to just ten minutes. I just can't be accurate in that little amount of time."

Stacy grew impatient. "You will figure it out when you're up there. Don't forget to mention that we BOTH worked on it equally or she won't give me a good grade."

Wiki assured her, "Yes, I know, don't worry; you are going to have that fantastic birthday party. I won't let you down."

Their teacher interrupted and announced it was time for the last few final projects of the year. One by one her classmates presented rushed, poorly planned, and sloppy presentations. The other students couldn't have cared less and were too excited that this was their last day of class. They did not even try to pretend to listen to the string of halfhearted speeches.

The olive-skinned girl nervously played with her dark hair by twisting it in her fingers as she waited. She had smeared orange-colored, cover-up acne cream on her face hoping to hide her new zits that arrived this morning. Of course, her white collar now had an orange stain from the cream, but Odessa Skouras did not notice. She was too focused on having to stand in front of the class wearing a tight dress that she had out grown with her last weight gain. Most of her classmates had started their growth spurts, but she was still waiting for hers to hit. Odessa had completely skipped the sixth grade and now was the youngest in her class being barely twelve years old.

The Greek girl had the unfortunate combination of being short and overweight. If she were only a foot taller, her paunchy build would not be so obvious. Her vertically-challenged stature amplified her obesity and made her dress skin tight and uncomfortable. The self-conscious young woman could not stop tapping her foot as her turn hurriedly approached.

The teacher invited Wiki to the front of the class to make her presentation. As she quickly stood up, her belly knocked her notebook and papers off the desk. Giggles and snide remarks could be heard quietly echoing through the class.

Wiki's face immediately turned a shade of lobster red. She especially felt awkwardly fat when she kneeled down to collect her papers. The curly-haired girl with the unicorn necklace, made her way to the front of the room while the crowd continued to snicker. Odessa took a deep breath and calmed down as she tried to focus on keeping her hands from shaking.

She cleared her throat and spoke up in a pompous tone. "My report is about the Pirates of the Lowcountry. Almost everyone knows something about pirates, but very few people understand the history behind them. Interestingly enough, pirates were actually created by the same governments that would later hunt them all down. England, Spain, and France all hated each other and would constantly attack each other's navies."

She wiped the nervous sweat from her forehead and continued. "It got so bad that those three countries were running out of military ships. So, the three nations each hired private ships to steal and plunder the enemy country's vessels. The governments gave the mercenaries their blessing and made them legal pirates called privateers. They were just as mean and rotten as regular pirates; the only difference is they were not allowed to attack their own country's ships. For example, an English privateer could murder and steal from any French or Spanish vessel, but was not allowed to attack another English ship."

Odessa Skouras relaxed a little as her confidence in her intelligence shined through. "The privateers loved the lifestyle and made tremendous amounts of gold and silver. So, when England, Spain, and France made an agreement to stop attacking each other, the rich privateers were suddenly out of work. There was one big problem the governments did not count on – none of the privateers wanted to give up their money and free lifestyles, so they started attacking every ship they saw, no matter what country they sailed under. The three governments declared them pirates, since they were no longer working for them. That is how privateers became pirates."

The unruly class grew quiet as talk of murder and pirates caught their attention. "The Golden Age of Pirates was between 1650 and 1720, but it really got going during 1716 to 1726 when a large amount of privateers were left without jobs. Almost all pirates led very short, violent lives. They were lucky if they survived more than just two years. The most famous southern Lowcountry pirates like Blackbeard, Gentleman Stead Bonnet, and Calico Jack Rackum had very short pirating careers before they were hunted down."

She smiled at the next part of the presentation. "The most famous pirates of their time were actually women. One of them was named Anne Bonny. The famous woman pirate plundered ships with another woman named Mary Read. Mary Read dressed and pretended to be a man for most of her career until she joined forces with Anne Bonny and Calico Jack Rackum. Eventually, all of them were caught and brought to the Caribbean to hang for their crimes. Mary Read died in prison, but it was rumored that Anne Bonny escaped back to Charleston with Mary's newborn baby, Nina. Rumors still exist to this day that Anne was never hung, but lived out a simple life as a mother in Charleston, South Carolina.

Wiki grew more confident as she started to notice that the class was really paying attention. "Of course, since we are in Savannah, we need to talk about some of our famous pirates.

Captain Flint was a famous pirate from the book *Treasure Island*. He supposedly died upstairs in Savannah's Pirates' House restaurant in 1754. His last words were 'Darby M'Graw – fetch aft the rum', as he succumbed to alcohol poisoning."

Savannah also boasts of Mary Read's half-sister, Admiral April Read. Admiral Read was very unusual because she had a very long pirating and smuggling career. She was famous for building her own fleet of free pirate ships. She led that famous pirate fleet of free men and women all over the seas of the world, but always came home to Savannah. The Admiral was an excellent swords-woman, but her weapon of choice was a very rare and terrifying weapon called a Swedish boarding axe-pistol. The heavy gun was half-axe, half-pistol with an eighty-caliber musket. Just the site of the fierce flintlock struck fear in her opponents and most surrendered without any bloodshed."

The students were now all on the edge of their seats, listening intently. Wiki continued, "Two of the captains under Admiral April Read were the most notorious scourges of Savannah. The two famous pirates were named Sam Scurvy and Shamus Red. Together they became some of the richest pirates of all time. By the end of their careers, Sam Scurvy and Shamus Red were so filthy rich that they had elaborate collections of ornate pirate gear. Sam Scurvy's most famous weapon was a sword made out of silver with a fancy hilt that was loaded with rare jewels."

Her eyes lit up with greed as she spoke. "Savannah's other wealthy pirate, Shamus Red, was missing many body parts by the end of his life. He had a whole set of lavish prosthetics made for him. His swag included an eye patch encrusted with diamonds, a hook, and a peg leg, both made out of pure gold."

"Nobody knows what happened to Sam Scurvy's or Shamus Red's treasure. Most folks think their fabulous pirate accessories are just a legend. But," she paused for effect, "accounts of Sam Scurvy's silver sword surfaced one hundred years after his death in the Civil War."

Odessa presents her research on pirates to her classmates.

Her teacher interrupted and corrected her. "You mean War for Southern Independence."

Wiki jumped right back on track. "Um, yes, I keep forgetting people call it that. Anyway, we can assume at least part of Sam Scurvy's treasure was found, but the silver blade was never seen again after the war. Shamus's gold hook, diamond-covered eye patch, and golden peg leg have never been seen since he passed on. Many fortune hunters have tried to find the fabulous prizes with no luck, but it is still rumored that all of the booty is hidden somewhere in Savannah."

A loud buzzer rang and the class shot up from their seats. The teacher yelled at the fleeing class, "Looks like we ran short on time! Have a great summer everyone and don't forget about us next year when you're big important high school students!" She turned back to Odessa and smiled, "Well done as usual, honey."

Wiki yelled back to the teacher over the noise, "Don't forget that Stacy did half the research, too."

The teacher nodded her head, relaying that she understood, and waved them on. Stacy grinned upon overhearing that she had just received credit for a report she did absolutely no work on. She did not even say thank you or goodbye to Odessa, but, rather, just ran for the door to meet her real friends. Wiki shouted, "Have a good summer, Stacy! See you in a week!" but the self-involved girl acted like she did not hear her former lab partner. The Greek girl watched from afar as Stacy joined up with her more popular friends who were waiting for her in the hall.

5 CHAPTER

MOHAMED'S LAST DAY OF SCHOOL

Odessa finished her story with sadness in her voice. The others could tell there was more to it, but she wasn't going to tell them yet. She redirected the group's attention to Mohamed. "Okay, Mo, you are the last one. I hope your day went better than ours."

Sadness also filled the Ugandan boy's voice. "Sadly, no. I did not have a very good last day either at my school. I guess it is my turn to share." His somber tone continued as he recounted his last day.

His nimble black fingers rolled across the valve keys and repeated their scale drills. His trumpet sounded just a bit off pitch and a little garbled. He blew into the mouthpiece while opening both spit valves. A puffing sound bellowed through the horn spray as saliva blew out into the grass. Mohamed then adjusted the tuning slide a little bit until his red brass instrument was no longer flat. He went over his fingering routine repeatedly until his hands danced across the keys without thinking.

As he looked into the large school assembly, Mohamed's mind drifted off. He recognized many faces, but even after an entire year he hardly knew any of their names. If his classmates were not in the band, they might as well have not even existed on this planet. Though the African boy had started out playing the violin, his whole life now revolved around his trumpet. Mohamed, or "Mo" as his very few friends called him, was somewhat of a musical prodigy. Practicing was never a chore to him. Unlike most kids in the band, he loved it. He sat for hours a day practicing scales, challenging himself to see how fast he could get his digits to move.

The Ugandan boy was starting to really sweat under the hot Savannah sun. The large, white, fuzzy cap was really getting steamy fast and beads of sweat were dripping onto the out-of-fashion polyester band uniform. Mohamed was used to wearing the traditional cap his father forced him to wear, but this huge, furry Q-tip felt like it had a magnifying glass built into it. He tried to focus on what people were doing in the graduation crowd, but kept getting distracted by his father. His dad was on his cell phone, agitatedly waving his arms around and looking generally annoyed to be there. Mohamed thought to himself, "He can't even stop doing business for twenty minutes. I bet if I was playing the violin like he wanted me to, he'd be paying attention."

When Mohamed's eyes met his mother's, she was smiling and waving at him as usual. The goofy sight of her using both hands at once to wave at him made Mohamed chuckle. She was always this excited to watch him play, whether his dad was interested or not.

Mohamed Obuntu mumbled to Cooper, a redheaded student who was playing second chair trumpet next to him. "I can't believe my father took off work just to come see this silly graduation. I mean really, do we need a graduation for middle school? We were only here three years; it seems very unnecessary and pompous."

He continued complaining to the oblivious kid in the second chair saying, "My father flew all the way back from Uganda just for this event. Seems like such a waste to me, but on the bright side, at least we get to play some music for this ridiculous ceremony. Of course, this music is way too easy; I wish the conductor had picked a much harder piece. I am so bored with this."

Cooper finally spoke up. "Quit complaining. You are the only one in the whole band who has a solo. Be grateful; you only got it because the teacher felt sorry for you that you don't have any friends."

Mohamed ignored the insult and kept complaining. "This is not even a graduation; It is just a pre-graduation ceremony. Heck, the graduating students don't even walk across a stage till tonight. This whole thing is so silly; who really cares about going from eighth to ninth grade anyway? Only parents and grandparents actually want to go to boring stuff like this. None of the students want to be here; it is pure torture for the rest of us. My father hates jazz so I know he's going to hate this piece, too. He'd prefer I was in an orchestra rather than a marching band."

The redheaded boy next to him rebuked, "Will you just shut up? One of these days we will be all alone and I will teach you to shut up, moslem."

The hundredth round of applause interrupted Cooper's threats. Another administrator Mohamed had never seen before got up to make a speech. The Ugandan boy's sweat was streaming down his collar now and dripping down the arms of his white band uniform. Mohamed rolled his eyes as another adult droned on and on about responsibility to one's school, how one should ask themselves every day what they can do to become better citizens, to always put others before their own wants and desires, and how it is one's obligation to sacrifice their own needs for that of the group.

Mohamed continued to pester to the angry redhead. "I saw this speech the other day when I watched *Star Trek II: The Wrath of Khan*. This is sounding like Spock's cheesy death speech after he burns his face off in that glowing light reactor thing and saves the *Enterprise*." He mimicked Leonard Nemoy's dying voice saying, 'The needs of the many outweigh the needs of the few, or the one.' He then replicated Spock's dying motion as he gave one last Vulcan salute and collapsed. "I bet this administrator forgot to write a speech and just decided to borrow this one from *Star Trek*. I am so on to him. I never realized how communist this message was until hearing someone other than Spock say it out loud now."

Cooper had reached his limit and shouted, "Please! Can you go one day without talking about *Star Wars, Star Trek, Stargate, Battelstar Galactica*, or any other dorky show with the word "star" in it? I am so sick of you having to show off how smart you are by talking about what you learn in civics class. I never wanted to hear you talking about republicans, democrats, socialists, libertarians, communist, and volunteerists all year long. You are such a nerd; I can't take anymore! What other thirteen-year-old on the planet even has a clue what that stuff is? Look at you; you are strong enough to be great at any sport you want, but instead you join the Mathletes, the chess team, and play in the band. You know, you might actually have some friends if you just played stupid and went along to get along. Haven't you figured that out yet? Man, you're so stupid! Nobody likes you because you're so different from us normal kids."

"Yes, I know! I hear that message from my father all the time." Mohamed sighed and stopped joking around. He sat quietly and returned to practicing his solo again in his mind.

Eventually, the parade of teachers and administrators stopped jabbering and they finally let the marching band do their thing. Most of the students had seen the same routine done a thousand times before. They had seen the same performance at every athletic event and pep rally that year, so the eighth graders ignored it and gossiped amongst themselves. The parents, on the other hand, watched their hot, sweaty children make patterns in the grass with choreographed marching. The music finally grew louder and Mohamed knew his time was quickly approaching.

The marching band formed a concave formation opening up to a large empty area in the middle. Mohamed marched into the newly formed void to draw attention to his solo. Although he had played it a hundred times before in front of many people, his dad had never seen him play a solo till now. His father was always too busy working and worrying with his import and export business to watch something as trivial as a band concert. Mohamed suddenly felt a nervous rush of uncertainty come over him. He did not know if it was the intense heat or the fact that his father was watching, but the anxiousness made him perspire even harder.

Mohamed calmed his nerves and started his solo right on queue. He tried to quiet his brain and just let his muscle memory in his hands take over his mind. The African boy's fingers had a subconscious mind of their own from years of drilling. The sun was so brutal it was causing the sweat from his arms to roll down his fingers and onto the valve buttons.

Mohamed sweats in the summer, Savannah sun.

All of a sudden, Mohamed heard a terrible off-pitch note come from his trumpet. He pushed forward, hoping nobody else heard the mistake, until another painful screech came from the horn. The sweat was making his digits slide off the keys and he was missing note after note. Mohamed was horrified by the sounds exiting the bell of the shiny brass instrument, but like a true professional, Mohamed just fumbled through till the solo was over.

The boy-perfectionist was so in shock about what had just happened that he slipped back into the crowd of the band and just stopped playing. All he could think about was how embarrassed his dad would be from his poor performance. He just wanted to hide in the band room forever, never to go home, rather than risk having to face his disapproving father.

6 CHAPTER

LEO • THIS SUMMER HAS GOT TO GET BETTER

"**R**eally! You got to be kidding me! These stupid, cheap pieces of dog squeeze." Leo's flashlight blinked on and off. "Odessa, is yours still working okay?"

"Yep, it seems to be fine. Check it out! It looks like that is a door or something way down at the end of this tunnel. Let's get closer; I can't tell what it is. It also looks like it is a good bit of a slow hike through this muddy slop."

Krystal reached out and put her hand on Odessa's shoulder. The Greek girl felt the excessive trembling coming through Krystal's palms and knew she needed to distract her from their dark situation.

Wiki attempted to focus the group. "Let's pick the next topic and each of us talk about it." She took charge and volunteered a victim. "Leo, you should go first. The topic is; what happened this summer before we met?"

The punk rock kid had no desire to share his private feelings with the group, but picked up on the fear in her voice. He breathed in and let out a large, annoyed sigh. "Fine, I will tell you more about this summer before I met you guys."

A week had passed since graduation and summer school was about to start. Leo had no intention of going and wasting his valuable summer repeating a class he hated. The young man was never gifted with good grades, athletic ability, or even a tangible talent; but he had one very valuable skill. Leo Stedman had a silver tongue and could talk his way in or out of anything. The boy figured out how the world worked at a very young age and somehow always wheeled and dealed to get whatever he wanted.

His 1980s, Santa Cruz, Jason Jessee Sungod, vintage skateboard is an excellent example of his real world skills at making money. Almost everything he owned he bought with his own cash he had earned himself. It all started one day when he was walking his dog, Linus, in one of the alleyways in Savannah. It was there that he saw piles of dead plants still in their pots by someone's garbage can.

Anyone else would have looked at it and just would have seen the expired greenery as trash. Leo, however, saw an opportunity. Within a week he had collected over one hundred dead plants from people's trashcans around town. He ripped the cadaverous clippings from the dirt and salvaged all the soil he could. He found a bag of fertilizer his parents never used for a vegetable garden they never planted and mixed it into the dead soil so he could reuse the dirt. The punk rock boy then saw another opportunity where other people would have seen a problem. His neighbor had a Sago Palm that was budding new baby palms all over the rootstalk. The clones were considered a nuisance by some people because they changed the look of the plant from a palm tree to a bush. He knew his neighbor paid good money to have their lawn guy cut them out every year.

So, Leo devised a plan. He approached his neighbor and offered to trim his Sago Palm for $50, half the price of what the landscaper charged. The neighbor was thrilled to save some money and was also impressed with the boy's entrepreneurial attitude. So, the young man carefully cut out twenty buds off the base of the palm and took them home. Not only did he make fifty dollars, but also, he now had twenty free clones to put in his empty pots. He repeated this process a few more times and even found some bonus wild plants that he transplanted to his empty containers. In a matter of just two weeks, Leo had a thriving plant nursery in his backyard.

Out of curiosity, Leo went up to the local home improvement store one day to see how much the same plants would cost brand new and was shocked by the high prices. He later took pictures of his new baby annuals with his cell phone and uploaded them all over the Internet's local, free, classified web pages. The boy gardener only charged half of what the stores did and completely sold out in no time. Leo had started out with no money and in just three weeks, with a little elbow grease and his imagination, had made over one thousand dollars. He used the money to buy a high-priced vintage skateboard. The boy with the jet-black hair even had enough left over to get a cool, antique Black Flag lunch box and an old, punk rock, leather motorcycle jacket.

Leo could see opportunity where nobody else did. For most of his short life, he was great at turning nothing into something. The fourteen-year-old now turned his resourcefulness into figuring a way out of summer school. He clutched his beloved skateboard in his lap and hummed "Kiss Off" by the Violent Femmes under his breath while he waited in the lounge outside the principal's office.

"Mr. Stedman, Mr. Hughes will see you now," said the secretary as she opened the door.

The young man strolled into the office with unexpected confidence. He couldn't help but notice a fur collared, leather trench coat and matching hat hanging on a stand in the corner. Leo thought to himself, "What the heck? Is Gordon Hughes a pimp or what?" The walls were covered in ancient and colonial mounted artifacts. He proceeded across the room filled with framed old maps to where the pasty, bearded man sat.

"Make it fast, Mr. Stedman. I am swamped with work today. And this better not be about...that," he whispered. "I asked you not to talk about that here."

"Oh, I think you will make time for this, Mr. Hughes," Leo challenged with a bit of attitude. "It seems I failed Mrs. Coleman's math class even though I had passing grades on all her tests. On the very last day I hit my tardy limit because your security officers made me late."

The principal skirted any responsibility. "Yes, I heard about that; you should have planned better and come earlier. I'm not sure what you want me to do about it. There are certain rules I can break and others I can't. You know I'm running for school board president so I can't be drawing any negative attention to myself."

Principal Gordon Hughes gets confronted by Leo.

"That's the thing; you don't follow the rules at all. I have seen you use your "discretion" to make exceptions for people you like all the time. I have seen you do things that would get an ordinary person in trouble, much less a principal-wannabe-school-board president. So, you are going to use your powers, whatever they may be, to fix my failed math grade so I don't have to go to summer school," Leo instructed.

The principal was taken aback by the young man's bold words and attitude. His eyes slanted evilly and his voice became low and dark. "Excuse me son, you need to watch what you say to me or I could make this a whole lot worse for you. I know people. My blood is old in this part and my money works for me. You do not want to threaten me," said the insulted man.

"Here's the thing, my man, you ARE going to do this and help me because I am going to help you. Do you see this cool little pen?" Leo held up a thick, black, formal Montblanc knock off. "Not only does it write, but it is also a camera. Look how small it is; you can't even tell it's recording right now." The boy smiled as he pointed it at the principal.

Mr. Hughes instantly became livid. His normally pale skin swelled and glowed like a flaming baboons butt. "You know all cell phones and recording devices are not allowed on campus! You are in serious trouble son!"

Leo ignored the irate man's threats and kept talking. "You see, Gordon, your crooked security guards have been harassing me all year, so I finally decided to use this wonderful device to secretly tape our encounters. It seems I captured two of your officers taking my stuff and keeping it or selling it. I have really clear video footage of Officers Bines and Gambit taking my lunch box, including all the food inside. That's just one video. I have more."

The principal's mood darkened as he slumped back in his chair and continued to listen.

"Officer Gambit isn't real bright. She immediately listed my expensive rare, Black Flag lunch box on eBay. It has some very distinct markings from wear and tear, so I can prove it is the same one. She was also stupid enough to use her actual name for her eBay account, so it was incredibly easy to track it back to her. Not to mention, I have an excellent video of her extorting me and taking it. I mean, she looked right into the camera so close I could see her pupils dilate. I assume you don't instruct your officers to steal whatever they want from students, right? Or maybe you do." Leo paused briefly, stared intently at Mr. Hughes, then continued.

"Seems to me that, right now, you should also be thinking about that little adventure you invited me and some of the boys from school on last month."

The administrator's swollen, red face suddenly turned a whiter shade of pale as he had to swallow his rage. "You know not to talk about that here!" he said.

Leo failed to care about that at the moment. He saw he had the upper hand in this conversation and used the man's own fear against him. "I know you weren't supposed to be digging in that area you had us digging in. There were 'no trespassing' signs everywhere. You don't have the right to dig on someone else's property. And what about all the gold and jewels we found? Does that stuff really belong to you?"

The superintendent sat stone-faced and said nothing. Leo continued. "I brought my "pen" with me that day, too. Funny how some of the boys said that they go off with you, Mr. Bines, and Ms. Gambit regularly, even at night. It's also funny that you all go dig up stuff on other people's land when they aren't looking and take all kinds of old silver and coins out of the dirt. I wonder how it would look to the voting public when they find out that a man who is running for school board president is taking little boys off into the woods at night on treasure hunts to trespass and commit violations against their neighbors; I'm pretty sure that would get you kicked off the board at the Historical Society for hoarding artifacts."

Mr. Hughes looked like he might throw up his five star lunch at any second when the young man offered a deal. "It's obvious by that look on your face that you are ready to meet my terms, so here is what is going to happen. You are going to save me from summer school by fixing my grade in math class. You are also going to fire Mr. Bines and Ms. Gambit from their security guard positions so they can't abuse children anymore. Then we will part ways and I will move on to someone else's school. I will be out of your hair forever and these videos will never get out. It is a win-win for us both."

The principal just could not let go of his authority complex and threatened the boy again. "How dare you! You can't speak to me like this; I am an adult!"

"You see, I think I can." The cocky young boy leaned back in his chair, threw his feet up on the principal's desk, and said, "Let me paint a picture for you. If you send me to summer school, this video of your trusted employees stealing from a fourteen-year-old boy and the videos from your little archeological dig last month will be all over the Internet in a matter of hours. Within hours of that, it will be picked up by all the local news stations and not only will you be publicly shamed, but I am pretty sure your bid for school board president will be over. Is all that really worth it just to stick me in summer school?"

The principal was so mad he literally could not speak. He wanted so badly to come down on this arrogant child and teach him to respect authority, but he knew he had been defeated...this time. He finally squeaked out, "Fine, I will fix your grade after you give me those recordings."

Leo accepted, "Very well; deal. But you will fix it right now in front of me." He opened the spy camera and pulled out the tiny SD card that the video was stored on.

The principal's shaking hand snatched the SD card out of Leo's hand and examined it. He smiled as he realized he just saved himself from a public relations nightmare.

"Okay, your turn. I want a print out of my new report card with your signature on it," young Leo demanded.

The head administrator plugged away at his keyboard and in just one minute a new report card was printed up and signed. The adult reluctantly handed over the new grades. "Here. I expect you will keep secret about it. Now get out."

Leo grabbed his ticket to summer freedom and headed for the door, smiling. "I also expect you to mail my Black Flag lunch box back when you retrieve it; oh and you owe me a lunch, too. By the way, if you somehow go back on our deal, I downloaded a copy of those videos to my computer days ago," he said, immediately slamming the door behind him.

As he walked out, Leo turned to the secretary gatekeeper and muttered, "This summer has got to get better!"

KRYSTAL • THIS SUMMER HAS GOT TO GET BETTER

Krystal was impressed with Leo's brashness and attitude. "Wow, I would never talk to an adult like that. I am surprised your parents didn't whoop yuh into next week fer that. My story doesn't end as well as his. Yuh sure yuh want to hear it?"

The group encouraged her with pats on the shoulder as they pushed down the long black hallway. "Okay, fine. Here is what happened about a week after my school ended."

Krystal's mom dropped her off at the stables on the way to her early shift at the diner where she waited tables. The tomboy loved horses so much that she volunteered once a week at a local horse charity called Horsin' Around. The rest of the week though, she took a job at one of the nicest stables in town.

The freckle-faced girl decided to sneak a sunrise ride in before she had to clean all the stalls. She had made a deal with the owner last year to muck the stables in exchange for the chance to practice riding. Her family was from very little money and owning a horse was extremely expensive. If she did a few hours of chores for the rich stable owners each week, then they, in exchange, would let her exercise any horse that needed to be ridden.

At first she was always supervised by an adult while she rode; now, however, she was so skilled that the owners never had to watch her anymore. Krystal Bennett seemed to be born to ride. She could get any horse to do anything she wanted. Somehow she innately understood their body language and knew how to subtly communicate with them. The small girl was always kind and calm around the massive animals and they seemed to be unexplainably attracted to her natural energy.

Krystal takes Clip Clop for a ride.

She borrowed one of the paint mares and took her out for some exercise. The sun was just coming up, but the merciless Savannah heat had not arrived yet. The thirteen-year-old pushed the horse to a full gallop and held on tight. The force of the wind blew her braids up causing her cowboy hat to fly backwards off her head. The string under her chin snapped it back against her shoulders, her braids flying behind her like tails on a kite. At that moment, nothing else mattered but the ride. Krystal Bennett did not think about rich girl bullies, having no dad, how bad she just wanted to be home-schooled, or that their family had no money. For this brief, early morning moment, everything was perfect.

When she returned to the stables she dove straight into work. She wanted to get the hard pitchfork work done before it got too hot. The tiny girl shoveled manure into a wheel barrel and repeated this process stall after stall. She moved on to putting fresh water out for the horses when she felt a cringe roll up her spine. Krystal heard the cackling of spoiled, plastic girls arriving. She immediately felt sick to her stomach when she recognized Gloria's voice coming into the barn. The freckle-faced girl hid herself in a stall to avoid the gang of annoying socialite harpies.

The owner of he stable arrived and welcomed the group of student riders. "Okay, ladies, I got you all for two hours, so tack up your horses and meet me in the ring. For those of you who don't own their own horse, you can choose any of those on the right side of the barn. I will double check that your tack is on correctly before we work on your posting."

Gloria was wearing a brand new, expensive English riding suit. The blonde girl made sure all the accessories matched, right down to her scrunchie and her nail polish. She wondered aloud, "*Hmmmm*, I think I want to ride Clip Clop today; do any of you see that Appaloosa?"

The owner responded, "I don't see Clip Clop either! Krystal! Krystal where are you? I need you!"

The small girl slowly emerged from hiding and presented herself to the stable boss. "Sorry, ma'am; I was busier than a pair of jumper cables at a redneck wedding. Boss, what can I do for yuh?"

A wicked smile of delight materialized on Gloria's face as she saw the manure-covered stable girl emerge from the stinky stable.

"Where is Clip Clop?" the owner asked.

"Ma'am, I put her out to pasture. I can go get her right now; she is just right over there in the lower paddocks," Krystal offered.

"Yep, bring her to Gloria here when you fetch her," the stable boss ordered.

"Yes ma'am. I'll go fetch the Appaloosa right now," Krystal said as she grabbed a lead and headed to the paddock.

When she returned with the horse, Gloria was all alone and waiting impatiently. "Finally! All my friends already have gear on their rides and I am standing here waiting for your slow behind. Help me saddle up Clip Clop."

A brief, uneasy truce was called while the girls worked together to tie down the complicated saddle and gear to the equine. But Gloria soon pushed Krystal out of the way. "You're too slow; I will finish it myself! The freckled girl shrugged her shoulders and returned to putting fresh water out for the horses.

Gloria rushed to finish tacking down the Appaloosa so she could join her friends. She impatiently dragged the horse out of the barn and into the ring.

Most of her friends had already started riding and Gloria was eager to get her gear checked out so she could join them.

The stable boss's voice echoed through the barn. "Krystal! Can you come out to the ring? I need your help!"

The tiny girl responded, running quickly into the ring. "What can I do for yuh, Ma'am?"

"I am running behind and need to start the lesson. Can you go check Gloria's saddle and tack to make sure it is tight and proper?"

"Yess'm." Krystal walked over to Clip Clop and started double checking the gear.

"I don't need your help, farm girl; I know I did it right," Gloria snapped as she moved the equine away from Krystal's inspection.

It was at that moment that the tiny inspector noticed that Gloria had fallen victim to Clip Clop's mischievous side. Krystal could tell by watching the horses' ribs as he breathed in and out that the saddle was too loose. Clip Clop liked to play a trick on new riders in which he would hold his breath and puff his ribs out while being saddled. This made the horse appear much fatter when the straps were tightened down. As soon as the tacking was over, the horse would let his breath out and the saddle would become loose.

The tiny girl grinned. "Looks like it fits like a saddle on a sow. I guess you got it all under control then. I will stay out of your way, Barbie." Normally, Krystal Bennett would go back to her barn chores immediately, but she decided to linger to watch the impending show.

Gloria was not skilled enough to mount her horse from the ground, so the instructor walked Clip Clop next to a hay bale and used it as a step stool. The moody girl awkwardly climbed into the saddle with the stable boss' help. Krystal snickered at the clumsiness of her mounting procedure. As the inexperienced rider practiced the timing of her posting, the saddle inched a little closer to the horse's right side.

The tiny stable girl grinned as she watched the eminent disaster unfold. The tricky equine, nerved by the unwelcome rider on its back, cut hard and stopped instantaneously, shifting the loose saddle forward.

As if gravity had stopped working, Krystal watched as Gloria seemed to fall in slow motion, head first, over the horse's lowered head. Clip Clop, seemingly in on the joke, had proudly chosen the largest, dirtiest, muddiest puddle to dump the snobby teen into. A large splash of mud and manure engulfed the downed rider.

Krystal couldn't contain herself any longer and started giggling aloud. As the giggle turned into a full-blown chuckle, Gloria stood up; her new outfit was completely mud-colored. The sounds of laughing infuriated the slop-covered girl and she screamed at Krystal, "This is your fault! You did this! You sabotaged my saddle on purpose!"

The owner came over to the snickering Krystal. "Is this true? Did you do this on purpose?"

The young Miss Bennett tried to control her laughter. "Ma'am, I saw it was loose and when I tried to help she yelled at me to leave her alone. She told me she knew how to do it and to get away from her."

"I don't care, you should have told me. Gloria could have gotten really hurt and this stable could have gotten sued. I want you to finish your chores and wait for your momma to come get you. I don't want to see you back here for a while," the stable boss scolded.

"That is so unfair!" the tiny girl shot back.

"You need to go, Krystal, before 'a while' becomes 'forever,'" she warned.

As the freckle-faced girl slowly meandered back to the barn, she mumbled, "This summer has got to get better!"

ODESSA • THIS SUMMER HAS GOT TO GET BETTER

dessa shouted with anger, "That is so wrong! I can't believe they fired you for that. Gloria had it coming; she sounds like such a jerk."

They continued slowly navigating the muck-filled passageway.

Krystal confessed, "The hardest part was telling my momma; I was so embarrassed. It really caused a big problem at our house. My momma had to stay at home with me and she missed working an extra shift. Losing that job cost my momma a bunch a money that we really needed."

The depressed little girl deflected the attention of the group by saying, "Okay, Wiki, it's your turn"

Odessa sighed with embarrassment, "I really don't want to share what happened to me, but you guys have been so open and honest. I will tell you, but please don't make fun of me. You guys are my best friends now." She began her tale and her voice crackled as she held back the tears.

"How about this dress? Does this one look good, mom?" Wiki stepped out of the dressing room. The yellow sundress looked wrinkled on top and too tight at the waist.

"No, Odessa, I think you need to try on a more sliming color like black or brown. Also, this one is too tight around the waist."

Odessa screeched in frustration. "I hate dress shopping! If the outfit fits on the bottom, it is way too big on top and if it fits on the top, then it is too tight on the bottom. I hate my body!"

Her overweight mother was sympathetic and gave her a hug. "We could try another diet this summer; we could do one together if you want."

A tear welled up in Wiki's eye. "It is so unfair. I eat the same stuff as everyone else at school and they are all thin. Why is it so hard for me to lose weight?"

"Baby, if I knew that answer I would be thin, too," her mother offered.

"It is just really important that I look good for Stacy's birthday party. Everyone is going to be there and it should really be fun because her parents are dropping a ton of money on it. They got her a DJ, an ice cream bar, and even a chocolate fountain. This party is the only thing Stacy talked about the entire last month in science lab. She was a terrible lab partner and I had to do all the work. We talked for hours about this shindig and planned it down to the last little detail. It is going to be so awesome," Odessa explained.

Her mother smiled at the idea of her daughter helping plan a friend's party. "I got an idea! I saw a cute babydoll sundress that should work for your body shape. You go back to the dressing room and I will bring it to you."

Odessa gave her mom one big hug. "Thanks for understanding! We still need to find Stacy the perfect gift. She has been talking about this designer pair of earrings forever. I think I saw them on sale in the front of the store."

A few hours later, their car pulled up to Stacy's house. Odessa's mom announced, "I guess by all the balloons on the mailbox and the decorations around the door that you are at the right place. I hope you have a great time! Oh, don't forget your gift. She better love those earrings at that price!"

"Thanks, mom. Remember, the party ends at four, so don't forget to come get me. You know, this would be a whole lot easier if you would just get me a cell phone. I swear I am the only kid in my entire class who does not have one. Stacy's little sister is only in third grade and even she has her own phone," Wiki pleaded.

"We are not going to have this discussion again. Somehow kids for thousands of years survived without one. I don't think you will be scarred for life if you have to wait till you're sixteen. Now go have fun. I will be back here in four hours to pick you up," her mother confirmed.

Odessa nodded her head in agreement and grabbed the neatly wrapped gift she had carefully decorated the night before. She shut the heavy door of the wood-paneled station wagon and watched her mom drive away. The Greek girl smiled as she looked down at her new, black babydoll dress that fit just right. For the first time in a very long time, Wiki was excited that she finally had a friend.

She walked up to the front door and rang the bell. Wiki could hear a whole bunch of noise coming from inside and figured everyone must already be in there. Odessa rang the bell over and over, assuming nobody could hear it.

Finally, the door flew open and Stacy appeared wearing a fashionable, new white dress. The birthday girl's face transformed from a large grin into a look of confusion. "Wiki, what are you doing here?"

Stacy's mom appeared behind her. "Who is it dear?"

"It is my lab partner, Odessa. What are you doing here?" Stacy asked again.

A look of confusion came over Odessa's face. "Um, I am here for your birthday party, of course."

Stacy's voice turned falsely sympathetic and sarcastic. "Oh, sorry, but you are not invited. My mom only let me invite fifty people."

"Not invited?" the Greek girl challenged. "I helped you plan this party for an entire month. I lied to our teacher saying you did half a project that you did nothing for. How could I have not made the cut when you got to invite fifty people?"

Stacy's mother stepped in to diffuse the awkward situation. "Look, Odessa, we mailed out the invites a month ago. If you didn't get an invite, you're not invited."

The hurt girl stuttered, "But, but, but I'm here...why not just let me in?"

Stacy stepped back in front of her mom. "Sorry, Wiki, we are all full!"

The door slammed loudly in Wiki's face. The confused girl sat quietly on the porch as she felt tears forming in her eyes. She heard a round of loud laughter inside and knew Stacy had just told her partygoers about the exchange. "I am so embarrassed, but I am not going to let them see me cry," the hurt girl mumbled.

Odessa was so upset that she decided to just leave the gift she had worked so hard for, on the porch for Stacy to find later. "Maybe when Stacy opens the earrings she will feel guilty for what she just did to me," Odessa thought.

Wiki stood up, straightened her new dress, and took a deep breath to slow down her out-of-control weeping. She started the long four-mile walk home as tears steadily streamed down her face. As the hot Savannah sun beat down on her, all Wiki could think about was how useful a cell phone would have been right about then. Through a stream of tears she cried out loud, "This summer has got to get better!"

Odessa leaving Stacy's house.

MOHAMED · THIS SUMMER HAS GOT TO GET BETTER

"**O**h darlin', I'm sorry." Krystal let go of Odessa's shoulder and hugged her roommate. "Some people on this planet are so selfish, and I can't believe her momma was that rude, too. I know that was hard to share."

Leo cut in on the uncomfortable, emotional moment. "You know what is creepy is that three of us said the same thing, 'this summer has got to get better.' What are the chances of that? I mean it is like we made some cosmic wish and fate threw us together."

"It is even creepier than you think, Leo; I also said that exact phrase," Mo confessed. A chill ran up their backs, but they continued to march slowly through the slop.

Leo's superstitious side took over. "That is crazy; now I am positive that greater forces are at play here. I am telling you, this is like supernatural stuff going on."

Wiki wiped the tears from her eyes and cut off the excited boys' ramblings. "Go on Mo; tell us what happened to you."

Mo really did not want to share is embarrassing story, but since the others had been so open, he took a chance.

He was in great form today and Mohamed nailed the new piece perfectly. The band camp teacher was so impressed that he pulled the boy-prodigy aside to talk to him privately at the end of class. "Son, I don't know what your father was talking about when he enrolled you. He told me that you needed a great deal of help."

"Well, my dad has never seen me perform but once. The only time he came and watched it was a disaster. Sweat got all over my keys and my fingers kept slipping off the valves. So now he thinks I am terrible and embarrassing to the family name. I already don't play a classical instrument as my Muslim father would prefer, and to be honest it causes a lot of tension around my house," Mohamed confessed.

"I will be happy to tell him you made fantastic progress during this camp. Don't worry, I will give you a good report and I hope that will help make things better for you at home. I had a father that was hard to please too, so I understand," the instructor related.

Mohamed was gracious. "You are a good man; thank you for your help. Now, I need to go to the band room and return my sheet music. It has been a fun week; I really enjoyed the pieces you chose for me. They were challenging, but still cool."

The teacher responded, "Thanks. I think you sure did nail those movements; you made everyone else look lazy!" He half-laughed at his own joke and continued, "Now go drop off your sheet music and have a great summer."

Mohamed ran to the band room to turn in his folder. When he arrived, four other boys had already dropped off their music and were talking in hushed tones. When Mohamed walked into the room further, the chatting stopped and all their eyes turned to the Ugandan wearing the Muslim prayer cap.

The boy-prodigy stopped in his tracks and looked questioningly at them. "What?"

Cooper, the redheaded second-chair trumpet player, snapped. "Why can't you just chill out? When you practice so hard, it makes the rest of us look bad. We are getting sick of hearing all the praises the teacher throws at you. Every time I screw up, he compares me to you and tells me to work harder."

The whole concept of laziness was lost on Mohamed. "So why don't you practice harder? Practice is fun!"

Cooper retorted, "No, practice is a pain; I hate practicing. I am only in band so I don't have to take other classes that are even worse."

Mohamed was confused. "So why would you sign up for summer band camp if you don't like it?"

"Because my stupid parents made me; I don't want to be here with losers like you." The three other boys jeered at his insult.

Mohamed suddenly became nervous as the group of boys slowly surrounded him. "I just want to drop off my music and be on my way," the African boy pleaded.

Cooper's gang rallied in closer. "I think we need to take you down a notch and remind you that you're not better than us. Fella's, grab the muzzie!"

The group of boys quickly overwhelmed Mohamed and his trumpet and sheet music flew across the floor.

"Okay, Okay! I will play worse! I will stop practicing!" the African boy shouted.

"I don't believe you!" Cooper shot back. "I am sick of you acting so smart. You talk about politics, sci-fi, and how great it is to be moslem. I'm plain sick of you! We are going to give you something to remember and remind you to just shut up from now on. Hold him down good, fella's, till I get back."

Mohamed struggled to get free, but the three boys pinned him to the floor. Cooper returned with his lunch box. Everyone in the room looked confused. His minions could not figure out what a lunch box had to do with humiliating their captive.

"Is it true you moslems can't touch anything from a pig or your God will get angry with you?" the redheaded boy smiled.

"Please, I said I was sorry. Don't bring my religion in to this, too," Mohamed begged.

Cooper took his time as he separated the ham from the bread in his sandwich. He enjoyed watching the young Ugandan boy struggle to get away.

The redheaded boy giggled with delight as he wiped the ham all over Mohamed's face. The captive boy screamed and fought, but could not get away from the greasy, unholy attack.

Cooper pressed the ham around his nose. "Take a good whiff of it, moslem, because you're about to eat every bit of this piggy! *OINK! OINK!*"

Cooper attacks Mohamed in the bandroom.

Mohamed bucked and wiggled. "Please, stop! Why are you doing this? Stop!"

"What's going on here?" the teacher yelled at the boys who were now squirming on the floor.

Cooper and his gang immediately let go of their victim and tried to pretend they were not just assaulting Mohamed.

Mohamed had tears in his eyes as he stood up and used his sleeve to wipe the pig juice off his face.

"Mohamed, were these boys just attacking you?" the man questioned.

The African boy looked at his victimizers. He wanted to tell the teacher what had just happened, but he knew the boys would just hurt him worse the next time if he told the truth. "No sir, I just fell."

"It didn't look like that; it looked like these boys were pinning you to the ground trying to force you to eat something." He turned to Cooper's posse. "Y'all need to get out of here, now; your parents will be hearing from me very soon."

The squad of thugs collected their things as they cursed their bad timing.

"Mohamed, I am going to wait with you until your parents come pick you up. I need to tell them what happened," his teacher informed with concern.

Mohamed responded, "No, please don't! It is hard enough being the only Muslim kid in school; I don't want to be singled out even more. Please don't tell my parents. They will make this into a huge thing about religious discrimination."

"It's your call, but I think you should tell them," the teacher urged.

The boy cried, "Please, don't say anything. I have a hard enough time making friends and fitting in. If my parents start a fight with the school board over this, it will never end for me."

"Okay, Mohamed, whatever you want, buddy. We can just wait here till your dad comes to pick you up," the instructor consoled.

Mohamed wiped the tears from his face and belted out, "This summer has got to get better!"

10 CHAPTER

THE MENDEL ACADEMY

The group grew excited as they could now make out a large, wooden door at the end of the long, murky, puddle-filled passage.

Anger filled Leo's voice. "That is messed up. I hope I run into that jerk Cooper soon. I am going to help you get some payback."

"Even if they had made me eat the pork, it would have been no sin on me. Allah would not hold me responsible for an act of aggression against me," Mohamed spoke in a sad voice. "Why does it matter so much to other people what god I believe in? I just want to be left alone, but people won't let me. It reminds me of a famous quote the immortal Ernest Hancock says..."

Wiki cut him off. "Who is Ernest Hancock? Was he a founding father or a philosopher I have never heard of?"

"He is a philosopher in a way I guess. He has one of the most popular radio shows about liberty in the world. He says there are two kinds of people in this world; those who just want to be left alone and those who just won't leave them alone. Which one are you?"

Wiki came back with a sarcastic tone, "So, wait, you are quoting a talk show host?"

Krystal interrupted, "I like that saying, Mo. It really simplifies people. He sounds very wise indeed. I think important messages need to be real simple because some people are about as quick as grandma runnin' backwards."

Even though nobody could see Mohamed in the dark, he was grinning ear to ear; somebody actually liked his interest in politics and liberty.

Squish, Squish, Squish could be faintly heard behind them. Odessa spun around and shined her light down the hall. She saw nothing but darkness. The inexpensive flashlight only pierced twenty feet into the black.

"I think that a ghost is followin' us, Mo, but it sounds like it's way back there. No worries, it won't ever catch us; nobody can move fast in this muck," Krystal whispered.

"You know I don't believe in ghosts, Krystal, but it could be a jinn, I suppose." Mohamed responded.

"Darn it! I lost my left boot in this maze of slime and sludge. This is more frustratin' than teachin' a mule to dance. Can y'all keep talkin' while I dig my boot outta this slop?" Krystal begged.

Odessa took charge. "Okay, the next topic is how did you get accepted at the Mendel Academy?"

"So, just to be clear, in exchange for gardening, grounds keeping, and a few odd jobs, you will let me attend this private school for free?" Leo confirmed.

Ms. Ruby Mendel replied, "Yep, that is the deal. Think of it as kind of like a scholarship for gardening. We grow a lot of our own organic food here and we really need someone to help work the garden. Our last student-gardener graduated and we need a new one. We will give you a room, meals, and even a small paycheck every week to help with expenses. I talked this over with your parents and they said the decision is yours."

The fourteen-year-old boy had negotiation skills that a Wall Street corporate raider would envy. Leo scratched his chin and looked to the high-priced, antique, crystal chandelier hanging over the head master's desk. "I think I can accept your offer for three hundred dollars a week."

The tall, thin woman with big, blonde hair like Dolly Parton smiled at the boy's boldness. "Let me repeat, you will have no expenses at all and you will get to enjoy the same benefits the other students get. You can use the entertainment room, the arcade, the gym, and the swimming pool; it's all included. In fact, you will basically be a student, but your classes will revolve around practical horticulture. So, my offer of one hundred dollars a week is more in line with what we were thinking.

Leo knew one very important rule to negotiating; never give away anything without asking for something extra in return. "Well, we seem to be two hundred dollars apart, so I will meet you in the middle. I would like two hundred dollars a week and a ten by ten square foot section of the garden that will be all mine. I will use it to grow veggies and sell them at the farmers market to make up the difference in pay."

Ruby was very impressed that such a young boy would think of such an inventive bargain. "Okay I will go up to one hundred and fifty dollars a week and you can have your own garden."

The tall, skinny boy followed that most important negotiating rule again; never give away anything without asking for something in return. "I will agree to one hundred and fifty dollars, but to make up that difference I want a larger twenty by twenty square foot garden. I will also borrow your tools and I want a cut of the seeds you buy."

The blonde in the sundress gave in and offered her hand. "Agreed!" she said. Leo accepted the hand, shook it, and said, "Deal!"

The punk rock gardener asked, "Now that negotiations are finished, why on Earth did you pick me to come here for the summer?"

"Well, at our little academy we are always on the lookout for exceptional children. Most kids today are content to just play video games and gossip about some reality show, but you are one of the exceptions. A friend of the Mendel Academy found out about your booming backyard plant nursery and was so fascinated with your entrepreneurial sprit, she recommended we take a look at you," Ruby explained.

Leo smiled, "Remind me to send her one of my plants to say thank you."

Ms. Mendel was impressed. "Ah, you already understand that giving special care to your best customers will keep them referring back to you. You really are quite the smart, young businessman. Anyway, come back tomorrow at 8 A.M. and you can move your things in and get started. It was nice meeting you, Mr. Stedman."

The boy in the Black Flag tee shirt and gray ribbon flashed one more smile then headed out of the office.

"Scott, can you send the next one in!" she yelled into the hallway.

A petite, freckle-faced girl and her mother came into the elaborate, but very old office. They looked around at the collection of antiques and expensive art and froze in place.

"Ladies, please have a seat," Ruby said as she pointed to the fancy wingback chairs in front of her desk.

"Sorry ma'am, we just had no idea this old building was so nice inside. We are kinda nervous about breakin' anythin'," Krystal Bennett explained as she twiddled her thumbs. The tomboy could not help but notice a large, stuffed porcupine behind Ms. Mendel's desk. "Um, ma'am, can I ask yuh why yuh have a large varmint mounted up behind yuh? I didn't think Savannah has porcupines; why do yuh have it?"

Ruby cracked a smile. "That is true; we definitely don't have porcupines this far south. This guy here is our school mascot."

"That seems a strange choice for a mascot; why did yuh pick him?" Krystal's mother put her finger to her mouth and hushed her child. Her mom spoke up, "I am sorry; she is always so full of questions."

Ms. Mendel smiled and laugh lines appeared around her lips. "It's good to be curious. The reason this academy chose a porcupine as its mascot is because of how it lives its life. It is a non-violent creature that just wants to be left alone. Our quill-covered friend makes its way through life peacefully, but you don't want to tread on it. At this school we try to remind children that violence against your fellow man is always the worst way to do things. We encourage and embrace non-violent solutions to all of life's problems. You will even hear people around town refer to our students as 'The Porcs."

The country girl and her mom stood in front of Ms. Mendel's desk and the Mother Bennett offered her hand. "Sorry, where's our manners? I am Ms. Bennett and this here is the joy of my life, Krystal."

Ruby stood up and shook their hands. "Thank you so much for coming. Please, have a seat. A friend of the academy informed us you might be a perfect fit for our school."

Refusing to sit, Ms. Bennett interrupted, "Wait, Ms. Mendel. Let me stop you right here. Since Krystal can't work out at that barn no more, I can't work double shifts waiting tables. So our money just got cut in half. Not to mention, I am a single mother who can't even afford a baby sitter. I am going to have to bring my daughter with me to the diner all summer long."

Momma Bennett sighed in frustration. "There is no way we can afford this place. Thanks for considering us; it was real nice to know my daughter is smart enough to get into a place like this," she said and offered a hand of thanks.

"Please sit, Ms. Bennett. I think there is a misunderstanding here. I am offering Krystal a full scholarship. You won't have to pay a thing. She will live here all summer and we will take care of all her expenses. This will let you work double shifts again and maybe get ahead on your bills a little bit," Ruby offered.

The girl with loosely braided hair and her mom shrugged their shoulders and finally sat down. Krystal interjected, "Why me? I am barely a C student. I am not very good at math or spelling. I am sure you also know I failed 6th grade and had to repeat it."

Ms. Mendel explained, "You see, we are not like the traditional government or public schools you are used to. This is a very different kind of educational center. We believe forcing children to spend years learning about topics they will never use or are not interested in is a waste and even damaging. Sadly it turns children away from their natural love of learning."

The mother and daughter exchanged confused looks with each other. Ruby went on. "Let me explain. We focus on something called unschooling. The students decide a topic they want to learn and we help them find the tools to steer their own education."

Ms. Bennett interrupted, "Wait, are you seriously telling me that these kids have no formal classes, but still learn anyway? Wouldn't they just sit around, watch tv, and play video games all day long if left to their own choosin'?"

"You would think that, but no. When children are allowed to learn what they are interested in they are very productive. Learning is fun and not dreaded like it is when it is forced on them in the traditional school model," the blonde, aging woman responded.

"How on earth do you get kids to learn about tough subjects like algebra?" Ms. Bennett challenged.

"Well, not all kids need algebra; it depends what they want to do. A good example is our space club. A group of kids decided they wanted to build a rocket. So we had a meeting and I explained to them that they would need to learn and understand a large amount of engineering, math, and chemistry to make the rocket work. They realized they needed a solid understanding of these tough subjects to reach their goal and they became very interested in learning them. All I did was help them find the resources and they figured out the rest. In fact, they will be launching their first rocket at Wassaw Sound this weekend," Ruby half-bragged.

"So, why would you want me? I don't know anything about rockets," Krystal questioned.

"No, you might not know about rockets, but I hear you know horses. You see, one of this school's more profitable businesses is our history tour business. We have built up a profitable horse and carriage tour company in downtown Savannah. Our horse and buggy are stabled here in the back of our facility. We are looking for someone who would like to learn all about running and operating a stable. This would be hard work and you would have to learn about all aspects of running a profitable stable. You would need to learn enough mathematics to deal with bills and expenses. You will also need to learn some basic veterinarian, farrier, and animal husbandry skills. We will supervise you of course, but this would be a little more like a job than a scholarship," Ms. Mendel explained.

Krystal giggled and jumped up and down. "Are yuh kiddin'? So my classes would actually be takin' care of horses? Oh, Momma! Can I, please?"

Ms. Bennett looked at her excited daughter and grinned. "So, you sure it won't cost us anything?"

"Not a thing. In fact, Krystal will actually receive a small cut of the profits based on how successful she is," Ruby smiled.

"If you really want to stay here all summer, it is fine with me," Ms. Bennett offered.

"YES! YES! YES! Thanks so much momma! And thank yuh so much, Ms. Mendel! I'm about as excited as Paula Deen eatin' an all-butter buffet!" The tiny girl launched herself across the desk and hugged her new benefactor.

Ruby blushed and then hugged the thrilled, small girl back. "Bring anything you will need for the summer tomorrow. I will see you at 8 A.M."

As the excited mother and daughter duo left, Ruby could not help but grin. "You don't see kids get that happy about going to public school. It is times like this when I know the Mendel Academy is really working," she thought.

"Scott, I am ready for the next family; please send them back."

A large Greek woman entered wearing a sweater with an untucked, button-down shirt sticking out the bottom of it and a plaid and pleather skirt. Her huge hair was adorned by a bow that was just as big as the massive tresses on her head. The Madonna-like outfit was a salute to 80s fashions and Savannah's finest yard sales.

Mrs. Skouras and her daughter took their seats in front of the large desk. Ms. Mendel greeted the two. "I take it you are Mrs. Skouras - and you must be Odessa. It is nice to meet you both. Thanks for dropping by today."

Mrs. Skouras tried to sell her daughter. "Thank you for the invite and considering my daughter for your prestigious school. I have heard about how hard it is to get into this place and we are thrilled you want to take a look at Odessa. She is super smart and a really hard worker. My daughter was so bright she even skipped a grade two years ago."

"Well, Mrs. Skouras, we do a lot of research before you ever get an invite. Odessa's reputation exalts her. All the staff at the Georgia Historical Society speak so highly of her. They say she spends hours a day there researching local history just for fun."

"It's true, Ms. Mendel. The only birthday present she wanted was a membership to the Georgia Historical Society so she can hang out there all summer."

"Odessa, we at the academy think you would be a perfect fit to intern at our Historic Carriage Tour Company. Our last student graduated and now we have an open position," Ruby offered.

"I have been researching your school and tours online and I know all about them. I would love to help out, but what would you like me to do?" Wiki queried.

Ruby continued. "To be frank, because there are so many tour companies in Savannah, we are starting to get lost in the crowd. I want to bring you in to dig up some new, interesting Lowcountry history to add to our tours. I am hoping that if we provide you a summer scholarship here, you, in return, will help us design the newest and best Savannah history tour ever. What do you think?"

Odessa looked at her mother for confirmation. "Sure! I think I can dig up some cool new stuff. I will need access to the Internet and a way to get to the Historical Society everyday; if you can give me that then I would love to do it."

"Fantastic. We will see you here bright and early at 8 A.M. I have gone over all the details with your mom already over the phone, but if you have any questions, Odessa, feel free to ask."

Her mother chuckled, "Oh, don't worry; she will. The one thing she knows how to do is ask questions."

Both mother and daughter shook Ms. Mendel's hand and showed themselves out.

"Okay, Scott. Send in the last family."

A large black man in a black power suit entered the room with an aura of authority. A woman wearing a vibrant, colorful African Dashiki dress with a matching hajib followed him in. Lastly, Mohamed entered wearing a polo shirt and khakis. The two males were wearing traditional kofias, or Muslim prayer caps. All three made introductions and had a seat.

"Mr. and Mrs. Obuntu, thank you for bringing your son by for us to meet. I have really been looking forward to finally meeting your family."

Mr. Obuntu responded in a thick Ugandan-Kitara accent, "Thank you for your invitation. It is a big honor in my country of Uganda to be accepted in a top school. Education is very important to our family and we make sure our children study very hard. Mohamed's mother spends many hours a day making sure our children excel at their school work."

"You both have done an excellent job. A friend of the academy heard your son play some very difficult compositions and was impressed. I think your son would be perfect for our school."

Mohamed's parents ate up the flattery and smiled at each other.

Ruby continued, "This summer program would allow Mo to rapidly excel his skill level. He would be able to study any kind of music he chooses, as well as other instruments-"

Mr. Obuntu pointed his finger at Ruby as he as cut her off, "Please call my son Mohamed, not Mo. It is disrespectful to our prophet to abbreviate his name. Our boy needs a strict lesson plan. He is too young to decide what he gets to do on his own. I am afraid our son is too lazy and disorganized to be trusted to study without supervision. He will reach the age soon that he won't have time for music and needs to learn how to make money."

Ms. Mendel tried a different approach. "Part of his training emphasizes how to make money doing something he loves. What if we could show him how to make money with his music skills? Would that be acceptable?"

The skeptical Ugandan man scratched his beard and changed his mood. "How would our son use what he learns here to make money?"

"Well, most musicians fail because they don't know how to run a business or market themselves. They could be incredibly talented, but die penniless. We will show your son how to embrace new media like the Internet to get his music discovered."

Mrs. Obuntu finally chimed in. "Can you guarantee he will make some money playing music this summer?"

"Yes, and I will tell you how. Our academy needs a new music entertainer. He will be responsible for playing at school events and our alumni banquets. He will also find other avenues of making money with his talent that he will have to discover. In return, our school will give him food and board for the entire summer, as well as a small paycheck based on his profit margin."

Mohamed's parents locked eyes, judging telepathically how the other felt about the proposition. Both nodded in agreement. "So this would be a paid internship?" the Ugandan man summarized.

"Yes. Think of it like a summer job where he learns new and useful skills," Ruby resummarized.

Mr. Obuntu scratched his bearded chin again. "We are very practical and we believe education should also be profitable. If you can meet all of Mohamed's other needs, I think I will allow him to try your program."

"His needs?" Ruby questioned.

"He will have to check in with his mother every night in some form. We also demand that he strictly follow and observe all our laws and to attend Friday prayer at the Mosque. He will need a private place to pray five times a day and we need your chef to respect his dietary requirements. We expect him to behave like a proper Muslim boy and he should be supervised around all girls. Can you vow this will be done, Ms. Mendel?"

"We have had Muslim children at our school before, so I understand how important it is. We will see to it he follows what you ask us to do."

The powerful man warned, "I have to return to Uganda for the summer and can not bring my family with me. I expect you to stay in constant contact with my wife and let us know immediately if there are any problems."

"Of course, we will contact you immediately," the blonde woman in the sundress responded.

"Mohamed is too young to be trusted with his own money; any money he earns will be mailed directly to his mother, understood?" the father demanded.

"We can do that," Ruby smiled.

"Very good. Now thank this nice woman for accepting you into her school," Mr. Obuntu commanded his son.

"Thank you so much for this opportunity; I can't wait!" Mohamed said with excitement in his voice.

"Please drop him off with everything he needs for the summer at 8 tomorrow morning."

The family said their goodbyes and saw themselves out.

A tall, bald, skinny man entered.

"What did you think, Scott, of our new scholarship students?"

Scott cocked his head while he was thinking. "Well, I think they have potential, but it could also be a disaster. I hope you know what you are doing and did not just make some decisions that will hurt the school's reputation. The alumni fundraiser is just around the corner and I would be careful not to do anything that would jeopardize our funding."

Siblings, Ruby and Scott Mendel, Directors of the Mendel Academy.

"Again, I really hope you know what you are doing." Scott stated.

Ruby retorted, "Think of it on the positive side; if these kids do what I think they can do, it will inspire donors to give money like they never have before."

FIRST IMPRESSONS

The four Porcs finally arrived at the large, wooden door and were brimming over with excitement. Leo reached out to the slime-covered oak entrance and pulled on the handle. Mohamed stepped up, grabbed the knob, and joined forces to give it a strong yank. Odessa shined the last remaining light on their hands while the boys continued to pull the handle. After a full minute of straining, the boys slumped down against the hatch, exhausted.

Leo panted, "I need a break. We're not getting around this door until I have rested for a few minutes." The tall teen boy looked at Mohamed. "Sorry dude, for calling you Mo. I had no idea I was being disrespectful."

"That's my dad's hang-up, not mine. It is acceptable for modern Muslims, but my father is very traditional. Feel free to call me Mo as much as you want," Mohamed offered.

Odessa took charge again. "Do you guys remember the first day we met? Let's talk about that."

As 8 A.M. approached, three cars arrived at the front entrance of the Mendel Academy. A beat up 1970 Dodge Dart pulled up to the front of the lavish entrance first. The old Dart was brownish in color and had gray primer sprayed on a few Bondo-ed spots. The vinyl roof had almost completely flaked off due to years of exposure to Savannah's merciless sun. A large crack ran up the back of the signature concave rear windshield. A tiny girl hopped out of the passenger side door

then leaned back in to hug her momma. She reached towards the back of the car and wrangled out two large, black plastic trash bags full of clothes and accessories. Dragging the large Hefty bags out of the sun, she cleverly made a seat out of them. Krystal wiped the sweat off her forehead and made a joke to herself. "Man, Savannah's summers are so hot I saw a dog walkin' after a cat." The small girl amused herself and laughed, "That's good; I'll have to remember that one."

The next car in line was the new Mercedes S class with tinted windows. The Ugandan boy emerged from the back seat of the luxury vehicle wheeling a large, aluminum Samsonite suitcase behind him. Slung over his back like a broadsword was an aluminum trumpet case. He waved goodbye to his parents, joined the country girl in the shade, and sat on his expensive, reinforced suitcase like it was a chair.

The third car to arrive was an early '80s, wood-paneled station wagon. When the car stopped, a large woman helped her daughter with her bright pink bags. The bags were the latest rage in the early 1980s, but now they were way past their prime. She helped her daughter drag the pile of "like, totally awesome" mismatched collections of old Esprit, Le Sac, Jordache, and Sportsac luggage into the shade. The neon pink pile was a salute to her mom's yard-sale addiction. The round girl squeezed her helpful mother goodbye and kissed her on the cheek.

The last new student did not arrive by car. Instead, the tall, skinny teen wheeled up to the entrance of the academy on his antique skateboard carrying a large army duffle bag strapped tightly to his back. He had jet-black hair with long bangs hanging just over his right eye. His torn jeans were adorned with his own crude doodles he had drawn himself when he was bored in class. Draped across the enigmatic boy's hip was an old, canvas messenger satchel. On closer inspection, the aged shoulder bag had the words "Zombie Bug-Out Bag" carelessly scribbled in marker across the flap. He skated in alone and pulled up next to the other three.

The first day at the Mendel Academy.

"Hey!" Leo nodded his head at the group.

Mohamed replied, "Hi there, my name is Mo."

"Sup Mo; do you skate?"

"No, but I would like to try someday. I have really strict parents and they won't let me get near anything with wheels. They are worried I will break my knees and knock my teeth out," the African boy admitted.

Leo offered, "Well, your parents don't look like they are here, so maybe later I can show you how."

"I don't want to anger my father, but thank you anyway." Mohamed took in Leo's vintage punk rock outfit. "Do you mind if I ask you something? I can't figure out what the gray ribbon pinned to your shirt is for. I have seen purple ribbons for Alzheimer's awareness, gold ribbons for childhood cancer awareness, and green for Lyme disease awareness, but I have never seen a gray one. What is it for?"

Leo responded, "It's for zombie awareness month. Although it's May, I wear it all year long to remind me to be ever vigilant. I made it out of my late grandfather's silk tie."

A look of confusion shot over Mohamed's face as he processed Leo's answer.

The girl with strawberry-blonde braids interpreted the exchange and asked, "Hi there. Do y'all think we should just wait here until someone comes to pick us up?"

Odessa spoke up, "Ms. Mendel gave very clear instructions to wait here until it was time. We probably should follow the rules."

"Well, if we are just going to be sitting here waiting, let's greet each other. My name is Mohamed; this is my first summer here."

"Mine, too!" Odessa announced excitingly. "I read all about this place on the Internet; it is really impressive. The building has been around forever and was used as everything from a hospital to a hotel and even a funeral home in the past. It sat empty for years until siblings Mr. and Ms. Mendel opened up this school in it."

"Well, thank yuh girl for that! I don't think I really ever wanted to know I am sleepin' in a funeral home; now I am really filled up with da creepin' shivers." Krystal shook her hands down her body as if to wipe off the spookiness.

Odessa awkwardly reassured, "Oh, don't worry. It has been like a hundred years since dead bodies where burned in here."

Leo slyly smirked, "Well I think we all still know that you have to always be on the look out for zombies. Keep your ears open and don't explore any groaning noises in the basement. Just remember, what you don't know can eat you."

"Zombies? I think those all live in Haiti; we should be safe here in Savannah." Mohamed concluded.

"No man, zombies are everywhere. Always keep that in mind. We have to stay together till we find a cure or a large supply of fresh brains we can distract them with. You're never safe; they are always hungry and waiting for you to slip up," the punk rock kid reasoned.

Odessa pompously interrupted, "Let me clear this up: zombies don't really exist. There have been cases in Haiti where people were poisoned and they appeared dead. So the local residents would think they are dead and buried them. A few hours later when the poison wore off, the mistakenly buried people would appear to come back to life and would dig out of their graves. So, you see, real history can explain away the myths; there is no such thing as real zombies."

Leo angrily challenged, "You're wrong. There are stories of the walking-dead from every corner of the world. There are records of real zombie attacks throughout history. How do you know so much about the undead anyway?"

Wiki backed off. "Well, I did a report about zombies, so I did a lot of research." She extended her hand as a peace offering to diffuse the argument. "My name is Odessa, but my friends call me Wiki."

Leo nodded his head emotionlessly. "Hey, I am Leo. This ain't over; we'll pick this debate up later."

The three then turned their eyes on the small girl sitting on the trash bags. "Oh, hi y'all. My name is Krystal."

Leo put her on the spot, "Krystal, do you believe the zombie apocalypse is coming?

"Ummmm, I am not really sure. I never thought about it before. By the way, do yuh know if horses can become zombies, too? I am sorta two brains about this; a zombie horse would be pretty cool, but I don't think they'd jump very good and they probably would constantly be tryin' to bite yuh."

Before Leo could answer the hypothetical question, they were interrupted. "Welcome folks! My name is Mr. Mendel and I will be showing y'all to your rooms. Grab your gear and follow me, please."

Odessa panicked. "Um, Mr. Mendel? My bags don't have wheels; can you help me move this pile?"

Scott replied, "Sorry, Odessa, no disrespect intended, but your education starts right now. This is a lesson in teamwork and self-reliance. You need to solve your own problems anyway you want. You're supposed to be very creative; I bet you can figure out a way to get your bags in your room."

She looked at the new group of students. "Can you guys help me out?"

Mohamed stepped up. "My bag has wheels and is very strong. I can put your large bags on it and wheel them all in together, but you'll have to put them into your room by yourself. It would not be appropriate for me to enter a girl's room."

Krystal and Leo were too self-absorbed with their own baggage and ignored Odessa's dilemma. They only focused on dragging their own luggage in and left Mohamed and Wiki to figure it out.

Scott was grinning while observing the group of new Porcupines awkwardly fighting and dragging their gear to the stairs. "Hey, you two - Mo and Leo - you are sharing room 202 and you ladies are sharing 306. Meet me back down here in a half hour."

Leo instantly grew irritated. "Sharing? Dude, I need to have my own room. When I took this job I assumed I would have my own room for the summer."

Mr. Mendel replied, "I have not been called dude since I was fifteen; please call me Mr. Mendel. I guess you should have asked more questions before you said yes to this academy. This is the situation; take it or leave it."

"Fine, I'll sleep here today, but I am going to talk to Ruby about fixing this as soon as I see her."

"First of all, you are to call her Ms. Mendel. Second, I am pretty sure she will back me up on this, but you're welcome to try," he smirked.

A slow, rhythmic thumping could be heard as the boys dragged their heavy luggage up step by step. They triumphantly pulled the dead weight into their rooms and let the bags crash to the floor.

Instead of hauling everything up in one heavy load, the two girls treated the event like a shuttle race. They took shifts carrying up one bag at a time until everything was inside their room.

The young men's dorm room was small and plain. It looked more like a prison cell than a dorm room. It had a bunk bed and a closet with two dressers inside of it. Leo dove onto the bottom bunk and yelled, "Mine!"

Mohamed looked very annoyed by this gesture and pouted. "Aren't we going to flip a coin or something? I wanted the bottom bunk, too."

"Nope! You snooze, you loose," the boy with the jet-black hair sang.

Mohamed schemed within himself and then giggled. "Well, if that is how you want to do this, I guess it is fine. Oh, but just so you know, I will be eating extra dairy tonight at dinner. Milk products make me very gassy, but I am sure the smell won't keep you up. You'll also be seeing my feet in your face every morning for my sunrise prayer. Hope you sleep hard enough that my recitation won't wake you."

"Oh, awesome. Hope I can find some earplugs around here somewhere," Leo said snidely.

Meanwhile, in room 306, the girls had solved their own bed dilemma without having to result to biological warfare. "So I was thinking, we both want the top bunk; I think I know a way we can both have it," Wiki proposed.

"How?" Krystal queried.

Wiki laid her plan out. "We rotate and switch beds every Sunday after we do laundry. That way we both get the top bed equal times."

"*Hmmmm*, that sounds a might fair. Sorta has a 'King Solomon' feel to it. Okay, yuh go ahead and take it the first week. Let's hurry up and unpack so we can get to our tour. I can't wait to see what kinda horses they got here."

12 CHAPTER

TOUR OF THE MENDEL ACADEMY

Leo smiled, "Well that seems like a life time ago, but I know it was just a few days ago. I guess time is flying by. Okay, let's figure this door out. Odessa, can you shine a light on this handle better; maybe there is a lock or something I am not seeing."

Wiki decided to keep Krystal distracted while Leo searched the door saying, "Do you guys remember our tour of the school?"

The four young adults finished unpacking and stood around at the bottom of the stairs waiting for Ms. Mendel to arrive. "Let me show you around our school."

She started walking through the old-world, elaborate woodwork. "We are a private school of only fifty students. Each of the students are exceptional in their own area of focus. We believe when children are born, they love learning. It takes years of forcing kids to study things they don't like or will never use to extinguish that natural drive. This academy is trying to reverse that trend in society by allowing students to teach themselves. Most educators refer to this idea as unschooling."

Ruby escorted them to a large dining hall. "We are very proud of our cooking program. We have found some of the finest student cooks in the Lowcountry and allow them to explore their passion. They can run their kitchens anyway they please and it allows them to experiment with ideas before they open their own restaurants in the real world. The student chefs are given a budget and they design their own menus. If they don't stick to their budget they have to spend their own profits to make up the difference, or folks don't eat. They can raise any personal funds they want outside this facility to keep as a profit for themselves."

The blonde woman in the sundress walked over to a tray of scones. "Here, try one of their amazing scones. Some of the Porcupine chefs have done quite well selling these to hotels and restaurants all over Savannah. It is hard work and the bakers here work over fourteen hours a day, but they don't seem to mind. The culinary crew is one of the most profitable ventures our school has and is a very competitive program to be accepted into."

The touring children grabbed the scones and tore into them. Audible moans of approval resonated from the group of new Porcs. "*Mmmmmmmm*...these are fantastic," Odessa mumbled with a full mouth.

Ruby waved her hand. "Come on; it is time we see our media department." The small group cut through a maze of hallways and arrived at a large oak door. Ms. Mendel looked at a little, red flashing light above the door that said, "On Air." "Sorry, it looks like they are recording and we can't go in. Take a look through this window here instead." The students peered through the window and saw three high school aged kids debating into a microphone.

"Oh, this must be your radio station I read about," Wiki mused.

"Yep, we are very proud to put in 8 hours of original programming a day. The students develop their own shows and each get a one-hour time slot. They must figure out how to make their shows lucrative. Some sell ads like a traditional radio station. Others use the time to record podcasts that they can then put out on the Internet. A few solely survive on donations and subscriptions. It is quite an unusual collection of productions. Some are gossip shows about teenage interests. Others are more daring like our sketch comedy troop. They also range from student-authors making hour long novellas to music and game reviews."

"Wow, I would love to get my music on one of those shows!" Mohamed exclaimed.

"Don't worry; if you are as good as you are supposed to be, they will find you. We also have some pupils who prefer video and filmmaking. They mainly publish directly to the Internet, but we do host a film festival once a year where they show off their stuff to the local public. Of course, they also have to find creative ways to earn a profit using this new media, or their venture is shut down and they have to try again with something new. Now, let me show you our acclaimed business department."

The eager children followed the head master into a large, open ballroom. "We use this space to allow children to explore business ideas. All you have to do is present us with a good business plan and we help get you started." She pointed to a corner of a room covered with large paintings.

"Over there is a student artist who paints old photos and sells his paintings online. If you look over in that corner you will see a stack of elaborate birdhouses and pet beds. That particular girl designs and creates custom, high-end pet houses and beds. You might also see her wonderful aviary creations all over campus as she tests them against the heat and weather. Currently, she is trying to make a stylish Purple Martin condo and we think it will be a very good seller."

What are Purple Martins?" Leo asked.

Ms. Mendel explained, "They are very useful birds. People around the world try to attract them so the birds will nest in their yards. They are beautiful and eat a ton of pesky bugs."

Odessa butted in, "The Native Americans used old, hollow gourds and would hang them up to attract the Martins. Through hundreds of years of this practice, the Purple Martins are now completely dependent on humans to make their nest cavities for them. There is a movement around the world to help these birds by encouraging people to put up Martin boxes in their yards."

Purple Martin box.

Leo snidely commented, "I see why they nicknamed you Wiki. You do seem to know answers to very random questions."

Ms. Mendel shot Leo a look. "Very good, Odessa. This student saw a need and designed a profitable solution. Her online sales are excellent and she is backed up on orders for six months already."

"You will also see some other business ideas students are trying. "At this desk is a group of high school students who do faux painting. The painting techniques are so good they trick the brain into thinking it is a different material. A good example would be those columns over there. They look like very expensive marble columns, but are actually made of cheap wood. This group of artistic students is making great money doing this all over Savannah and Tybee Island."

"Then we have one of our more imaginative businesses. This student here hosts flash skate mobs and makes money by throwing skating parties. He has designed his own mobile roller park and all his ramps and half pipes can be easily assembled just about anywhere. He has a cool, new, secret location he sets up every weekend and hosts his own private skate park. The teenager is excellent at social networking and his events are always crowed," Ms. Mendel explained.

Leo paid homage. "I have been to those roller raves; they're totally awesome. I wish I had thought of that."

"The businesses constantly change here and new stuff is tried all the time. Most people's first businesses fail a few times, but they keep trying until they find one that works. Now let me take you to the area you guys will mostly be working in," the older blonde woman said as she took the group to the estate's enormous backyard.

"Hot Darn! Look at those stables! I'm as anxious as a one-eyed cat watch'n two rat holes!" Krystal exclaimed. "It is amazin' that yuh have miniature paddocks and riding rings all in this area so close to downtown Savannah."

"I agree. We can't believe we found such a large chunk of property in Savannah either. I guess the fact that it had a darker history scared off other buyers. We are not real superstitious; I feel we got it for a steal."

Krystal was struck slack jawed as a gigantic draft horse walked in her view and began eating sweetgrass at the fence line.

Ruby continued, "Well, I am glad you approve of our equine faculties, Miss Bennett, because you will be spending most of your time out here. We are very proud of our carriage tour program and it has been very successful until the last two years. I expect you guys to help turn that around. I am confident, with the help of Odessa's amazing research skills and your horsemanship skills, you girls will do something really special. You two are going to develop a new history tour that will bring profit back into the carriage program and keep it from closing down."

"Come along, I want you to meet your mentor."

13 CHAPTER

JAH LOKO

The group escaped the heat and walked into the main barn. Inside, attached to a carriage, was a giant draft horse drinking water. "Jah! Are you in here?" Ruby shouted. A large, sweetgrass hat popped up from around the side of the buggy. "Yes, Miss Ruby, jus' waterin' me haw'ss Harricane and cleanen dis yez."

"Weh hunnuh dag wine?" Ms. Mendel questioned in a strange language.

"Yu be talk'um goodfashion, Miss Ruby. I be gone'way 'nodduh tour n ten minutes," Jah Loko replied in the same odd language.

Odessa interrupted, "Is that Gullah you two are speaking? I've never heard it spoken before."

"Very good, Titi. Yes, I'm Gullah. I tol' Miss Ruby I was givin' water to my haw'ss, Hurricane and cleanin' out his ears. Then Miss Ruby asked where was I goin' and I tol' her I was goin' on another tour in ten minutes," the old black man in the sweetgrass hat replied.

"Umm, what is Gullah?" Mohamed questioned.

Wiki took it upon herself to answer for Jah Loko. "The Gullah is a large culture group of African slave descendants who live in the Lowcountry. Eighty percent of the Gullah slaves in Charleston and Savannah came through a famous British slave castle called Bunce Island in the African country of Sierra Leone. Today, their culture is rich with art and history. Interest in Gullah culture is growing very fast through festivals, books, and artwork. They still try very hard to preserve their own distinct traditions and language."

Jah Loko and his horse Harricane.

"Dat was very good, Titi. I am impressed yu know so much about me ancestry. I don't speak Gullah too often anymore because da tourist get a might confused. So I will try to remember to speak da king's tongue with ya," Jah explained.

"What does 'Titi' mean?" Odessa asked?

The old man smiled at the two young ladies. "Oh, it be a nice way to say "little girl" in my language."

Ruby dropped her hand in a formal motion. "Jah, let me introduce your new help. This stable hand here is Miss Krystal and you already met our new history expert, Miss Odessa. I want you to take them out with you today and show them the ropes. Over here is Mr. Leo, he will be your new grounds keeper and gardener. Please take him along to explain to him ideas you have for growing our own hay for Harricane and the other horses."

The last gentleman here is Mr. Mohamed. I want you to take him with y'all today to see how the tours work, too. Perhaps he can throw in some ideas that might help. I will see you four at dinnertime. Your first assignment is to take what you see out there today and figure out why it is not making a profit like it should."

The blonde woman in the sundress hurried back inside to get out of the heat before her make-up ran down her cheeks.

The four sweating Porcs stared intently at Jah Loko, waiting for directions. "Well chillun, I mean children, might as well get up into the buggy," the old man offered.

Krystal pushed past the other three children and yelled, "Shotgun! I get to sit up front."

Wiki interjected with an unsolicited historical story. "Funny you should call shotgun when we are about to take a carriage ride. These days people yell "shotgun" to claim the front passenger seat in a car, but 'riding shotgun' is a very old concept. People had to carry guns everywhere with them in the old west and colonial days to protect themselves. So the passenger seat at the front of the wagon was traditionally reserved for a guard who carried a shotgun to protect everyone. I find it uber cool that you are using the historically accurate term for riding shotgun right now."

Krystal pushed past her and claimed the prized seat. "Umm, thanks for that completely unnecessary story. Harricane looks like a well mannered horse; can I pet him?"

"O'course, Miss Krystal. He likes bein' scratched wid ya nails da most." The rest of the group loaded onto the buggy and relaxed while the tomboy ran her chewed nails behind the draft horse's ears. Then the mammoth equine pulled the group effortlessly toward downtown Savannah.

Mohamed whipped out a small notebook and searched his body for a pen. "I want to take notes on the tour today, but I forgot my pen. Does anyone have one I can use?"

Krystal offered, "I got a #2 pencil you can use." She pulled a knife-sharpened pencil from her overalls' chest pocket.

The Muslim boy stared at the pencil with a confused look. "I don't understand this country. If 99% of people use a #2 pencil, then why don't they just call it a #1?"

The question stumped the group and they exchanged puzzled looks. The African boy continued, "And what happened to single A and B size batteries? They have AA, AAA, C, and D, but no A or B. What does your country have against these size cells?"

The moving carriage of students pondered his deep questions, and then shrugged their shoulders.

He continued his line of questioning. "Also, why do Americans park in a driveway, but drive in a parkway? The English language makes no sense sometimes."

Krystal cut his hard-to-answer questions off with a frustrated groan. "Because America has their own way of doing things; that's what makes us so great. Now, if yuh don't stop askin' anti-American questions, I'll have to take my pencil back."

The Porcs giggled at Krystal's mocking, ethnocentric answer.

Jah spoke up and changed the topic. "I liked your story, Titi Odessa, and I can tell ya more about shotguns back then if ya want."

Odessa was taken aback that someone had given her positive feedback for one of her stories. She had no idea what to say to a compliment, so instead she just nodded yes.

"Although folks been stuffin' shot into rifles since the 1700s, da shotgun was really not in use till after the War of Northern Aggression in the 1850s."

"You mean the Civil War?" Odessa challenged. He bit back saying, "I said what I meant, Titi. Dat war was for southern independence, despite what your skoo' books say, but we can get into dat deeper some other time." Jah then waved his hand to dismiss the topic. "Anyway, da shotgun became so useful in da Wild West dat just about everyone started carrying dem." Odessa listened intently about the shotgun history while the sounds of horseshoes striking cobblestones rang through the air.

Jah went back into a calm teaching voice. "Double barrel shotguns were 'specially prized since dey could be loaded wid two diff'rnt kinds of shot. One barrel'd be stuffed with tiny balls of metal ta hunt birds. Da other barrel'd be loaded wid larger balls ta shoot big game. Guns were extremely important tools back den. Widout a good gun, most folks'd starved ta death. Also, if ya were out in da wild west, ya could not exactly pick up a phone and call da police back den if ya be in trouble. Ya protected yourself."

The story piqued Mohamed's interest. "I have seen all the Hollywood western movies; wasn't it was so violent back then because everyone owned a gun?"

The Gullah man countered. "Well, Mr. Mohamed, da movies want ta make da stories exciting, so dey play up da killin'. Real history is much less violent. In fact, da Wild West wasn't so wild at all. If ya compare da most murderous town back den to a modern city like Baltimore, Maryland, ya'd be surprised. Any average year da murder rate per person is thirty-six times greater den da most murdering town in da old west. So, ya should be a lot more scared ta live in Baltimore den Tombstone," he said as he laughed at his own morbid joke.

The old tour guide concluded, "Despite what da Hollywood shows ya, a well-armed society be a polite society.

Da fact dat everyone had guns back den made da criminals think twice 'bout robbin' folks. It was a much safer time back den, compared ta now.

Okay, chillun, we be here. Dis be our first stop ya need ta be knowin'. I plans on teachin' ya 'bout some important sites of Savannah." The crew surveyed the area. A lush green square scattered with ancient live oaks was sprawled out in front of them.

"Dis be Wright Square. It be famous for da grave of da great Indian Chief Tomochichi. The chief help make peace wit da local Indians when da British invaded Georgia and founded da town of Savannah. So loved was da chief by da founder of Georgia, General Ogelthorpe, dat he got a full military funeral right here in dis square almost three hundred years ago. Oglethorpe promised da Creek Indian tribe dat people would always know his name. Only a hundred years later dat promise be broken and his grave be desecrated."

"That is messed up. Did they at least dig up his body and move him first, or just move the headstone and leave the body behind? I sure hope they moved him first to make sure he would not come back as an angry zombie because they replaced his grave with some rich dudes," Leo warned.

Harricane lumbered around the square as Jah grew surprisingly serious. "It was o'er one hundred years ago, but da Central Railroad built dat monument dere ta honor dere founder Mista William Washington Gordon. And while it's a grand monument, in order ta build it, dey had ta remove da original grave dat was dere. Da Creek Indian chief Tomochichi was buried dere in da center under a pyramid o'rocks, as was da tradition of da Creek people. Removin' his grave was a direct n' final insult ta da Indians, as some years earlier da same railroad desecrated and destroyed two of dere ancient burial mounds. Da workers was takin' home Indian bones and da offerin's to da gods dat da Creek had buried wit dere dead."

Jah stopped at the great granite rock and finished his tale. "Dis man dey be honorin' wit dat monument had a daughtah-in-law. She weren't none too happy wit da way da Central Railroad be treatin' da Creek people and didn't want God ta hold her family responsible for defilin' graves. Miss Nellie Kinzie Gordon and da Georgia Society's Colonial Dames of America bought dat piece'o granite from da Stone Mountain and put it dere. Now, da tourist tink dat be da place where Tomochichi be buried, but us locals know better den dat. We know Tomochichi's spirit be hauntin' dis square because his restin' place was disturbed all dose years ago."

The children became focused on the old superstitious man as he learned in to speak quietly. "If ya show Tomochichi respect, he will answer any question ya ask 'em. But he only answers ya if ya ask 'em da right way!"

Leo leaned back into the old man. "How do you ask him? How does one talk to the dead?"

The Gullah tour guide questioned them in a surprised tone. "You chillun don't knows? I thought e'ry chil' growin' up in Savannah know. Ya must run around da rock three times yellin' da chief's name. Oh, and ya have ta do it runnin' backward," he shared in hushed tones.

"Man, I have so many questions for that ghost; how much time do we have?" Leo mocked.

"Mr. Leo, ya should not make fun of dat; ya da not understand. Us Gullah take spirits very seriously. Ya don't wanna be makin' light of da dead or ya anger dem. Ya should learn ta be respectful, boy."

Leo nodded in apologetic way. "I will try to watch what I say around you, Jah."

"If ya be respectful, I will let ya meet da chief tonight. He be easier ta talk ta after da sun go down. Now, tis time to see some of da sights 'round Savannah, so ya can learn what da tour does.

Da next stop be Forsyth Park. Dere is some very ghastly hist'ry dere. Y'all might not be ol' enough ta hear all da bad and scary tings dat happened dere," the man in the sweetgrass hat warned.

14 CHAPTER

SAVANNAH'S DIRTY SECRETS

The Porcs breathed in the stale air as they stood in the tepid, stinky mud puddles and stared at the large imposing door.

"Did you hear that noise again? Sounds like it's getting closer," Mohamed warned the group.

Odessa continued to deny the faint noises. "You guys, there are no such things as ghosts. I think what you're hearing is the sound of groundwater seeping into the tunnel. Let's not forget we are probably below sea level and we live on the coast of the Atlantic Ocean," Wiki concluded with a sarcastic tone.

Leo sighed aloud. "I am stumped! I cannot figure a way around this old door. It is still surprisingly strong after all these years."

Mohamed tapped into his vast nerd math knowledge. "Maybe we can use some of the boards from the tunnel walls to build a lever and pry this entrance open."

Odessa snapped him back to reality. "Look, Archimedes, if you start harvesting the wood from the supports to build fulcrums and levers, you will collapse this passage and drown us all!"

After hearing the phrase "you will collapse this passage and drown us all," Krystal's fear started to completely over take her. "I think we need to head back and come down here another day. Let's turn around and come back better prepared."

Wiki was too close to her prize to give up now. She knew she had to keep Krystal calm till they figured out a way around the forbidding portal. Not wanting to give up yet, she distracted Krystal. "Do you guys remember our big day out with Jah?"

The mammoth horse and tour carriage arrived at Forsyth Park. The huge, rectangular green-space was loaded with ancient, live oak trees that sprawled across its thirty acres. Spanish moss dangled on the huge oak branches like tinsel on a Christmas tree. Large fields rolled across the middle of the park and were being enjoyed by sunbathers and rugby players.

The old man pointed out the group of men and women passing around a large, oblong ball. "Dose are rugby players ya see out dere. Savannah hosts one of da countries largest n' oldest rugby tournaments on St. Patti's day weekend."

"That game looks so cool. I can't wait to finally be old enough to play next year," Leo dreamed.

The man in the sweetgrass hat continued. "Da world famous St. Patti's day parade also goes around dis park. Many concerts, weddin's, and events happen here every year."

Odessa bubbled over with curiosity. "So what dark things happened here that you think we are too young to know?"

"I really not be sure ya chillun are old enough yet ta hear da horror stories dat happened here," Jah joked with the four kids.

"We can handle it, right guys?" Wiki looked to the other students for support.

The group all mumbled in agreement and began pestering Jah Loko into telling his tale.

"Okay, chillun, but don't be tellin' ya parents I tol' ya dis. Forsyth Park is one big graveyard. All da folk walkin' 'round and playin' don't know dey be treadin' o'er dead men's graves.

Savannah is called da world's most haunted city for good reason."

The group of students exchanged spooked-out and frightened looks at each other. Jah knew he had their full attention and continued. "In colonial times, da end of dis park be a duelin' ground. Folks who done angered each other come 'ere and fight to da death. But dat little bit a'dyin' don't mean much compared t'what happen' 'round da war and durin' da yellow plagues. Under dis park is a maze of tunnels; most of ol' Savannah has tunnels under it. Dey made dis park bigger right 'round da time of da War for Southern Independence."

Mohamed cut in, "You mean the Civil War?"

Jah snapped back. "I know what I be callin' it, boy." The Gullah man continued. "Durin' dat great war, disease, and death visited da troops campin' at dis park. At first da soldiers started buryin' da fallen bodies all over dees grounds. Den so many soldiers be dyin' dat dey just toss'd da bodies in da tunnels and mass graves. They built dat big statue dere in da middle on dat hill ta stop people from snoopin' and diggin in dat area."

Cold shivers ran up the young student's spines as the tour guide continued. "Savannah be da victim 'a three major yellow fever outbreaks. Da first in 1820 killed six hundred and sixty-six people and folks blamed it as da devils doin'. Dere is a mass grave for dat outbreak at Colonial Park Cemetery a few blocks from dis park. Later, in da plague of 1876, dey built a secret tunnel from dat hospital over dere down ta dat womens' hospital on da south end of da park." Jah first pointed at a run-down looking hospital adorned with a gigantic live oak and a plaque that read Warren A. Candler Hospital then pointed down to the south end of the park where another similar structure sat. "Da yellow fever was killin' folks so fast dat da city tol' da hospital to hide da deaths from da public. Da city knew dat if folks foun' out how many people da yellow fever really done took, it would cause a panic. So dat hospital dug out an underground morgue and more secret tunnels ta dispose of all da dead bodies under da park where nobody could see dem. Da outbreak got so bad dat dey didn't even wait for some of da victims ta die. Dey locked over one hundred live, infected people in dat passageway and let dem all die down dere."

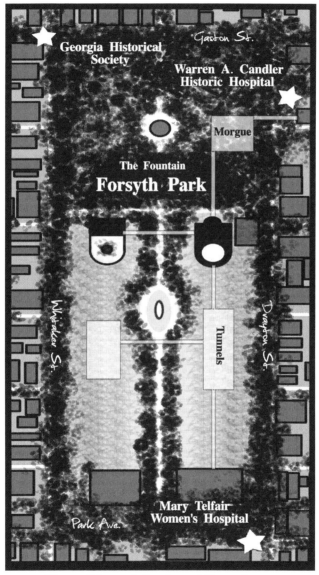

Map of Forsyth Park and Tunnels

Odessa officially became completely frightened. "You mean the hos   pital and city murdered all those sick people to keep yellow fever from breaking out worse?"

"Titi, da city or hospital never admitted dey did da horrible acts, but some of da people doing da deeds let da secret slip out. All da evidence is dere if one looks hard enough. Dis park be one of da most haunted places in all da world."

"Holy cow! I will never be able to enjoy another evenin' of movies and music here ever again; thanks a lot, Mr. Loko!" Krystal sarcastically announced.

The zombie-obsessed fourteen-year-old boy warned, "Dude, there has to be so many walking-dead down there; they better keep those tunnels really locked up tight."

Jah ignored Leo and changed the subject. "Alright, I tink I scared ya chillun enough. Let's go get some lunch at da Pirates' House Restaurant." The kid's minds quickly shifted from zombie-filled secret burial tunnels to lunch.

The odd group of five made their way through a maze of ancient, cobblestoned back streets. They slowly turned back onto pavement when they saw a cylinder of fire from a torch shooting into the air. A sign in front of the flames read "The Pirates' House" in old English font.

The Gullah man spoke up. "Dis buildin' is huge and tis made up of some very old, small structures up front 'n' more modern structures were built out in da back. The parkin' lot and surroundin' areas is built over da historic Trustee's Garden. Da garden was an expensive exper'ment ta grow food and plants from all o're da world when da English first settled 'ere almos' three hundred years ago. Now it's a parkin' lot wid some buildin's and a grass field. We'll put Harricane in da shade over dere while we eat. I gotsa nice spot set up for him wid some water and feed. Da owners of da Pirates' House are very nice ta us and let us park in da grass over dere."

Krystal dismounted and helped hitch the draft horse in a cool, breezy location. Once the equine was secured well, the crew strolled into the large restaurant. The little country girl confessed, "I know I have lived outside of Savannah my whole life, but I've never been in here; only just driven by. I'm happier than a newborn tick on a fat hound. I always wanted to eat here."

"I've never been here either," the Ugandan boy admitted.

Odessa cut in with her know-it-all attitude saying, "This is my thirty-third time here. I can give you a better tour than the pirate that works here." In her typical, presumptuous style, Odessa started her unsolicited tour. "To the right of the front desk is the original building of the Pirates' House. It was an inn built shortly after Savannah was founded." She pointed to a crooked little house that was now a dining area that the restaurant enveloped. "That little section over there is the Herb House. It is the oldest house in all of Georgia; it is on the national historical registry and everything. They left the house where it was and just built the restaurant around it. It is so hard to believe that tiny room was an entire family's house back then."

"Very good, Titi. I see why Miss Ruby gave ya a scholarship for hist'ry," Mr. Loko said and nodded his head in approval.

The overweight, curly-haired girl turned bright red and blushed; she was not used to getting compliments.

A bubbly waitress interrupted them, "My name is Jena! Let me get y'all a seat. Oh, hi Odessa! Are you back again? Is it already your birthday?"

"No birthday, Jena. I just love this place. Can you please seat us in the original section right next to the secret Shanghai closet? I love that table," Wiki begged.

"I think we can arrange that for our most loyal customer," Jena winked.

The group was seated in the oldest part of the restaurant. It was nearing three hundred years of use and still had most of its original woodwork.

"What is the secret Shanghai closet?" Leo questioned the history nerd.

"Do you see the wall there by the fire place?" the Greek girl pointed.

Leo shrugged his shoulders. "Yea, I see it. So what?"

Wiki smiled a devilish grin. "Look closely at it. Do you see a tiny doorway or hatch cut into the right side of the wooden wall? It really blends in; look for the little latch and you will see it."

The punk kid stared and searched the wall for a minute, but did not see it. He finally took Odessa's advice and searched for the latch first. Suddenly, he saw an out-of-place black latch on the surface. Immediately, the frame of the small door finally appeared plain as day to him. "Dang! How did I miss that before? I never even noticed it and I have sat at this very table twice in the past. Interesting that they would hide a secret door in plain view."

The old man finally cut in, "Dat little hatch has a dark secret, chillun. Da pirates would bribe da bartenders ta drug people who were drinking. Da drugged folks would pass out cold and da bartenders would take da sleeping bodies and stuff dem in dat secret lil' hatch. When da tavern closed, dey would pull da bodies out and sell dem to da pirates. Da pirates would sneak da bodies outta dat secret tunnel under dere to a boat waitin' down by da river. Da po', hung-over souls would wake up a day later aboard a pirate ship and be forced ta work as one of da crew or try to swim home."

Wiki cut Jah off and said, "Sometimes the smuggling vessels would go around the world as far as Shanghai. So they nicknamed the kidnappings and referred to it as 'being Shanghaied'."

The group sat quietly and stared at the inconspicuous hatch on the wall. Mohamed finally spoke up. "I hate to be the one to say it, but that is pretty awesome. To think we are sitting so close to such an interesting piece of history. Do they really have pirate smuggling tunnels under the Pirates' House?"

The Greek girl beat Jah to the punch. "They sure do. If you go right outside this room you will see some very old steps that lead to the original rum cellar. There is a haunted tunnel that leads down to the river in there. You can also see right down into the tunnel if you stand right next to the Herb House."

Jena, the waitress, returned and interrupted their discussion to take their orders.

Jah Loko pulled out the academy's credit card. "Dis meal is on da school, chillun', so eat up." The kids all smiled at each other and dove into their menus.

Krystal grinned ear to ear. "I am hungrier than a hostage. I would like your most expensive steak and bring me a dessert menu please!"

When their food arrived, they all ate like they'd never seen food before. Mohamed moaned as he rubbed his full belly while he walked to the buggy. "I think I ate so much dessert I just gave myself diabetes!"

"Yuh know, in the country we call havin' diabetes 'gettin' the sugars'. So if yuh ever leave the city, yuh might need to know that if yuh want to crack that joke," Krystal giggled at her own advice.

The tomboy helped the slow, old man get the carriage ready to go and everyone loaded in.

"Next stop, chillun, is da oldest graveyard left in Savannah."

15 CHAPTER

COLONIAL PARK CEMETERY
&
TOMOCHICHI'S ROCK

The dark, wet passage really started to gnaw at Krystal's nerves. "Look, I would really like to just turn around and get out of this place. I am hot, stinky, wet, and we can't get through this giant door. I can hardly breathe in here. Let's call it quits and get topside."

Odessa, not wanting to leave, made an excuse. "I think I dropped my retainer; my mom will kill me if I don't find it. Look, let's finish the story about Jah's tour and then we will head up. Fellas, while I look for my mouth piece, you guys keep working on opening that door." The tomboy conceded. "Fine, finish your stories while we look for this tooth-straightenin' device. Did yuh know the toothbrush was invented in rural Georgia?"

Wiki pondered, "No, I never heard that; how do you know it was invented in Georgia's countryside?"

"Because if it was invented anywhere else, it would have been called a teethbrush!" the farm girl howled, laughing at her own joke.

Odessa shook her head. "I can't believe I set you up for that and walked right into it. You know what? I am just going to go back to telling the story."

Harricane towed the group down some twists and turns and arrived quickly in front of a six-acre graveyard. "Dis is da second known graveyard in Savannah. Da first was in da corner of Wright Square where we were earlier wid Tomochichi's rock. Folks buried so many bodies in da first days of Savannah dat dey quickly run out of room in dat square. So da city made dis graveyard which is now called Colonial Park Graveyard," the old man informed.

"Is it true, Jah, about the number of people buried here? You know, about how there are only six hundren grave stones, but the underground ultrasound showed over nine thousand skeletons?" Odessa questioned grimly.

The man in the sweetgrass hat spoke in hushed tones. "It be true, Titi. Grave markers and stones were expensive. Many people were buried in da same grave. It was custom to reuse da same spots over and over. After a body done decay for ten years, da tomb could be used again. Dey kept buryin' peoples here all da way up to da Northern War of Aggression. So many of dese graves been disturbed and dug up, causing dis to be da most haunted area of da most haunted city in da world."

Odessa educated the rest of the group. "Do you guys see all the grave stones set up against the wall over there?" She pointed to an old brick wall with broken grave markers bolted on to it. "All those gravestones were vandalized or simply knocked down when General Sherman's troop camped in this graveyard during the Civil War." The Gullah man huffed and shot the Greek girl a nasty look.

"Oh right. Sorry, Jah. I mean the War for Southern Independence, not the Civil War, or whatever name we are calling it today." The old man nodded his head with his approval and she carried on. "Well, the Union troops knocked over and destroyed many of the grave markers here. Since people did not know where the original gravesites were, they just pinned the loose tombstones to that wall. It has been over 150 years since that war and people down here are still mad about this massive display of blatant disrespect here on this wall from the northern troops."

"We have lots to see today, chillun; we can come back 'ere some udder' day. It is startin' ta get late and we gots ta get movin' if y'all goin' ta be back for supper." The old man pushed the carriage on. The group of young adults spent the rest of the afternoon learning about Savannah's historic squares. As the sun set, Jah drove the students down to River Street. The carriage became extremely bumpy as the thin wheels maneuvered across the large cobblestones. "I know y'all probably been down ta River Street ta shop, eat, or get some candy, but lots o' history took place here. Dis be da landin' spot of da first settlers. Everythin' from old pirates and gigantic supertankers been down dis historic river. Y'all can see even old and new artwork up and down da street." He pulled up to a statue of a girl waving a sheet over her head and standing next to a collie dog. "Dis here is my favorite artwork. Dis was made ta honor Savannah's famous Wavin' Girl. She was the daughter of the lighthouse watchman and she waved ta every ship dat came in for many, many years. She was so loved by sailors dey used ta bring her gifts from all around da world."

Leo interrupted, "That is some interesting history, but what is most important about this statue is that it is the meet-up point for Savannah's famous Zombie Crawl."

The carriage exchanged confused looks until Mohamed spoke up. "What is a Zombie Crawl?"

Leo replied with passion in his voice, "Hundreds of people dress up like zombies and for one scary night, they invade River Street. I can't believe y'all have never been to the Zombie Crawl. It's loads of fun."

Kyrstal smirked, "Shouldn't you really call it a Zombie Stagger to be more correct?"

The group of Porcs giggled at the joke. "Come on, chillun. It's startin' ta get dark. It be time ta get ya back for ya supper," Jah said. The old man then led the buggy back out of the rocky road and onto the paved streets.

As nightfall approached, Odessa spoke up. "Mr. Loko? You said we could go back to Tomochichi's grave at sunset and ask him a question. Can we still do that? Something has been bugging me and I want to ask him something."

"I can drive by, but y'alls have to be quick. Just ask your question and go." Jah accommodated. The carriage made its way back to Tomochichi's rock and Wiki hopped off and waved to the group. "Come on guys. Let's go ask him a question."

Tomochichi's Rock

Mohamed spoke up. "My parents are very strict Muslims and I am sure they would not agree with me being involved in this sorcery. I do not believe in ghosts, but I do believe in spirits called jinn, or what you might call a genie. They are not spirits of the dead. They are free willed entities, but will occasionally impersonate the dead to make a point. Sometimes jinn are mischievous and sometimes they are messengers for Allah. It can be difficult to tell between the two. I don't want to go messing with the spirit realm today."

Krystal added, "I agree. My momma is Pentecostal and quite superstitious. I think she might get mad, too. I'ma stay here with Mo."

Odessa shot a look of desperation at Leo. "Well, are you coming at least?"

Although the punk kid really wanted to do anything that revolved around the undead, he was more worried at how ridiculous he would look doing the silly ceremony. Leo shrugged his shoulders like he was too cool to be involved in such a thing. "Meh," he said, "this all sounds super lame to me."

Wiki grunted. "Fine, I will go alone." She made her way to the large granite rock while the carriage continued slowly to circle around Wright Square. The Greek girl spoke her question quietly and nobody but her could hear what it was. Then she started the sacred ritual of running backwards around the rock.

The group on the buggy got a great chuckle at the site of Odessa yelling "Tomochichi" at the top of her lungs and trying to run backwards around the rock. As she chanted, Odessa ran past a few confused tourists who obviously had never heard of the local ritual. The bewildered tourist's stares, of course, made the scene even funnier to the other students. They howled with laughter as Odessa climbed back in the carriage.

"Thanks for that, Wiki. I really needed a good laugh to brighten up this boring day," Leo smirked.

"Shut up! You are just too chicken to let other people see you doing something foolish," she barked back.

"Did ya gets an answer from the him, Titi?" Jah asked in all seriousness.

Odessa blushed with embarrassment. "Um, no, I did not hear an answer."

"Well, da dead have lotsa different ways dey be answerin' da livin'. Keep ya senses open da next few days and da answer will present itself to ya."

The other three Porcs continued to poke fun at the Greek girl on the return trip to the stable. Krystal stayed behind and helped Jah break down Harricane's tack while the other three returned to their rooms to change out of their sweaty clothes.

In a short time, the group of four misfit students made their way to the dining hall. They quickly discovered this was much more like a restaurant than a school cafeteria. The crew of students were then greeted by a host and shown to a table.

The host informed them how dinner worked. "Since this is your first time, each of you will be allotted a certain budget for dinner. The amount of money you get will be based on the amount of work you have done that day. You can spend your budget anyway you see fit. Here is a menu and your money." The host placed a menu in front of each person. He then handed each of them a small bag of coins.

The confused group of misfit children opened their menus and was stunned by all the choices. "Holy cow, there are like thirty things I can order here. This is way better than my school's egg-roll Thursday's and fish-stick Friday's. And look how cheap everythin' is; it is priced in dimes. These steak nachos are only forty cents!" Krystal explained with excitement.

Mohamed questioned, "These prices can't be right? This makes no sense; why are things so cheap?" He opened his small bag containing five old dimes.

The host smiled and explained, "Take a good look at those dimes, you will see they are all pre-1964. Most coins before 1964 are made of ninety percent silver. So, with silver prices what they are today, those five dimes are actually worth about $20. We try not to use paper money at the academy. The school has a policy to only use real money like copper, silver, or gold when we do business with each other. The groups of students who run the restaurant have decided to set prices in silver dimes to make it easier for everyone."

"Wow, so these are real silver coins...I kinda don't want to spend them now and just want to keep them," Leo confessed.

The host understood. "When I first got paid in silver I wanted to horde them too; but after you see it being used everyday all around this school, you realize it is okay to spend them because you will get more shortly. So, have fun tonight and spend away; you will get more silver tomorrow."

Krystal did not wait. She slapped down all her coins and said, "I am about to cry like Richard Simmons at a salad bar if I don't get somethin' good to eat. Please bring me a large order of nachos with everythin' on it and spend whatever I have left on cookies."

The group followed the tiny girl's lead and ordered as much as they could until their dimes were all gone.

After the big meal, the boys and girls separated and returned to their own rooms. They wanted to stay up late and explore the school, but the Savannah sun had sucked all the energy out of them. Within fifteen minutes of returning to their rooms, everyone was fast asleep.

The next morning, as the sun rose, Odessa shot straight up out of her bed and fell onto the floor.

Krystal mumbled in a sleepy voice, "What is going on? Wiki, are you okay?"

The Greek girl was covered with sweat and was shaking. "I think so. I just had the most vivid dream of my life. It all seemed so real."

The country girl rubbed her eyes. "What happened? What was your dream about?"

"I think Tomochichi answered my question. I heard some old Indian chanting and then I saw myself walking into a library. I walked over to an old section trying to find something - I think the chief's ghost wants me to find a book."

Krystal rubbed her eyes again. "That is kinda creepy; I warned you not to mess with that stuff. Look, treat your nightmare like a booger on your dress; just flick it off and forget about it. Now go back to bed. We can talk about it over breakfast."

As the tomboy rolled over and went back to sleep, Wiki mumbled in disbelief, "I am telling you, Tomochichi is trying to lead me to something, I know it."

PTERYPELGIA: OR THE ART OF SHOOTING FLYING

T he Porcs were starting to get waterlogged feet and the air was getting hard to breathe. Odessa finally pretended to find her retainer in her pocket. "Oh here it is! I found it! Okay, let me take one last look at this door before we go, Krystal."

Krystal grew impatient as she watched Odessa examine the edges of the door. "Y'all, I seriously can't breathe; the air feels so dense. I think we need to cut our loses and head back up to warmer pastures."

"It feels hard to breathe to me, too, but can you hang in there just a few more minutes? I think we can figure a way around this door," Leo pleaded

Wiki offered up, "Well, I am sorry. I know a big part of this is my fault, but if we can escape, think about the awesome bragging rights we will get when we show off this treasure."

"Well, it is kinda all our faults darlin', don't y'all remember?" Krystal reminded them.

When Odessa came down to breakfast, all she could think about was her dream. It seemed so real, so vivid, like her spirit had left her body and flown over to the library. Her dream spirit watched herself walk into a section of the Historical Society that was off limits to the public. The dream was almost like an outer body experience with her peering down on herself with a bird's-eye view. Odessa could see the section, but as she picked up a book, her dream became cloudy and broke up. All morning it was driving her crazy; she could almost make out the book. What was it? Something was abnormal about the old tome, but Wiki could not figure out what.

The four students joined each other and passed around the menu. Krystal licked her lips as the tiny girl's ravenous appetite took over. "Wow y'all, they got apple puff pancakes! It's official; I love this school."

A curious look came over Mohamed's face. "What is so special about an apple pancake?"

She educated the foreign boy. "Oh, it ain't no normal pancake darlin'. This puppy fills the entire plate and is about four inches thick when it comes out of the oven." Krystal's accent disappeared while she explained the entrée as if she were a world-renowned food critic. "It is one giant pancake smothered with sautéed apples and cinnamon sugar baked to perfection. This mouthwatering delight is topped with a deliciously rich Sinkiang cinnamon sugar glaze that satisfies even the pickiest palates." The small girl quickly returned to her country twang and said, "It's really unbelievable y'all, and totally worth gettin' 'the sugars' for. The only place you can still get one in Savannah is the Original Pancake House. I am happy as a goat that they make them here."

Mohamed was sold. When the waiter arrived he said, "With that kind of recommendation I have to try this diabetes-inducing American pleasure." The other three chuckled at Mohamed's attempt to be amusing. All four ordered the sugary breakfast.

Mohamed wondered, "So, Leo, I heard you get up late in the night and leave our dorm room. Where did you go?"

"Sorry, I didn't mean to wake you. I just wanted to check out the arcade. It's awesome up there. They even have all the gaming platforms free to play. I jumped on the Xbox and decided to try dungeon crawler. I decided to be an archer for once instead of a wizard. What I don't get about all these role playing games is why monsters leave their gold and valuable items just laying around in barrels."

Mohamed laughed and added, "I love how you can just walk into any character's house and take all their stuff as if they don't mind that you are stealing them blind."

"Well, I guess if the monsters were smart enough to use the weapons in the barrels instead of guarding them, the game would be a lot harder," Leo surmised.

Wiki cut them off. "I totally had something weird happen to me last night, but I don't want you to make fun of me."

The other three students stopped and focused on the Greek girl, their eyes demanding the story to continue. Wiki went on. "I had the most vivid dream of my life; it seemed so real. I think Tomochichi answered my request and showed me a clue."

"Do not treat jinn lightly," Mohamed responded. "If a jinn visited you in your sleep, you should pray for protection."

Leo was the most superstitious of the entire group, but pretended not to care. "I'm sure that running-around-the-rock ritual was made up by locals so they could laugh at the tourists. I don't think it really works."

Odessa challenged him saying, "I did not tell any of you what I asked the chief for, did I?" She paused for dramatic effect and for them to focus their full attention on her. "I asked Tomochichi to help me find Savannah's lost pirate treasure. Nothing happened at the rock, but I really believe he answered my question in that dream. I have to get to the Historical Society's library ASAP; the curiosity is killing me."

The blonde, head master interrupted the conversation as she sat down.

Leo jumped with surprise at the sight of Ruby. "Where did you come from? Nobody told me the principal here was also a ninja."

Ruby chuckled having been taken off guard by the offhanded compliment. "That is correct, Mr. Stedman. All the faculty here have super human skills, don't forget that." She then turned her focus to the group. "So tell me about your day yesterday."

Krystal spoke up, "I liked Jah Loko; he was real pleasant. Harricane was such an impressive horse. Y'all did well to find him. I also learned a good bit about drivin' a carriage yesterday, but it was so hot I had to pour a McDonald's scaldin'-hot coffee in my lap just to cool off."

Ms. Mendel did a John Ritter style spit-take with her morning tea as she snorted at Krystal's joke.

In her controlling style, Wiki butted in. "We took in many of the historic sights and learned a good bit."

Ruby cut right to the chase as she wiped up the table in front of her. "Do you have any idea why the tour is not selling that well anymore?"

Leo reflected, "Ruby, I think it is all played out. Too many other companies are doing a similar tour."

The blonde woman looked annoyed. "I prefer Ms. Mendel, please! Anyway, I think you might be right, Mr. Stedman. Do you guys have any fresh ideas?"

Mohamed added his take. "Well, you asked me to come along to see if music could somehow be worked in and I think I have two ideas. The first is to do a romantic tour, say a violinist would play for a couple during a carriage ride at night. It should bring a great deal of attention to the tour company if you did it downtown or on River Street. The second idea is to have the tour stop at a square where you could have musicians playing historical tunes. You know, you could have them dress in period costumes while they played old music. They could make extra money with tourist's tips and even make tips off other tour companies."

Ruby was impressed. "That is a brilliant idea, Mr. Obuntu. I can't believe you came up with that so quickly. I think you have a much better head for business than you lead on. We need to talk more about this later and explore those ideas further." She turned to Wiki. "What did you come up with?"

The clever girl used the situation to exploit her own agenda. "Savannah has history tours, food tours, movie tours, and ghost tours, but I noticed nobody is doing a pirate tour. I think we need to research and develop a pirate tour."

The blonde woman scratched her chin. "You don't disappoint, Miss Skouras. I want you to do more research and see if you can make one interesting enough that will sell well."

The curly-haired girl jumped at the opportunity. "Well, if you want me to do it right, I will need to go down to the Georgia Historical Society's library and do a lot more research."

Ms. Mendel nodded her head in agreement. "Very well. Have Jah drop you off down there today."

"Mr. Stedman, what have you come up with?" Ruby asked.

Leo, of course, hardly ever planned anything ahead time, so, as usual, he made up something on the fly. "Um, I need to do more research, too. I need to find out what will grow in this heat. It would really help to talk to the Savannah Garden Club here and see what would be smart and profitable to grow."

Ms. Mendel smiled proudly. "You all have done very well; kudos. You know, other kids your age are just sitting around watching TV or playing video games right now, but you four are learning skills and thinking about business. I want you to report back in three days about the progress you have made."

The head master flashed one more smile to her new projects then excused herself as the massive apple pancakes arrived at the table. She walked over and quietly conferred with the host.

The host came over to the table. He dropped a small, blue, velvet bag embroidered with gold porcupines on it in front of each student. "Here is your pay for yesterday. Y'all must have done something right because Ms. Mendel instructed me to bonus y'all today. You will see five extra silver dimes in each bag."

The four new Porcupines gleamed at each other and then dove into the pancakes. After they gorged themselves, they said their goodbyes and went off to their respective jobs. Mohamed left to inspect the music department and take inventory of what instruments they had. Krystal headed to stables to try to beat the heat and start her chores. Leo got online and tried to find out what would grow successfully in Savannah. Odessa headed straight for Jah to pester him into leaving early so she could be at the Georgia Historical Society when the doors opened.

As the day started, the students immediately noticed the differences in this academy compared to their public or government schools. The excitement of studying their own curriculum was really kicking in. No uncomfortable rows of wooden desks. No ridiculous schedules and being shuffled from place to place like cattle. No classes they had zero interest in. No mystery government meat for lunch. No raising their hands to use the restroom or to speak. No doing mindless hours of homework that they would never use. No bullies or forced social situations. It did not take long for the young adults to realize how free it was to be independent and to teach themselves.

The four students unconsciously worked harder than they did in their previous schools, mostly because it did not seem like work at all. The group enjoyed what they were doing and that made all the difference to their education. No task master was needed to supervise them and harass them to finish their work. All of them agreed; it felt good being treated like an adult, even if it was just for the summer.

Odessa grew impatient as she sat on the front steps of the Historical Society. She looked at the beautiful French fountain that anchored Forsyth Park. She watched the grackles and mockingbirds fly in and out of the ancient, giant live oak trees. If it were any other day, the curly-haired girl would have thought this would be a wonderful place to sit and read a book. Finally, the first volunteer arrived at the front doors of the Georgia Historical Society, interrupting her thoughts.

The employee spoke up. "Wow, you are here early! Give me a few minutes to set up and I will let you in."

The Greek-looking girl nervously crossed her arms and shifted her weight from foot to foot. The large, heavy, ornate portal swung open and Odessa burst inside. "Finally!" she huffed in an impatient tone.

Wiki closed her eyes and tried to recall her dream. She saw herself walking into the back section of the library where it was off limits to the normal public. Odessa was startled back to reality when a thin, wrinkled woman with tobacco-stained fingernails knocked into her. "Oops, sorry little girl," the cleaning woman apologized and then went back to dusting. The young lady was so consumed with her task at hand that she never even noticed the cleaning lady entered with her.

Even though Odessa practically lived in this building, she played it stupid and pretended not to know she was entering a forbidden section. The young lady looked over her shoulder and took notice of the volunteer that was now missing. A second scan of the place revealed that the cleaning woman also had her back to Wiki and was too busy working to notice. Wiki quickly made her move into the employee-only area. She worked her way deep into the back of the room to hide herself as best she could from the staff.

Wiki closed her eyes and tried to remember her dream. After a minute of flashbacks she concluded she was in the right section. If Odessa could only remember what the book looked like. The curly-haired girl nervously scanned the shelves of the old tomes. Some were very old and Odessa knew the books should not be handled, except by experts. She was hoping something would catch her eye and remind her exactly what the mystery dream book was. After a few minutes of frantic searching, the young lady calmed her nerves and looked around again.

When she finally quieted her mind, she noticed something. A box on the floor full of books rattled her memory. The corrugated box had the word "Donations" sloppily written on the side of it. It was then that it struck her – she had seen this box before. Odessa lowered her lids and with her mind's eye she remembered seeing the same box in her dream. In her vision she saw herself digging through the donation bin and finding a book. Odessa's eyes flashed open. Cautiously, she snuck around the room and opened the large brown cube as quietly as she could.

The donations box had a mix of new and old books carelessly thrown together by someone who clearly did not appreciate them. Everything from *Hitchhikers Guide to the Galaxy* and *Angel Star* to some Civil War books on surgical procedures were in the box. Wiki carefully took the old books out and stacked them with respect. "Darn, what did that book look like? Come on, think girl," she mumbled to encourage herself. The Greek girl dug through to the bottom of the box and then stopped in her tracks.

"Is this it?" She lifted a very old, tanned, leather-bound book. Wiki blew off the heavy dust caked on the cover and a brown cloud bellowed forth. The cover revealed a woodcut print of a colonial man shooting a shotgun at a bird.

She held the unimpressive book to the light to get a better look at it. *Pteryplegia: or the Art of Shooting Flying* was etched on the front in worn-out lettering. "What the heck? Why would the old chief lead me to a book about bird hunting?" she whispered to herself.

The sneaky, young woman cracked open the old manual quietly. "Whoa! Published in 1767. This is so old, I need to really be careful with it," she warned her clumsy self. Odessa started flipping page by page through the tome. "*Hmmmm,* what does learning about how to host a birding party have to do with pirates?" She stopped turning pages and stared at what was in her hands.

The treasure hunter was only about a quarter of the way into the book when she found the little wooden compartment cut into the pages. Odessa knew she had just found something big. She cautiously looked over her shoulder, left then right. Wiki dug her chewed fingernails into the wood until the panel reluctantly gave way with a defiant creaking sound.

Inside the secret compartment was a small, sheepskin book. Odessa slowly lifted it out and examined it, noticing that there was no writing on the cover, and opened the tiny journal. It was very aged, but Wiki could make out "Property of Admiral A.R." on the inside cover.

Odessa finds April Read's Diary.

Odessa got goose pimples all over her body; she knew this was it. This was big! She reasoned to herself, "It would not be right to steal this journal; I won't do that. But, I can't exactly take this up to the Xerox machine and copy it, either. *Hmmmm*...oh yes! I have my camera with me." The Greek girl dug in her pocket and pulled out her outdated digital camera. She carefully focused the old camera and captured the ancient cover. *Flash, click. Flash, click. Flash, click.* She repeated the process over and over until the entire sheepskin book was captured forever in digital form.

Wiki knew she was pressing her luck and started reassembling the hidden clue to return it to the way she found it. As Odessa closed the aged book about shotgun techniques, she noticed the wrinkled cleaning woman approaching her from behind.

"Excuse me, little girl," a deep, gravelly, tobacco-infected voice resonated from behind her.

Odessa spun around to find she was only inches away from the unhappy-looking cleaning woman. Her skin was leathery and wrinkled and she looked angry as she said, "This area is for employees only; what do you think you are doing back here?"

Noticing the book in Odessa's hands, the weathered-looking cleaning woman said in a gruff smoker's voice, "What's ya got there, girl?" Her tobacco-stained digits snatched the book from the curly-haired girl's hand.

"*Hmmmm*..." the woman held the aged book up to the light. She spun around and stared down the small, round girl. "This section is not open to the public. You can't be back here."

Odessa played it dumb. "Oh, sorry. Is this a restricted area? My bad. Let me get out of your way." The Greek girl did not allow time for an inquisition to start and calculated an escape route from the scene of the crime.

Odessa stumbled with her voice. "Oh, alright, sorry. I will just go." She quickly slid the camera into her backpack and made her rapid departure.

The wrinkly woman studied the old book now resting in her hands. She opened up the pages with her stinky, brown fingers and found the hidden compartment. "Well, well well, what do we have here? What did that meddling little girl find?" she muttered to herself while flipping through the tiny book with little care. "Mr. Hughes is sure going to be happy I found this before the curator did. I gotta go find Mr. Bines and hand this off. Should be worth a pretty penny," she thought to herself as she stuffed the little book into her cleaning apron.

ADMIRAL APRIL READ
&
AIR DROPS

Wiki finally joined in Krystal's conclusion and accepted defeat. "I can't figure a way around this old oak door and I am starting to suffocate."

"I hate to give up. I was hoping this treasure would be worth enough money to help the old man. I hate to say it, but I am spent, too" Leo confessed.

Mohamed was torn. "The old man deserves better than this, he needs our help. I don't want to give up, but I don't know what else to do."

Krystal's flashlight illuminated her friend's disappointed faces and a fire lit in her heart. She shook off her fear and found her second wind. "Look, I know y'all are supposed to be much smarter than me, but are yuh willin' to listen to my idea?"

The three other Porcupines turned their heads in curiosity. "I never said I thought you were dumb!" Mohamed challenged.

Leo added, "Neither did I. Tell us what you got."

The tomboy smiled and, for once, felt accepted. "Well, I saw y'all tug on the handle like a stubborn mule till y'all were blue in the face. Did any of y'all try to push it instead of pullin'?"

Odessa butted in, "Of course we did...at least I think we did...did we?"

Mohamed, Leo, and Wiki all searched their memories. "No way, how did we overlook that?" Leo said as he drove a shoulder into the door. Mohamed dropped down low and joined the combined shoving effort.

The ancient door started to crack and tremble with age. Krystal found an empty spot on the door and joined in. The portal wavered and creaked with the combined force. The farm girl shouted, "Come on, Odessa! We need you! Come push." The Greek girl charged the door with excitement and her added thrust rocked the entryway open, throwing them all into the filthy ground as the gateway flew ajar.

The students simply laid in the mud and the slop and looked with amazement at the giant chamber that Odessa's flashlight was now lighting. There lying before them was a huge, arched room made of old Savannah brick. There were rusted, copper barrel hoops lying in the corners and piles of dust and debris was everywhere.

Mohamed sprung to his feet and helped the others up. "Since we only have one working flashlight, let's stay close and search this room together." As they slowly sifted through the giant chamber, Leo started laughing. "This is all Tomochichi's fault, do you remember?"

Wiki returned to Forsyth Park overflowing with excitement as she contemplated her find. The girl spent the rest of the morning hunting down Jah and begging him to return her to the school so she could upload and enlarge the digital pages of the secret book to study.

Two hours later, the Greek girl stared at her computer screen examining the electronic pictures. Not even a visit from her favorite author could break her focus right now. After a few hours of study, she knew she had to share these amazing discoveries with her friends.

Odessa Skouras grabbed her notebook off the desk and caught up with the others who were already eating dinner. "Guys! I got something to tell you!"

Leo ignored the Greek girl and continued his *Call of Duty* debate with Mohamed. "Your kill streaks are so lame. Who would have care packages and emergency air drops as kill streaks?"

Mohamed came back saying, "My kill streaks are not lame; they're brilliant. I watched Martin's videos on YouTube and this is what he said to do for more achievement points."

"Whatever! You know as soon as you drop those care packages the enemy will kill you and take them from you. So, good luck with that, chump!"

Odessa spoke louder. "Hey guys, I have really important news."

Krystal chatted calmly with Wiki. "It is no use. They have been speakin' nerd for like a half hour. This argument is somethin' 'bout some video game they are playin' together." Krystal barked at the two, "If y'all want to live on this planet, yuh need to learn to speak like the rest of us!"

The two boys were oblivious to the two girl's quiet conversation. Mohamed defended his strategy. "You are not thinking this through. They won't take my care packages - I'm a Ninja! If they even come near them I'll use my throwing knife to take them out before they even knew what hit them."

Wiki cleared her throat. "Excuse me! I know where April Read's hidden treasure is located in Savannah!"

The boys stopped their debate and stared at her to process what they just heard. Then Leo turned back to Mohamed and continued speaking in gaming language. "Do you have lightweight pro and marathon pro activated?"

"Of course, I am not a complete idiot like you are," Mohamed snapped back.

"Well, I am going to just run around knifing and using my spaz then. We're gonna really own them! Let's do this strategy tonight!" Leo let out an evil laugh.

"This is going to be great; what time should we start playing?" Mohamed inquired.

"GUYS!" Wiki yelled. "I am not joking! I found something big today." She barged her way between them and opened her notebook computer.

The Greek girl finally got the table's attention when she added visuals to her presentation. "I know it sounds crazy, and I would not believe it if it did not happen to me, but I found that book that was in my dream. It was a super old book and inside that one was a secret hidden book. I assume someone had donated it and probably had never even opened the thing or they would have found it. I found a tiny hidden book inside that bigger book. I took pictures of the ancient, hidden, sheepskin journal and that is what these pictures are that you are looking at."

The friends squeezed around the computer and started reading. After a minute, Mohamed interrupted, "Is this in a different language? I barely understand any of this."

Wiki explained, "It is in old English and is very tough to understand. You got to remember, back then there were no standard rules for grammar. There was no such thing as sentence structure and the same word could be spelled five different ways on the same page. It took me a very long time to translate this and I have been studying old English as far back as I can remember."

Leo took a jab, "Um, you're only twelve, so how many years equals 'far back' for you?"

Wiki came back, "Oh, was that a joke? I am sorry; I didn't get it because I was too busy reading Old English while you were playing video games."

Mohamed moaned, "If I don't play these games, how else am I supposed to learn how to trash talk each other and really understand the complexity of your language."

Odessa finally smiled at Mohamed's attempt to make a joke. "Anyway, what I figured out is that this is a very old shipping record from the infamous woman pirate Admiral April Read. It mentions the names of a few of her ships in these records, like the *Mary Read, the Black Hound, Archibald's Vendetta*, and the *Robin*. Not to mention, it also says this book is the property of A.R. on the inside cover."

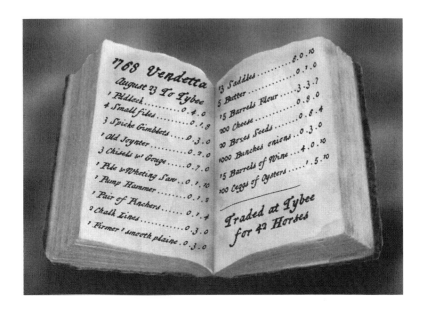

Shipping records from April Read's Diary.

The small group focused on Wiki intensely. "Mainly, this book is simply a shipping record, but look at this entry. It looks like she stashed a bunch of her personal effects and there is no record she ever went back for it. It might still be down there if we can find it. The Admiral mentions stashing her swag in a secret underground location under Savannah."

Wiki flipped through her digital presentation until a picture of a faint map appeared. "Look here, there is even a map of the secret location. The problem is it never says where the start of the map originates from."

Everyone's eyes lit up with excitement as they zoomed in closer and examined the digital drawing.

18 CHAPTER

BARREL OF SECRETS

"**M**ost of these are completely ruined and are just dust now," Odessa grunted as she kicked a lump of dirt that used to be a barrel.

"Well, there are a few of the barrels that sort of survived over in that dry corner over there. Let's see what is in those," Leo offered.

The chamber was at least 50 x 50 feet wide and half of it was still in good shape. A pile of rotten barrels, rusted copper hoops, and fallen bricks were strewn across the west side of the room. It appeared that, over the years, the west wall had given way and moisture and time had claimed any prizes that could have been found.

The Porcupines made their way to the east wall where a few storage containers still survived the march of time.

"Shine the light better on this barrel, Odessa. I think it says something on it," Mohamed pointed.

The word RUM was carved into the wooden cask. Mohamed reached out and shook the cylinder keg with his hand to test its weight. The ancient drum slumped over and crashed into a pile of kindling.

"I guess this one was not air tight and the rum all evaporated," Wiki surmised. "Try the next one." Mohamed reached out and shook the next barrel, but it did not budge. "This one is still full," he reported.

Odessa shined the light on all the barrels and examined them closer. After a minute of intense searching, she concluded, "It looks like they all say 'rum' except that one barrel in the back. Let's go take a better look at it."

The students arrived at the mystery keg and debated about what to do. "Y'all think it is right to open this thing after all these years? Once a jar of peaches is open you got to put it in the fridge or it will go bad. Don't y'all think the same thing might be true about whatever is in there?" Krystal challenged.

"Well, you are probably right, but gold don't spoil, so I am willing to take that chance," Leo countered.

"Being a history buff, I should be agreeing with Krystal that we should preserve it the way we found it, but the curiosity is killing me. I have to know what Admiral April Read left behind. I say open it."

The three turned to Mohamed for the final vote. "Well, our friend needs money right now for his operation, so I don't think we have a choice. Let's open it."

"Stupid democracy," Krystal pouted. "I just hope we aren't making a mistake that we will regret later."

"How do we open this thing? The top is sealed with old tar," Mohamed questioned as he tugged at the lid.

Leo reached into his Zombie Bug-Out Bag and pulled out a very large knife.

"Whoa," Odessa stumbled back, "are you telling me you have been carrying that huge thing around this whole time?"

"Of course. What good is a Bug-Out Bag without a Zombie Apocalypse knife? Now stand back, I am going to cut through this waxy tar seal and see if I can pop the top off." The tall boy cut carefully like a surgeon around the top of the barrel then wedged the thick blade into the thin opening.

POP! A rush of putrid, ancient air rushed out of the top as it lifted open. The group coughed as the blast of musty stank filled their noses. The four friends surrounded the barrel and leaned in to see what wonders it held. The light from the flashlight reflected off the top of a large clay pot and Odessa steadied the light as the other three carefully lifted the earthy jar out of the cask. As it was placed at their feet, the waves of curiosity were overwhelming. The clay urn had a large mouth and was sealed with wax. It had no writing on it at all, but did have a picture of a cat's silhouette carved on it.

The party held its collective breath as Leo cut free the lid from the large jar. He stuck his hand in the mouth and retrieved something. The punk rocker held it to the light. It appeared to be a journal identical to the one Odessa had found at the Historical Society. "Wiki, I believe this is for you." Leo handed her the book as she squealed in delight.

Krystal sounded disappointed, "Is that it?"

Leo stuck his hand back in the large urn again. "Nope, there is something else heavy and big in here." Using both hands, Leo cautiously guided out something wrapped in a canvas. The skater carried the bundle over to the top of an adjacent rum barrel and slowly unwrapped the prize. The band of friends watched in silence as Leo treated the find like a very expensive Christmas gift. A collective gasp echoed through the chamber.

Odessa mumbled, "Can it really be April's legendary Swedish boarding axe-pistol?"

"I don't get it. My granddaddy has all kinds of muskets. What's so special about this one?" Krystal queried.

"Take a close look at it; it is half-pistol, half-axe. This is extremely rare. I would guess the only one left in the world." Odessa broke her normal mannerisms because she was so excited. "In addition, it is Admiral April Read's superbad axe-pistol; how cool is that?"

"You're right on the money. It is totally awesome." Leo picked it up and balanced it his hands. "I can't believe how heavy this thing is! Can you believe they classified this as just a pistol? Man, they were hardcore back then." He smiled as he passed their treasure around for each person to hold."

Odessa handed the weapon back to Leo. "Here, keep this safe. Now what else is in that pot? Mohamed, you have the long arms. Make sure we did not miss something on the bottom."

Mohamed gladly did as he was commanded and, to his delight, retrieved something small. He asked Odessa to shine the light on his hand to get a good look at it. "I think it is an old key, but to what?" the Ugandan questioned. "It has April's mark of the three circles and the cat on it so we must be on the trail of something good!"

April Read's famous Swedish boarding axe-pistol.

Mohamed gladly did as he was commanded and, to his delight, retrieved something small. He asked Odessa to shine the light on his hand to get a good look at it. "I think it is an old key, but to what?" the Ugandan questioned. "It has April's mark of the three circles and the cat on it so we must be on the trail of something good!"

"That's not all, y'all; shine your light back on that cloth the axe-pistol was wrapped up in." Wiki illuminated the area and giggled aloud. "I can't believe this! Is that really April's flag? I just can't believe we are looking at the jack of the *Archibald's Vendetta*." The pack of friends gazed on a faded, yellow and black flag adorned with a dagger, skull and bones, and a heart. "We need to be extra careful with that. Hey, Leo, please tell me you got a plastic bag in your pouch of greatness," she teased.

Leo did not take his eyes off the impressive weapon that he was holding and dug into his satchel without even looking. "Here! I have a few trash bags in here that I use as ponchos when it rains while I am gardening."

Odessa handed the trash bags off to Krystal. "Please wrap that jack up carefully." The Greek girl kept repeating, "I seriously can't believe we found a cloth flag this old!" Wiki turned and yelled across the chamber. "Hey Leo, do you have anything I can use to protect this book we found?"

"I got a Ziploc bag that my lunch is in, will that work?" He walked over and handed her the lunch.

"Sorry to be the worry wart, but we are completely unprepared for this. I say we head topside with our finds and come back down for another search. If that last flashlight dies, we all be in a world of hurt," Krystal warned.

Odessa reluctantly agreed, "Look, I think we got the best stuff. Let's get out of here, restock, and come back down."

The boys grumbled with discontent, but agreed with the cautious logic. The four secured their finds and started the long trek back up the muddy passage.

Leo burst out into an awkward laugh "Mo, I can't believe the irony. We actually found treasure in a barrel just like a dungeon crawler game."

Mohamed chuckled in agreement.

"I am still in shock that we found this stuff. The people at the Historical Society would never believe us if we didn't have the proof," Odessa bragged.

Mohamed pondered, "I think my parents would be proud, but also upset I took such a risk. Look at this place it is...*ugggghhh!*" Mohamed's body flew back, into the darkness.

"My zombie bag!" Leo shouted as something in the dark cut the strap and swallowed it.

"MO! LEO! What's goin' on? Where are y'all?" Krystal yelled as Odessa spun the light around in a panic.

Wiki could see a large, fat man shoving Mohamed into the tunnel wall. Another figure ran down the hall making an escape with the Zombie Bug-Out Bag.

A scratchy voice yelled, "Give me what you found, boy!" as the obese attacker slammed the African teen hard into the wall.

Leo was too stunned to help and was screaming, "Where is my bag?" Krystal, on the other hand, reactively sprang into action. The scrappy teen approached from behind and jumped up on the attacker's shoulders. She dug her dirty fingers into the heavy man's eye sockets and yanked his head backwards.

A pain-wrenching scream could be heard echoing down the tunnel as the attacker dropped Mohamed to the ground.

Krystal squeezed her legs around his back like a jockey and dug her digits in harder. The noises in the tunnel no longer sounded human and were now shouts of pure agony. The goliath man spun wildly in circles as he tried to buck the tomboy off. He desperately crashed his back into the wall of the passageway to dislodge the small girl. The fat man's desperate move worked and she was crushed by his massive weight. Her body fell limp to the floor.

Mohamed screamed, "Krystal!" and dove on his savior to protect the unconscious girl. A terrible cracking noise filled the area as the ancient wall gave way to the repeated assaults. The last thing they saw before the rush of water hit them was Odessa's flashlight blinking out.

19 CHAPTER

WATERLOGGED
&
JAH'S SECRET

The small girl was blind. She opened her eyes and could not see a thing in the absolute blackness. *CRASH! CRASH! CRASH!* A loud pounding echoed in the chamber. She screamed in terror, "I'm blind! I can't see! Where am I? Someone answer me!"

A soft hand gripped her shoulder and she recoiled from it. A small amount of light appeared. "Relax; you're safe! It is just me, Mohamed. Hey, everyone, I think she is awake. A soft glow revealed Mohamed's bloody face smiling at her. Hugs from the group quickly embraced her and helped her to her feet.

Mohamed held his cell phone up higher to maximize the light it was putting off. Odessa hugged Krystal again. "Are you okay? We have been so worried."

The small tomboy got her bearings and checked her self out. "I am seriously dizzy and my ribs really hurt, but no worse than when I was learnin' to barrel race and cut. I got thrown, bucked, and kicked every day; I will be fine. Where are we? What's goin' on, y'all?"

Wiki took it on herself to recount their plight. "Mo was right; we were being followed, but it was not by a ghost. We were attacked and robbed in the tunnel when we were heading back to the Pirates' House cellar. The man who assaulted you accidentally knocked a wall down that was holding back a whole lot of water. We got blown all the way back into the chamber where we found the treasure."

"Where is the man that attacked us now?" Krystal asked. *SLAM! SLAM! SLAM!* The rasps on the thick oak door answered her question.

Leo finished the tale. "Somehow Mo held onto you and dragged you to safety. When the three off us realized we were all in the chamber and the thieves were not, I rushed to the door and locked it. I am thankful that these pirates thought to put a lock on the inside."

The water from the hall continued to pour under the door, creating a small creek in the middle of the vast room.

"Now what?" Krystal asked rhetorically.

Wiki took charge saying, "Well, think of all the trouble we had with that door. They are not getting around it anytime soon. Look, let's all calm down and take inventory of what we have left. Let's take a minute and collect our thoughts. Mo, can you see if you can make a call for help using your phone? In the meantime, why don't we think about something else to help us try to relax? I think you guys should remember all our reasons we needed this treasure. Come on; think back to our conversation this morning."

The boys had finally stopped arguing about their game *Call of Duty* and focused on the notebook computer. Wiki pulled up the map and they all studied it.

Leo confessed, "Well, you're right. It sure looks like a secret underground room, but where do we start from?"

Wiki tapped into her legendary book smarts. "Let's use deductive reasoning and see if we can narrow the search down. I use this technique all the time when I do research on hard to find information."

"Okay, the map is dated 1769. So we need to focus on what structures would have existed back then that had tunnels." She continued, "Savannah was still getting a foothold and was not real big yet. The pirates were smugglers, so they needed to be close to the ports. They would also need a place that would be a good business front with lots of activity, so as not to draw attention to their comings and goings. All that being said, I think that drastically narrows down our search."

Leo still stared dumbfounded at the Greek girl until she recognized his gaze. "Come on you guys, really? None of you figured it out? This has to be the notorious Shanghai tunnels under the Pirates' House. Look at the map again; it even shows a set of stairs leading to a little room that looks just like the Pirates' House's rum cellar. This has to be were we start!"

Map of tunnels in April Read's diary.

Krystal interjected, "Well, yuh heard little Miss Research; what are we waitin' for? Go grab yer gear and meet me in the barn. Hopefully Jah has not left yet and we can hitch a ride with him."

The students jumped out of their chairs and ran to their rooms. Mohamed took his cell phone off its charger and put his tennis shoes on. Leo, in the meantime, prepared his Zombie Bug-Out Bag. The tall boy took inventory aloud. "Okay, it is almost packed. Oops! I almost forgot my Apocalypse knife. I also have these other flashlights, but no new batteries. Oh well, I will take them anyway. They might have a little life in them." He jammed his Elvis-style, peanut butter and banana sandwich in a plastic Ziploc bag and carefully placed it in his satchel. "Okay, let's go meet the girls!"

Mohamed stalled. "You go ahead. I have to pray before I meet up with you guys."

Leo nodded while shoving on his Doc Martin boots. The skater shut their dorm room door as Mohamed pulled out his grass-cloth prayer mat.

Leo stopped at the girl's room to pick them up. "You chicks got everything you need? I brought a few flashlights in case you don't have one."

Odessa agreed, "Yes, we will need them. Neither of us have anything like a flashlight. I did, however, print out this map. I have a copy for each of us."

"Cool idea, Wiki! Krystal, are you ready?"

"Well, I don't have anything to take; just my glowing smile," Krystal responded.

"Neither of us have mobile phones, or else we would bring them. I do have a little money in case we need it. Where's Mo, by the way? Wiki questioned.

"He had to pray again; he will catch up with us at the stables," Leo informed.

The three hightailed it down to the barn, hoping to catch Jah Loko before he left. Krystal took a survey of the area and instantly knew something was wrong. "Wait, y'all! Harricane is not properly tacked and he is just aimlessly walkin' around. Something ain't right here; come on."

The small stable hand calmly approached the mammoth equine and gently reached out for his bridle. The huge horse was mouthing at his bit that was not situated in his mouth correctly. The draft horse bucked his head as Krystal tried to fix the improper gear.

"This tack was only half on his head and he is outside the barn. Let's go find our Gullah friend. Mr. Loko? Mr. Loko? Where are yuh?" the farm girl yelled into the stables.

A groan came from a dark stable. The students ran over to find the old man lying on the ground, holding his gut. Krystal threw her arms around Jah. "What's wrong? Can I help?"

"Oh, chillun! Tank goodness you're here. Help me ta my feet," the Gullah man pleaded. "Is Miss Mendel with you?"

The stable hand responded, "No, but I can run and get her if yuh like."

"No! Don't do dat, Titi! I have a secret, chillun, but ya must swear on your mother's life never ta speak of it." Jah looked each teen in the eye to confirm they would keep his information confidential. One by one the teens gave him his word.

"I be at the end of my life, chillun. I have a sickness in my stomach that strikes me down like dis a few times a week," Jah confessed.

Odessa asked an obvious question, "Have you seen a doctor? Isn't there anything that can be done?"

"Yes and no, Titi. I am very sick and I can't afford da treatment. I just want ta keep workin' until da Lord comes a callin'."

Wiki did not accept his explanation. "Wait, don't you have insurance or something? Somebody has to help you."

The old man looked upset. "Sadly no, I am on da government's insurance and dey have deemed my surgery as too costly and unnecessary. Dere be no way I can come up with dat kinda money, so I just want ta enjoy da time I have left."

Wiki blurted out, "That's so unfair! They should take care of you! Why don't you ask the Mendel's for a loan? I am sure they would help you if they knew how serious this was."

"I can't do dat. It would put da skoo out of business. I don't like tellin' other's business, but ya needs to know. Da skoo has no money. Dey need every penny dey have to stay afloat. Miss Ruby be puttin' her faith dat da four of ya will help her turn it around. So ya see chillun, I can't be askin' dem for help. Dis be my time I guess, and I wanna meet my maker doin' what I love. Y'all promise ya never speak of what I be tellin' ya."

The Porcupines nodded their heads again to reassure the old man they would keep his secret.

A look of alarm shot across the tour guide's face. "Oh, my maker! Did ya find Harricane? I collapsed in da middle of gettin' him ready and he done run off."

Krystal assured him with a hand on his shoulder. "Don't worry, I found him. He is fine."

The barn door rattled as Mohamed popped his head in. "Are you guys all ready to go to the Pirates' House?"

Jah stumbled to the opening and welcomed Mohamed. "Yes, we jus' have ta finish a few tings. Ya three go ahead and catch Mo up; I trust him. Now, I need ta get da buggy ready or Miss Ruby gonna come 'round and start askin' questions. Miss Krystal, can ya give me a hand?"

Krystal and Jah disappeared to ready the horse while Leo and Odessa filled Mohamed in on what he had missed.

THE PIRATE TUNNELS

A s the tepid seawater rose over his Doc Martin boots, Leo ran his finger across the ancient weapon. "Still sharp after almost three hundred years; unbelievable," Leo thought to himself.

A voice behind the thick, oak door yelled into the secret chamber. "Just give us whatchya found and y'all can leave without gettin' hurt!"

The four terrified students could barely make out each other's faces in the glow of the useless cell phone. The Greek girl stood by Leo's side and sighed with defeat. "Why should this be any different from any other thing in my life? I never win."

Meanwhile, the other girl in the underground room climbed onto some loose rocks trying to escape the water that was pooling at everyone's feet. Krystal grew nervous after she surveyed the situation and realized there was no escape. Although the tomboy showed no fear in almost every other aspect of her life, she was still horribly afraid of the dark. The small girl stared nervously at the illuminated cell phone as the low battery light began to flash. The anxiety of being in complete blackness gripped her. She continued, however, to play it brave. "I don't want to give it to them either, Leo, but we can't stay down here the rest of our lives. I don't think we have much of a choice; we're trapped, y'all. Let's unlock that door and try to run through them. One of us might make it back up to the surface with at least some of this treasure."

The group was surprised at what came out of Mohamed's mouth next, for he was always so polite and thoughtful. "Don't give them a thing, Leo! We have come too far! I so am sick of bullies ruining our lives; this is where we dig deep and make a stand!"

Leo cut back in, "Guys, guys, guys! Let's not forget why we are doing this. We need this treasure to save Jah. Do you want to see our friend and say, 'Sorry, we had enough money to pay for the surgery to keep you alive, but we handed it over to some jerks who trapped us?'" He held their deadly prize aloft and said, "This is just the first piece of the puzzle. It proves the stories are real. This is the key to lead us to the rest of the booty and I am not giving it away to some spoiled idiots. Let's put our heads together and think of a way out of here."

The sound of threatening shouts and pounding on the other side of the thick door increased as the secret room slowly filled with more water. The cell phone finally died and the four reached out and held each other's hands. As the room became completely black, strangely all each student could think about was how they ever got themselves into this mess to begin with. The damp room grew eerily silent as if their pursuers knew the group of treasure hunters had just lost the last of their light.

Krystal drove the carriage since Jah was not finished with his painful intestinal episode. "Don't look so afraid, Titi. I have one or two of dose attacks a day. It ne'er seems ta happen in da day, just wakin' up and fallin' asleep. I'll be fine on my own today. Ya chillun have fun doing your pirate research."

The tiny girl laid a caring hand on the sick man's shoulder. "Are yuh sure, Mr. Loko? I will stay and drive the buggy all day if yuh ask."

"I am fine, Titi. Ya need ta find somethin' good to save dis skoo; dis skoo is more important den my comfort." The team pulled into the Pirates' House and unloaded. "Can you swing by here after every tour to check on us?" Odessa asked.

Mohamed added, "I have a cell phone we can call you on to let you know when we are ready. But I forgot to charge it enough and it looks like it's low on cell power. It might be a good idea if you come look for us, too."

The old man gave the Porcs a nod of affirmation and pulled the carriage away.

All eyes fell on Odessa. She surveyed her team and looked confused. "What?"

"We all thought yuh had a plan to get us into to the tunnel. It is closed off to the public. I don't think we can just stroll right in," Krystal informed the history nerd.

She smiled and turned to Leo. "Correct me if I am wrong, but finding ways around rules is your area of expertise, isn't it, Leo?"

The tall boy accepted the offhanded flattery then smirked. "Well, I can't stand authority always trying to tell me what I have to do. I think you're right. I am your man for this."

The skater thought for a minute. "Well, I don't think our plan has to be real elaborate. All we have to do is wait for the big lunchtime crowd. There is a table in front of the steps going down to the cellar. We wait for that table to be empty and make our move. We just need a good, old-fashioned distraction so people are not looking at us. Let's go in and do some reconnaissance and get a feel for the comings and goings of the staff."

Mohamed became uneasy. "I am not real comfortable with the whole breaking-and-entering thing. In my country you can be killed for such a crime."

"Dear Mo, this is research; not a crime. Technically, nobody owns the tunnels, so we would not be trespassing. The cellar is part of the restaurant and it used to be open to the public when my dad was a kid. So, I look at this as more as a retro tour, not a B and E," the tall teen said as he flashed a devilish smile.

The four students walked into the restaurant and eyeballed the busy atmosphere. Leo casually walked right past the hostess heading into the interior of the establishment. The other three looked like they were robbing a bank. Mohamed was already sweating through his collar and the two girls looked very conspicuous as they awkwardly walked past the hostess. Fortunately for the three ungraceful and amateurish trespassers, the hostess was too busy to even notice them sneaking passed.

"Relax. Just act like we are tourists looking at the sites in the restaurant. Now let's watch for that table to open up so we can get behind it. I need to think of a good distraction," Leo said, easing the gang of amateur criminals.

The students took a few minutes to observe the comings and goings of the staff. Leo continued to stroll around the main room, playing the part of the tourist. He walked over to the Herb House and inspected the ancient architecture. He then directed the group's attention to a large hole cut into the floor that was fenced off for safety. The pit allowed tourists to look directly into a cross section of the tunnel from above. At the bottom of the thirty-foot shaft laid a skeleton grasping a bottle of rum.

The mood was broken by the touch of boney fingers on Leo's shoulder. He recoiled from the frosty touch and stopped dead in his tracks as he stood face to face with his nemesis.

A pair of emotionless, coal-like eyes cut straight through Leo as the woman's monotone voice jittered his nerves. "Mr. Bines, come over here and look who I just ran into!" A tubby man in a tight shirt pushed forward and stared at Leo. A bubble of spacetime seemed to appear as silence fell around Leo and the two former security guards. The only sound Leo could hear was the asthmatic breathing coming from the heavy man.

Leo Stedman assessed the strange standoff. He came up with two choices; either A, maturely walk away, or B, antagonize the situation and make it worse. True to his nature, Leo poked the beehive with the stick. The skater finally broke the silent confrontation and said, "Thanks for mailing my lunchbox back. That must have been a mess trying to get it back from the guy you sold it to on eBay."

Mr. Bines lurched forward in anger, but Ms. Gambit restrained him with her corpselike arm. Her tobacco-ruined voice flashed with anger. "Boy, you caused a good bit of trouble for us with your little stunt. We both lost our jobs at the school because of you!"

"Wow! I didn't think Gordon Hughes actually had the guts to fire you two thieves. I must have scared him more than I thought," Leo announced smugly.

The rhino of a man charged forward again, but the gaunt Ms. Gambit held him back. The leathery-looking woman coughed and cleared her throat. "Who are your new friends? Do they know what kinda screwed up kid you really are? I doubt they would hang out with you at all if they knew everything I know about you."

The comment rattled the teen. "Whatever!" He changed the subject and deflected her comment. "I am sure you two crooks will find stellar careers at whichever job you steal from next."

"Boy, you're so lucky we're in a crowd or I'd teach you some respect," Mr. Bines snorted.

"Respect? The only thing it looks like you respect is half-price buffets," Leo taunted the irate man.

The cold woman slowly pulled her angry companion away. "Don't worry, my friend; this is not over."

"We'll be waitin' for you in the parkin' lot. Can't wait to hug it all out, boy," the fat man spit in fury.

Leo continued to throw gas on the fire and yelled loud enough for the rest of the patrons to hear, "You are such a loser! Did you seriously just challenge a fourteen-year-old boy to a fight outside?"

A great number of eyes suddenly focused on the tense situation. Mohamed grabbed his friend's arm and whispered, "Lower your voice. You're bringing too much attention to us."

The tall skater shook Mohamed's hand loose and pouted, "I know. Those two have made my life miserable for the last three years. I thought now that I graduated I would never have to deal with them again."

The hostess walked over to the four and began her investigation. "Excuse me, where are your parents?"

Odessa tried her best to play it cool. "They're coming in later after they check out the Trustee's Garden."

"Well, y'all will have to wait up front for them. We don't allow kids to just run around without supervision. Come with me!" the hostess said as she escorted the crew to the reception area and made them wait.

The three companions gave Leo the stink eye as they sat waiting for nonexistent parents to show up. Krystal turned to him and spat with anger, "Yuh couldn't just leave the situation alone, and yuh had to ramp it up so we got noticed. How are we gonna get to the rum cellar now?"

The group stood and exchanged defeated looks with one another. "How are we ever going to get to the treasure now? I don't think we can go outside and just dig our way in," Mohamed sulked.

A Cheshire Catlike smile flashed across the Greek's face and it caught the other three's attention. "Wiki, what did your big beautiful brain just figure out?" Leo grinned.

"I just realized, there is an entrance and an exit to every tunnel. I know where the back door is! You guys ready to find Admiral April Read's treasure?"

A wave of excitement spread over the four as they just realized they had a second chance. Leo surveyed the parking lot. "I don't see any signs of the fat man and his corpse bride waiting for us outside. I guess they were all talk." He smiled and patted his messenger satchel. "I left plenty of room in this bag so we can load it up with gold doubloons if we find any."

As the four excited teens exited the lobby, all failed to notice the tobacco-stained hand lurking above them in the stairwell leading to the gift shop.

21 CHAPTER

TREASURE IN 200 PACES

The water continued to rise up over the Porcs' ankles. *Blam! Blam! Blam!* The knocking on the large oak door became louder. "Just give us what you found and we will let you all go!" an asthmatic shout rang through the underground chamber.

Leo felt Krystal's hand trembling in the pitch-blackness of the room. He gave it a squeeze to reassure her, even though he was starting to get scared himself. "We gotta get outta here! I can't breathe! We gotta do somethin'. At least if we had light in here we might be able to figure somethin' out," Krystal said in a panicked voice.

Mohamed raised his voice in desperation. "Let me see your flashlight, Odessa."

"It's no good; it stopped working when the water overtook us," the Greek girl said, but offered the waterlogged torch anyway.

Mohamed waved his hand back and forth in the pitch black searching the air until his digits struck a plastic tube. He carefully took the dead light out of her hands and desperately flipped the switch on and off. *Click, click, click* was heard, but nothing happened.

Krystal shook as the darkness started to overwhelm her courage. "I feel like I am blind in one ear and can't see out the other," she said. Although too dark to see, her three companion's sighs reflected their confusion to that musing. "Can we at least talk about somethin' while Mohamed tries to fix the flashlight?" Even though Krystal's voice was brave, Leo picked up on her trembling tone. "Who the heck are these people, and how did they find us down here?"

Odessa confessed, "It is my fault; I think I gave them the map."

The students climbed the hill behind the Pirates' House until they stood before a stone staircase. The steps were blocked off to the public by a large fence, but at the bottom of the enclave were three doorways. One had been bricked up and the other was padlocked. The third, however, was bricked up with a large section that had collapsed, now offering an opening.

Odessa pointed, "Even though it is rumored they bricked up all the entrances and exits, one of the walls has crumbled open. We just got to jump this fence and head down."

Leo nimbly jumped the fence, followed by Krystal and Mohamed. Odessa needed help and the three ungraciously pulled her over onto the steps. As the sun was setting, Mohamed interrupted, "I am sorry. I know you guys are eager to start, but according to my phone it is time for my lunch prayer."

The excited group let out a collective audible sigh as they watched the boy use an application on his phone that pointed towards Mecca. The application alerted him of times to pray as they were constantly changing with the seasons. Mohamed complained about getting his new name brand, khaki pants dirty as he knelt down on the landing pad to pray. The other three studied Odessa's map of the tunnels as they waited for him.

"If we follow this passage to where the rum cellar starts, we should be able to back track down the tunnel two hundred paces. I think we can get close to this marking of a cat and three circles. Can you imagine how cool it would be if we really found something down there?" Wiki dreamed out loud. They watched the sun start to hang lower in the sky as Mohamed finished his prayer.

The Ugandan boy turned to the group. "That should hold me for a few hours; let's go!"

Leo opened his favorite bag and handed Odessa a flashlight. "You have the map, you should take this. Let me go first. I have everything I need in this kit if we find zombies. Remember, if we get in trouble, you guys should be able to out run them while I fight them off."

Savannah's underground tunnels.

The four slowly entered the opening and were enveloped by darkness. "That is very brave of you. I will be sure to tell the school you went out fighting the undead like you always predicted would happen," Wiki mused.

The skater responded in a compassionate voice, "That would be real sweet if you did. I want you to burn my body so I don't come back to life. Oh and throw my ashes into the river. I don't want my name to be forever linked to the teen who infected Savannah. I won't be Savannah's own Patient Zero."

The other three tried to keep their chuckling under control so as not to hurt Leo's feelings. The Porcs turned the corner and the light from the entrance completely vanished. The walls were stone and the passage was larger than expected.

The group found themselves walking two by two through the darkness. Then something clicked in Odessa's mind while they were walking. "Leo, I think I have seen that skinny woman you were arguing with before."

The tall boy stopped. "How do you know Smokey?"

"Well, I think she has a job at the Georgia Historical Society," the Greek girl responded.

"Oh, so she probably doesn't have a clue who you are. I doubt she would mess with you," Leo said.

"Wait Leo, there's more. She ran me off when I found the secret book and she took it from me. I am not sure if she knows what it is, but she doesn't seem like the kinda woman who would give a rare book to the library. If you know she is a thief, I would assume she has the book and the map."

"*Hmmmm,* if that is the case, I guess we need to make sure that we beat them to it. Besides, I don't think those two are smart enough to figure out what they have. Not everyone has a brain as smart as you, Wiki," the tall boy flattered her. "But..." he paused and considered, "Mr. Hughes is that smart. Ms. Gambit and Mr. Bines, they worked for Principal Hughes at my old school as security guards. They robbed me of my vintage stuff at least once a month and I would have to buy it back on eBay. Mr. Hughes is also on the board of directors at the

Historical Society and I know he is an artifact thief. I have video of it. They all work together and, with the help of naive little boys, go dig up treasure on other people's property. I have no doubt that he used his connections to put Ms. Gambit in that job after I made him fire her from the school."

Odessa considered all that Leo said then suggested, "Let's push on." The group finally arrived at a walled-up doorway. "I think this is where the tunnel connects to the cellar, but it looks blocked. I guess they closed the cellar up. It's a good thing we did not try to go through the passage from the Pirates' House."

"So now what, Wiki?" Krystal questioned.

"Let's just follow the map!" she snapped back.

Krystal piped up, "Wait, before we set out and do this y'all, I have a proposition. I say whatever treasure we find we use at least some part if it to help Jah Loko. We split whatever's left equally."

"Are you sure you want to give all our money away to a man we barely know?" Leo asked the harsh question.

Krystal reasoned, "It is the right thing to do, we are young and we have all the time in the world to make more money, but Jah needs it right now if he is going to live. Who's with me on this?"

Mohamed spoke up first. "It is a noble thing to do. Allah would want me to help."

Odessa thought for a minute. "I already love the old man like a father; he actually likes my stories. So I'm in."

All eyes fell on Leo. "Fine, but there better be tons gold left after we help him. Let's get moving!"

Wiki studied the map under her flashlight. "Okay, it looks like the map says two hundred paces this direction. One, two, three…"

THE CELLAR OF THE WALKING-DEAD

The pounding on the door continued. "We are going to find a way in eventually, there is no way out. Just give up!"

Wiki took over and redirected the group, "Any luck on that flashlight, Mo?"

"I have disassembled everything and used my shirt to dry it all off," the boy in the dirty polo responded.

The pounding on the oak door became less threatening as the captors grew tired. Halfhearted threats would occasionally be heard, but they were showing exhaustion in this cat-and-mouse game.

Mohamed was extremely careful to reassemble the flashlight. He knew if he dropped any of the pieces in the water they would be near impossible to find. He screwed the top of the light back on and made an announcement. "Come on, Allah, help us out on this one." *Click!* For one-second, a beam of light shot out and illuminated the watery floor.

Mohamed shook the light and it blinked on and off, thus randomly interweaving moments of excitement and terror within each member of the group.

"I think this little post is bent from when you got washed away. I can only get it to stay on if I hold it in a certain position," Mohamed said, demonstrating how the light flashed on when he bent his wrist in an awkward yoga pose.

"Man, I can't believe I lost my Zombie Bug-Out bag. I had so many things we needed in there. I guess that old bat thought it was full of gold when she stole it. Plus, this place is at least a zombie-level orange down here. It is just reckless and crazy to be down here without any walking-dead protection," Leo warned.

Krystal laughed at Leo's obsessive, undead fear. "Well, darlin', we do have this if the undead come," she said and held up the nasty looking weapon in the light.

"You found it! I lost it when the water blasted us down the tunnel." He hugged Krystal and laughed, "I thought those idiots out there had it! I am so happy!"

Krystal continued, "I would rather try to give a pedicure to a wolverine than to fight someone holdin' that." She then handed the tall boy the boarding axe pistol.

Leo responded in all seriousness, "You stay close. If you hear any groaning, I got you covered."

Wiki interrupted, "Okay we got some light. Let's all keep talking as we inspect this large room and look for a way out." The students were reenergized now that they had light.

The flashlight blinked on and off. "Hold your wrist still!" Odessa snapped at Mohamed.

The Ugandan snapped back, "I am trying! Look, this torch is barely working."

Krystal giggled and relaxed the tension. "Yuh call a flashlight a torch; yuh foreigners are so silly sometimes."

Leo examined the wall as Mohamed slowly moved the beam across the large chamber. His toes were getting so numb that it was hard to stay on task. He encouraged Odessa again, "Okay, Wiki, use your big brain to get us out of this one."

The Greek girl blushed and ate up the praise. "Well, whenever I need to solve a puzzle, I go all Sherlock Holmes on it. What does deductive reasoning tell us about this place? The first odd thing I can think of is why there is a lock on the inside of the door and not the outside. That means the pirates not only used this as storage, but also as a safe room. If they were in trouble, they would run back this way and lock themselves in. Logically that means there should be another exit in here so they would not trap themselves. All we have to do is find the secret exit."

Krystal clapped. "That is some good mind noodle-in', darlin'! I think I know where the exit is."

The group paused. "Well, don't keep us in suspense! Where is it, Krystal?"

"Oh I thought the answer was obvious; we just follow the water, y'all. We got blasted by a huge amount of it and now it is all practically gone. Where did all that water go?"

Mohamed shined the light down the stream running from under the door, across the middle of the chamber, and to a wall on the east side. "Look at that area of the wall. The water is runnin' right under it," the farm girl pointed.

The Porcs approached the section and examined it. Krystal had no fear of cleaning the many years of caked-on green goo off the wall. "This looks like an old barrel hinge here," she pointed. "If they work like old barrel hinges in a barn, you should be able to push right here for leverage." The gang banded together and with a combined shove, freed the rusted hinges from the wall. A section of the brick wall slid open and a blast of rank-smelling air hit them in their faces.

"Yes! We are out of here. Everyone, take inventory; do we still have our booty?" Odessa commanded.

"I still have the key," Mohamed started.

"Thanks to Krystal's sharp eyes, I got the axe-pistol," Leo confirmed.

The country girl chimed in, "I sure am glad I wrapped this flag up in a couple of yard bags; it's bone dry still."

"I should say the same thing about the sandwich bag; it kept this journal nice and dry. Now let's get out of here before those awful people find their way around the door." Odessa rallied.

The only remaining working flashlight blinked on and off as the four treaded down the long passageway. Krystal's hawk eyes picked up on it first, "Look! There is a tiny bit of light at the end of this hall. Let's keep goin'!"

As they continued onward, the light grew brighter and brighter. When the Porcs reached the end of the hall, they finally realized that the light was coming from under another secret door. The group quickly found the hidden hinges and pulled on the opposite side. With a squishy sound, the door flung open, freeing itself from years of slime build up.

Although the light was very dim by normal standards, it was still blinding enough and all four tried to cover their eyes. As their eyes adapted to the low-level light, neon glow-in-the dark paintings of '70s roller disco scenes were revealed on the walls. They could see they were in a basement full of aluminum beer kegs and soda dispensing boxes with plastic hoses running from them up through the floor. There were boxes of plastic cups and napkins strewn about. "What the heck is this place?" Krystal mumbled aloud.

"I am not sure yet, but the one thing I do know is that we need to close this door back to how we found it so others won't discover it." The students worked together to conceal the sliding wall by pushing it back into its original position.

Leo pointed, "Looks like the only way out is up those stairs. I think we should..." He was interrupted by a long moaning sound. The four students froze in place. "Brainnsssss!" The sound originated from the top of the stairwell. *Thump, thump, thump* could be heard, as something from above seemed to be dragging its leg down from the top of the stairs. It was then that they realized the sound was slowly heading directly toward them.

The other three students panicked and turned to Leo. "*Shhh!* Everyone, hide behind these barrels and don't say a word." The group did as they commanded and scattered for hiding places.

Thump! Thump! Thump! A single gimp leg wearing rotten jeans appeared at the top of the stairs, banging loudly as it dragged against each step. *Thump! Thump! Thump!*

Leo became petrified as a bloodstained body with a rotten-looking head suddenly appeared. "Brainsssssssssss!" the figure moaned louder.

The creature staggered toward the keg that Leo was hiding behind. The tall boy thought to himself, "I bet the others are not laughing at me now; I knew I was right about zombies."

The walking-dead zombie moved closer to Leo's hiding place, snapping the teen back to the task at hand.

Leo prepares to strike!

"Brainssssssssss!" it screeched as its rotten teeth caught the dim lighting. Leo started to breathe heavy and began to sweat. The frightened boy tightened his grip on the axe-pistol and waited for the zombie to get close enough for him to administer a deadly blow.

"You have to take the head clean off to stop it; swing for the neck. You only get one chance! Let it get as close as possible," he reminded himself

Mohamed, with a terrible fear in his eyes, looked over at Leo as the tall boy slid both hands down to the end of the axe-pistol to gain the maximum amount of strength needed to execute a razor-sharp blow. Leo watched in terror as the undead thing stumbled closer. Odessa held Krystal as they watched Leo prepare to strike.

He gave himself one last pep talk to muster his courage. "This is it; just one more step closer and swing for the neck."

The zombie stopped dragging its leg, stood tall, and shouted back up the stairs at the open door, "Hey, Bob! I forgot which one ran out. Was it the Mountain Dew or the 7up or both?"

The talking zombie completely unraveled Leo's deadly concentration.

The sound of hurried footsteps running down the stairs filled the room and a second zombie appeared. "It's the syrup for the Mountain Dew and the soda on the 7up! I assume you need me to come down and help ya."

The original undead-walker answered, "Thanks, but check this out first. My zombie stagger is the best. I'm going to win The Best Zombie Competition for sure. Brainsssss..." he moaned as he dragged his leg and stumbled in circles.

"That's awesome! You got your stagger down good. Now let's finish this; we got a ton of people to serve up there. Grab some garbage bags, too. We're gonna need them." The men exchanged the boxes of soda and syrup and headed back up the stairs.

The three burst out laughing. "That was epic! You almost took that worker's head clean off!" Odessa chuckled.

The zombie stopped dragging its leg, stood tall, and shouted back up the stairs at the open door, "Hey, Bob! I forgot which one ran out. Was it the Mountain Dew or the 7up or both?"

The talking zombie completely unraveled Leo's deadly concentration.

The sound of hurried footsteps running down the stairs filled the room and a second zombie appeared. "It's the syrup for the Mountain Dew and the soda on the 7up! I assume you need me to come down and help ya."

The original undead-walker answered, "Thanks, but check this out first. My zombie stagger is the best. I'm going to win Best Zombie Competition for sure. Brainsssss..." he moaned as he dragged his leg and stumbled in circles.

"That's awesome! You got your stagger down good. Now let's finish this; we got a ton of people to serve up there. Grab some garbage bags, too. We're gonna need them." The men exchanged the boxes of soda and syrup and headed back up the stairs.

The three burst out laughing. "That was epic! You almost took that worker's head clean off!" Odessa chuckled.

Leo turned white as he realized he had almost chopped down an innocent man. "I can't believe it; it looked so real. I saw how scared you guys looked. You thought it was real, too."

Krystal and Odessa gave the shaken teen a hug. "Thanks for protecting us anyway, even if it was just a bar keep."

The embarrassed zombie slayer shook the girls off. "I don't want to talk about it! Let's just get back to the surface."

The group continued to snicker as the discombobulated teen vented with frustration. They chuckled all the way up the stairs. When they opened the door to the room above, they found themselves standing in a restaurant full of the walking-dead.

"Oh, yeah! Face-palm!" exclaimed Leo. "Today was the Zombie Crawl I was telling you about. I forgot all about it in the excitement of our adventure!"

One of the waiters looked at the kids standing in the doorway. After noticing that they were covered from head to toe in mud, blood, and gunk and holding the formidable-looking axe-pistol, the waiter enthusiastically shouted, "Hey Kids! Awesome costumes! You guys even smell like zombies!"

The haggard-looking group was attempting to look for an exit out of the jam-packed room full of bloody, rotting corpses when Mohamed noticed Mr. Bines and Ms. Gambit bursting through the basement door into the crowd of people. Mohamed frantically shouted, "We need to run! They are in here and will see us soon!"

Wiki thought for a millisecond and said, "No! Sit down right here. Just sit at this table right here with the other zombies. Chances are better that they won't see us mixed into this crowd. They will certainly know who we are running down the street, just the four of us, looking like this."

The four of them sat at a large table near the window, crowded in by hundreds of zombies. They lowered their heads and tried to blend in as Ms. Gambit and Mr. Bines surveyed the area, looking for them with no avail. It felt like forever, their hearts were beating hard inside their chests, but Ms. Gambit and Mr. Bines finally left.

They looked at each other sitting there covered in gunk when Krystal said, "I know that y'alls used to seein' me kinda nasty and smellin' bad, but this is ridiculous. How are we gonna make it back to the Pirates' House lookin' and smellin' like this?"

Wiki thought for a minute, figured out where they were and suggested, "If we go out the back door, there is a fountain in the courtyard of a church not too far away. We can take the back alleys there, jump in, clean off a bit, and try to go find Jah."

The four headed out the back near the bar when Leo spotted a stack of empty garbage bags. He hollered at the bar keep, "Mind if I grab one of these?" The bar keep replied, "No problem." Leo grabbed the bag, wrapped the axe-pistol up in it and the four of them, very cautiously, headed out the back door into the alley.

SECRETS SHARED

The filthy, bedraggled quad of students made their way down the alley back towards the Pirates' House. They stopped by the fountain at the church and hopped into it for a second to try to remove even the slightest bit of the yuck they were covered in. Everyone was keeping a vigilant look out for Ms. Gambit and Mr. Bines when Krystal commented, "Well, we look a LITTLE better, but we smell worse than pigs rollin' in slop. I wonder where those two ended up at after they left. I swear they seem as crooked as a barrel of fishhooks. That woman is so mean, I bet even her own dog bites her when she gets home."

The students chuckled at Krystal's attempt to lighten the mood when Mohamed confessed, "It is times like these I wish I would remember to charge my cell phone." The small group hid themselves behind bushes in the parking lot of the Pirates' House as they waited for Jah to return.

Leo offered his wisdom regarding their situation. "I have been thinking. I don't think we should tell anyone about what we found yet."

Mohamed looked confused. "Why would we not tell Ms. Mendel about our progress and report those two for assault and robbery?"

"Well, it's kinda like playing chess; you have to think a few moves ahead before you ever move your piece. I see it like this; if we go back and show everyone what we found, people will take it. I remember watching this news story about how these guys spent years of their lives searching for a shipwreck. They finally found it and the government stepped in and took almost all the gold. If people find out we have this stuff, adults will take it from us," he paused, made his fingers into air quotes and then spoke, "'for our own good'."

Mohamed scratched his chin and went into a deep thought. "Now that I think it through, you are probably right. I know my parents are greedy and would demand their fair share. It would probably end up in a legal nightmare with everybody and we would all end up fighting over money."

Leo agreed. "There is that, too; since we are minors, we are not allowed to legally own this stuff. Our parents would take ownership. Also, let's not forget, we have not found any real treasure yet; all we have found so far are some antique trinkets. This stuff might not be worth much at all."

"I hate to say it, but I think you're right. We can't talk about this stuff to anyone yet. If word gets out we found a piece of the legendary treasure, Savannah will become over run with other treasure hunters overnight. Our best chance to find the rest of the stuff is to stay quiet and study what we just found for clues," Odessa added.

Y'all, let's not forget we are in a race against time. We need to find somethin' good to sell before Jah gets even sicker," Krystal reminded them.

The group sat in silence as they thought about their next move. Fifteen minutes later the man in the sweetgrass hat pulled into the parking lot in a buggy. The anxious teens ran out of their hiding spot and flew into the carriage. "My lord, what happen ta ya, chillun?"

Krystal grabbed the old man's shoulder to emphasis the importance of the situation. "I need yuh to trust me right now. Please get us outta here now. I will explain this to yuh later."

The Gullah man understood and snapped Harricanes' reigns. The wagon took off at a fast clip and within minutes they were heading back towards the academy. Jah Loko turned to Krystal Bennett. "Okay, Titi. What dis all about?"

Krystal spoke from the heart. "Yuh remember how yuh made us all swear to keep your secret? Well, I need yuh to promise yuh will do the same. I can't tell yuh everythin' right now, but I will when the time is right. Yuh just got to trust me, Mr. Loko."

"Okay, Titi, I promise. Harricane and I will ne'er tell a soul what we hear."

Odessa butted in, "Well, all you need to know right now is we are looking for some lost stuff to help save the school. We got into a tough spot today, but got ourselves out of it. I have a feeling we will need your help a few more times before this is all over."

The old man roared with laughter. "Don't tell me ya chillun are lookin' for dat silly pirate booty, too. People done been lookin' for dat treasure for hundreds a' years wid no luck. I even went lookin' for it when I be your age. I be afraid y'all be on an impossible hunt; nobody has ever found anytin'."

Krystal bragged, "Until now." Odessa swung her hand over and swatted the tiny girl's shoulder. "*Shhh!* We all agreed not to talk about it."

The tomboy turned to the group. "Look, I know we can trust him. Besides, he could be a great deal of help. He knows everythin' there is to know 'bout Savannah. Leo, show him what yuh found."

The tall boy sighed. "Way to keep it secret, Krystal. That lasted a whole five minutes." He reached into the black garbage bag on his lap and produced April's legendary weapon.

Jah stopped the carriage and gasped, "I don't believe it! Is dis really what I tink it is?" Leo handed the old man the ancient axe-pistol.

"My goodness, chillun, do ya have any idea what a find dis be? I take it all back; y'all keep doing what ya doing." He ran his fingernail across the razor sharp blade. "Ya chillun be smart ta keep dis a secret. Many people will try to take dis wonderful find away from ya."

He handed the unusual firelock back to Leo. "Ya need's ta hide dis good boy. Ya have my word; I won't say nuttin' ta anyone about dis. I will help ya whenever ya ask. Dis be very excitin'. I can't believe after all dis time da rumors be true."

The old man grinned ear to ear with pride as the carriage pushed on toward the school.

When they arrived, the new Porcs cautiously tried to be inconspicuous, avoiding all the other students on the way to their rooms. Once inside their respective dorms, the immediate consensus was to shower and wash their funky-smelling clothes. The group covered for each other until everyone was finished cleaning up.

Leo hid the weapon behind his clothes in the closet. "I know I need a better spot, but this will have to do until I can think of something else."

Mohamed tried to help. "I saw a book on the Internet called Stash Your Swag. It teaches you the best places to hide anything. I say we download it tonight."

"Brilliant idea! We will pick up the eBook later and share it with the girls. Okay, let's pick them up and head to dinner."

"You go ahead; I have to pray again and video chat with my mom to check in. I will meet you at dinner in thirty minutes." Mohamed dug in his closet and pulled out his grass-cloth prayer mat.

Leo took his time going to the girls' room, but when he arrived he discovered that they were still getting ready. He knocked on the door and shouted, "You guys almost ready to get some dinner? I am starving!"

Odessa joked with him through the door, "Yep, just about ready. By the way, do you want to go back down to the Zombie Crawl tonight?"

The embarrassed teen mocked, "Hardy har har. You know dang well I don't want anything more to do with zombies today. I can't believe I am saying this, but I am zombied out!"

Giggles could be heard from the other side of the door before it flung wide-open, revealing Krystal in her old, beat-up cowboy hat and Odessa in a sundress. "Alrighty, we're ready to go. Where's Mo?" Krystal asked.

"Take one guess," Leo challenged.

The girls answered in unison, "Praying!"

"*Ding, ding, ding!* You ladies win a prize," Leo joked.

The three exchanged experiences about the day's events as they walked to the dining room. They got a table for four and ordered sweet teas and lemonades.

Mohamed finally appeared in a clean polo and a small bandage on his forehead. "I was surprised my mom did not ask me about my bandage. I guess she assumes I am trying to cover a runaway zit or something. My mother would kill me if she knew I had been running around underground unsupervised with girls."

The friends enjoyed the joke and were pleased to see Mohamed trying to come out of his shell more. "So what should we do tonight?" the Ugandan boy asked, changing the subject.

Wiki jumped in, "Well, you guys know I am dying to start going through this new journal looking for clues."

Leo nodded his head. "I am surprised you have waited this long. We kinda figured you would be busy tonight. What should the rest of us do?"

Odessa replied, "Not much you can do until I finish this. Go find something fun to get into."

Mohamed announced, "I do believe it is *C.O.D.* night. Krystal, would you like to join us as we shoot each other and talk about each other's momma?"

"No, computer games ain't really my thing. I need to finish readin' *Angel Star* so I can figure out which hunk the main character ends up with. Will she fall in love with the good angel, or the bad one?"

Wiki interjected, "Oh that's one of my favorite books! Hadrian sounds so dreamy. I really like how. . . "

Krystal blurted out, "Don't ruin it! I am still readin' it! Let's just relax and have a good meal; we have earned it y'all."

As the group enjoyed their dinner, the newfound friends recounted all the adventures they had been through together that day with great relish and utter amusement.

PIRATE FUNERALS
&
PEG LEGS

AM! BAM! BAM! The boys woke up to a pounding on their dormitory door. "You're on the bottom bunk, you answer it," Mohamed said to Leo as he covered his ears with the pillow.

Leo tried to ignore his roommate and pretended he was still asleep. Mohamed was on to this ruse and hit him with his pillow. "You had to have the bottom bunk, now go answer the door!"

The tall, sleepy boy dragged himself out of his slumber and stumbled toward the dream-wrecking noise. He peeped through the crack of the door and shouted, "What?"

Odessa had an enormous smile on her face. "Hurry up and get out here; it is almost lunch time already! I have come by and knocked on your door twice already and you never answered."

Mohamed looked at the clock on his wall and sprang out of his bunk. "My goodness I overslept and missed my morning prayer. My phone must be dead again; I must pray immediately!" The Ugandan boy scrambled to find his hat and prayer mat while Leo scratched the sand out of the corners of his eyes.

"Sorry, Wiki we stayed up all night gaming. We went to bed right before sunrise. I'm sure I was sleeping so hard that I didn't hear you. What's so important any way that you had to come wake us?" the exhausted skater asked.

Odessa could barely contain herself. "I think I found another clue! I want to get everyone together to tell you guys about it."

"Awesome, great work. Where is Krystal anyway?"

The Greek girl blushed at the compliment. "She is finishing up the morning stable work. She should be meeting us for lunch in about twenty minutes. So hurry up and get ready. I have something so exciting to show you."

Leo did his best not to disturb Mohamed's praying while he cleaned himself up.

Odessa sat at the dining table flipping through the sheepskin journal, reading it again for the eighth time trying to commit it to memory. The tiny girl in her large, straw cowboy hat sat down next to her. "How did Jah look this morning?" Wiki asked.

The tomboy removed her giant hat and sighed. "Not so good, darlin'. He was clutchin' his gut all mornin' while we were doin' chores. We need to help him soon. Can't we sell this stuff we just found and give him the money now?"

Odessa shook her head. "No! Leo is right; when people know we have this stuff they will all try to take it away from us. Also, even if we sold everything we found, I don't think it would come close to paying for an operation. I was doing research and operations are stupid expensive."

Krystal waved her hands in frustration. "So what should we do? I hate seein' him suffer like that."

"The only solution I can think of is to find a lot more treasure, and I think I might have found another clue," the acne-faced girl said with a smile.

"Well, spill it girl! What'd ya find?"

"I can't tell you until the boys get here; they should be here any minute."

"I can't wait. Come on, yuh can tell a girlfriend," Krystal pushed.

"Here, order another giant, apple puff pancake," she distracted her friend with the lure of decadent food.

The calculated move worked and the small girl instantly became distracted as she focused on the daily menu.

The boys finally arrived and took their seats at the table. "Okay, spill it girl!" Leo demanded.

Odessa leaned in and lowered her voice, "Here's what I figured out so far."

The other three students huddled in tight and focused.

She continued. "It looks like Admiral Read kept a couple of these journals, but I think this might have been one of her last. It is mainly a mix of her rum-running schedules and contacts. Part of it is a personal journal. She talks about her husband Patrick and their daughter Tracy a good bit, but nothing real helpful."

Leo let out a sigh of frustration. "Well, that is some cool history, but that does not help us find any buried treasure."

The Greek girl raised her hand at the impatient teen. "Hold on, there's more. The last few pages are all about Shamus Red's funeral. It seems Shamus and Sam Scurvy were both so rich that they became the most wanted men in the Lowcountry. All kinds of people kept trying to kill them to take their booty."

The group edged in tighter and listened as Wiki's voice dropped to a whisper. "The book doesn't say anything else about Sam Scurvy and his silver sword, but it does say a good bit more about Shamus. To avoid all the assassination attempts, the pirate faked his own death. April helped him stage an elaborate funeral over at Colonial Park Cemetery. The great thing about this journal is April's sense of humor. The Admiral talks about how Shamus blew his own leg off in a drunken stupor during an attack on a ship. Later in life he had a custom peg leg made for him out of solid gold."

Odessa began to snicker. "April goes on to say what a terrible idea that peg leg was. The pirate, Shamus, was so drunk when he commissioned it that he did not remember doing it. When the peg leg arrived, it took two men just to carry it in. Even though a gold peg leg sounds awesome, it was so heavy it was completely useless to walk with. The only time Shamus could wear it was when he was sitting down and wanted to show it off to women. He would sit himself down at the parties he hosted and have his servants strap on the heavy prosthetic. Then the guests would be allowed to enter and he would try to impress women with it. April said he was not strong enough to have even taken one step with it on."

The group chuckled at the pirate's poorly thought out predicament.

"April goes on to say he also had a diamond-encrusted eye patch and a gold hook, but never mentions how he lost his eye or hand."

"Does she say where the golden peg leg, diamond-encrusted eye patch, or hook ever ended up?" Krystal questioned.

The Greek girl shook her head in frustration. "No, all the book says is that he wanted April to make sure it was passed down to his son. He gave her everything to hold on to during the fake funeral. So, I know April had them all in her possession at one time, but this journal ends with Shamus's fake funeral."

"Well, that doesn't help us that much. Now what?" Mohamed emoted.

Odessa smiled. "Don't give up; I do have something that might help us. I forgot to tell you the best part. Shamus knew that grave robbers would dig up his body when they could get away with it, so he planted a surprise for anyone digging up his grave."

"A surprise? What did he go and hide?" Krystal said, demanding an answer.

Wiki shrugged. "I don't know if I should tell you, it was really crude and gross. Apparently, Shamus Red was world-renowned for his pirate foulness."

"Come on, tell us already!" her companions demanded.

Odessa sighed and flustered with embarrassment. She stared at the ceiling so she would not have to look them in the eye while she told them. "The pirate, Shamus, filled a coffin with jars of his excrement and had April bury it in his place."

"Ewwwww! That is nasty!" Mohamed pretended to vomit.

Leo smiled with delight. "I bet that taught those grave robbers a good lesson! That is hilarious!"

"Although that was pretty darn funny, that does not help us find Shamus Red's treasure." Krystal remarked.

"Well, he commissioned a special gravestone that was supposed to have a clue leading his son to his real gravesite. Apparently, Shamus knew he was really sick and had April make plans for his real place of rest," Odessa finally revealed.

Mohamed looked up and thought aloud, "So, let me get this straight; are you saying Shamus Red had a fake burial plot, but the gravestone at the site has a secret message on it leading to his booty?"

"Yep, that is about the summary of it. This whole time hundreds of thousands of visitors at the Colonial Park Cemetery have probably been walking right past the clue and never knew it. We need to get down there right away and find his gravestone," Odessa pushed the others with excitement.

"Wait, wait, wait! I really want to go down and look around, but I have to get a little work done. It has been days since I have maintained the garden. If my garden fails, they will throw me out of here. I need the rest of the day to catch up, and then we can roll," Leo offered.

Mohamed added, "I want to go, too, but for once I have to agree with my friend. I have an entire music program to put together and if I don't show any progress, Ms. Mendel will be disappointed and dismiss me. If I have to leave this place in shame, my parents will be very mad with me. I need to work today."

Krystal threw her two cents in. "Sorry, girl. We gotta help shoe Harricane today. I can't go either until my work is done."

Odessa looked disappointed, but understood. "Okay, I will keep doing research. But I say we leave tonight after dinner and look around. I don't want to wait another day."

"Will we be allowed out that late? I don't think they will just let us off campus unsupervised to roam around a graveyard at night," Mohamed challenged.

The group grew quite as they realized Mohamed was correct. "I gots an idear, y'all. I will see if Jah will take us out to explore the idea of makin' some night tours. Let me ask him; I doubt he would say no to little ol' me," Krystal said as she batted her eyelashes and threw the group a look of childhood innocence.

Krystal's friends giggled at her little display. "I will meet y'all at supper and I will tell yuh if Jah said yes."

The four Porcupines were filled with such grand expectations of treasure that they stuffed their food down quickly. With visions of gold dancing in their heads, each Porc went joyously to their respective jobs.

25 CHAPTER

RENE'S GHOST

O dessa, Mohamed, and Leo all crammed food down their gullets and waited impatiently for Krystal to arrive. "Where is she? We are ready!" Wiki stated agitatedly.

A tan, well-kept blonde woman in a brightly colored dress arrived at the table. "How's y'all's work coming?" Ruby interrupted.

The three had no idea what to say and just answered with blank stares.

Ms. Mendel tried again. "I am asking y'all to report your progress. I know we give you complete freedom to make y'alls own classes, but you are accountable you know. Catch me up. Miss Skouras, you go first."

The Greek girl tried to stop thinking about the treasure for a minute and focused on answering the aging woman's question. "Well, I have been digging up a tremendous amount of good information on Admiral April Read and the pirate Shamus Red. I think I am about to uncover some great stuff. I will have something for you soon."

Ruby flashed a nervous smile. "Well, don't take too long. I am hoping to hear what you have soon. Mr. Obuntu, what did you come up with?"

Mohamed explained, "Well I was thinking of making the upcoming alumni ball a swing music theme. We could ask the guest to dress in clothes from the 1920s-1950s and even give a brief dance lesson. Since the world famous Johnny Mercer is from here, I think we need to make an entire feature around his best swing-era songs. What do you think?"

"I love the idea, well done. I will take any chance I get to wear a flapper dress. I need you to come up with an expense report for the supplies you will need. Also, I will give you a list of some music alumni to help you make up your band. Mr. Stedman, how is our garden?"

"Well, I have planted some peppers and watermelons. I am also trying to grow strawberries, blueberries, and raspberries. Unfortunately, it got so hot so quick it has been a real fight keeping them alive. We really need some shade back there so they are not in direct sun all day. It is frying everything. I also want to use an empty stall in the barn to try to grow mushrooms," Leo explained.

"I think the mushrooms sound very promising. I also think it is already too hot for berries and you missed that window. Make sure you rotate the watermelons and keep them from getting too hot, or they will explode. Oh, I see Krystal is finally here," Ruby said as she pointed at a dirty girl in a cowboy hat approaching the table.

"Hello, Miss Bennett. I told Mr. Loko that you four can go out tonight to study the feasibility of night tours. Did he tell you?" Ms. Mendel asked.

The tomboy flashed a grin to her friends, "Yes ma'am! I am about as excited as a monkey on a mule. I can't wait to see the town at night."

"Very good! Mind yourselves out there and follow whatever Jah Loko tells you to do; he is in charge. Next time we talk I am hoping we have made some more progress. Enjoy your meal folks." Ruby waved her hand that was adorned with many rings and moved on to talk to another table of kids about their progress.

"Jah agreed to take us to the cemetery, but we are not supposed to go very far without him. He only said 'yes' with the condition that we do not leave Colonial Park Cemetery for any reason!" she squealed with excitement.

Wiki gave her a hug. "Great work, girl! Now hurry up and eat so we can go. Leo, did you get what we needed?"

The tall boy held up Mohamed's expensive designer backpack. "Well, since my Zombie Bug-Out Bag is still missing, we had to improvise. I bought some new flashlights and got you a book of tracing paper and some coal from the art department. Do you plan to sketch a portrait of us while we are out there?"

"I will explain it later. Just make sure everything stays dry this time," Wiki warned. To speed things up, Krystal just ate the other three's leftovers instead of ordering. The gang watched the small girl sock away some food, while Mohamed disappeared for his sunset prayer. When the Muslim boy returned, they all hurried to the stables.

As the group made their way down to Jah Loko, Krystal turned to Mohamed and pointed to the brimless, cylindrical hat on his head. "Do you have to always wear that? Is that, like, a religious thing?"

Mohamed informed her saying, "No, not a religious thing. Many Muslim men wear them to show respect and for fashion. The cap is called a kofia and I wear it because it is popular where I am from. Sometimes when I pray I also wear a white shirt with a tassel called a kanzu. It is also very popular in Muslim Uganda. I wanted to stop wearing it when we moved here two years ago, but my father insists I keep wearing it. Unfortunately, it brings much unwanted attention from the bullies in my school."

Krystal sighed. "I know a thing or two about bullies, also. They were always teasing me about my cowgirl hat. Sure, I think they are cute, but if I did not have it I would be continuously sun burnt. I just don't understand why other kids care what I wear. I don't care what they wear."

"You said you are from a Christian family; how often do you pray a day?" Mohamed questioned.

The country girl explained, "Well, that is left up to the person doing the praying. Like, my grandmomma prays all the time. She be talkin' to Jesus all day long like 'Jesus, give me the strength not to choke the daylights outta that girl!' Then there be folks like myself. I mostly pray when I'm in church. Let me tell yuh though, we Pentecostals pray real hard on Sundays.

Our morning service done run like three hours and then our night service run for another two. I get nothin' done except for church on Sundays. But since my momma is havin' so many money problems, we've not been goin' like we should."

Leo responded, "I don't think I could spend that much time praying."

Mohamed shook his head. "I enjoy prayer. I feel relaxed and connected to Allah every time I do it. Why wouldn't I want to feel good at least five times a day?"

"Leo, I have to admit, there are definitely days when I don't want to be in church that long, but what can yuh do? Like Mo says, yuh feel really good afterwards, so I do really like going," Krystal admitted.

"You know when you say 'Jesus' backwards it sounds like sausage?" Leo joked with her.

Krystal snorted. "That's hilarious! But, I'll not be pointin' that out to my pastor. What 'bout you, Leo? What do you believe?"

"Oh, I don't go to church or believe in a God," the tall boy confessed.

The Muslim looked taken aback by this news and Krystal looked uncomfortable.

"Do you think that just because a person doesn't believe in God that they cannot be a good, honest, and faithful friend?" Leo challenged.

"That is a tough question, my friend. I would like to think you could, but I don't know," Mohamed admitted. "What I do know, Leo, is that even with the lack of a God to believe in, you have been a good friend and you are not mean or spiteful. You are respectful of our religions and of us. Also, my views on liberty teach me that for yourself to be truly free, one must let others live however they want, even if you disagree with them. So, yes, I would say that it is possible to be good without a religion."

"Well, I am glad you are open-minded and able to be my friend without religious differences stopping that. It shows a level of good nature in you," responded Leo with a smile.

Odessa interjected with her unsolicited opinion. "Us Greek Orthodox know how to do it. We are in and out of the service in one hour and then we go eat amazing food. Sometimes it is really great being Greek."

The group of religious philosophers finally arrived at the stable. They quickly found Jah and Harricane ready to go. As the waxy moon started to rise, the carriage pulled out. The four could hardly contain themselves as Colonial Park Cemetery came into sight. Jah warned the children saying, "Chillun, ya got's thirty minutes ta do ya snoopin'. Da cemetery be closed now, so don't be gettin' caught. I be waitin' right here if ya need me for anytin'"

The crew nodded their heads indicating that they understood his terms and departed. An old iron gate surrounded most of the cemetery. The grounds normally were backlit by streetlights and the police station, but some mist rising from the hot ground already made the area hazy. Compounding the blackness was the fact that about half the lights from the street were not on. Two of the lights that were working were having some sort of issues and flickered in the haze. The malfunction caused a strobe light effect on the mist.

"What the heck is with the lights? Is the cemetery having a rave tonight?" Leo joked.

Not being cool enough to even know what a rave was, Odessa faked it anyway and laughed with the others. Slowly they entered the blackness through the wrought iron archway.

Odessa took charge. "This is a big place; we need to split up to cover all the gravestones. Leo and Krystal, you go that way and Mo and I will go this way. Holler if you find something."

Krystal confessed, "This might take some time. I got a bad habit of lookin' for my own name on the tombstones."

Leo snickered, "I guess that is sort of a Goth way of Googling yourself, huh?"

The tiny girl hit him on the shoulder with her cowboy hat. "Shut up. Who yuh callin' Goth?"

Before entering the cemetery, Mohamed removed his shoes. Odessa looked at the Muslim boy in confusion. Sensing the Greek girl's stare, he explained, "One should not wear shoes in a graveyard; it is disrespectful in our religion." He then recited a prayer in his native language before entering.

"I never knew that, but if you don't mind, I will be leaving my boots on. Now come on, we don't have much time and it is getting really dark." Wiki beckoned the boy to follow her into the flickering, lamplit mist.

Krystal and Leo made their pass and examined the first few grave markers. "Man, some of these are so old I can't make out the names at all."

"Well, Jah and Wiki said these graves go back hundreds of years and there are bodies piled on top of bodies that we are treadin' on," the girl in the straw hat shot back.

"It's times like this when I really wish I hadn't of lost my Zombie Bug-Out Bag. We are totally defenseless," the tall boy groaned in frustration.

Krystal shined her light on an ancient tombstone. "Well, I am not worried about zombies as much as I am worried about ghosts. Now, I believe in ghosts and right now we are all alone at night, in the fog, in the most haunted place on the planet. If I see one iota of a spirit or Rene's ghost, I'm runnin' outta here. I don't care how much gold we lose, I won't go back in."

On the other side of the graveyard, Odessa's excitement overwhelmed her fear of the forbidding cemetery. Her flashlight burned through the mist as she quickly searched the names on the tombstones. "I am starting to wonder if Shamus's body is actually tucked away in Rene's catacombs."

Mohamed shrugged his shoulders, not following her reasoning.

"You know the twisted maze of tunnels under this cemetery is supposed to be haunted by Rene Asche Rondolier, right?"

Mohamed continued to look dumbfounded.

"How many years have you been living here and you have not heard of Rene's Playground?"

Her companion threw his hands in the air to express an apology.

The Greek girl continued to eagerly search while she explained. "Back in 1777, a seven foot, five inch, hairy ape-like man named Rene lived in Savannah. They say he was psychologically messed up. He hung out all the time in this graveyard and is even rumored to live in the catacombs under it. He had a reputation for torturing and killing animals and then moving on to doing the same to two young girls. He was lynched and hung out in the swamps, but people have been seeing his ghost here for over two hundred years. He normally appears as a tall, massive black shadow that follows little girls around the graveyard."

Mohamed tried to appear brave. "I don't believe in ghosts, so I am not worried," he said, though his hands quietly trembled.

The night mist seemed to have thickened since they started their search and now the two groups could no longer make out a visual of each other. Sea breezes blew in hard and the Spanish moss hanging from the live oaks rustled making an unnerving sound.

As Leo and Krystal made their way through the graveyard's six acres of land, examining yet another aboveground brick crypt, Leo, without warning, put his arm out. "*Shhh!* Did you hear that?"

A low-pitched moan was audible in the fog. Leo called out, "Odessa! Mo! Is that you guys?"

The groan grew louder as an incoherent mumbling could be heard heading straight for them. Krystal slipped behind the tall boy, using him as a human shield.

"Come on you guys, stop fooling around! You are creeping Krystal out!" Leo shouted into the fog.

A long, black shadow grew larger in the mist until the figure of it finally rested, pointing at the tomboy's feet.

Rene's ghost in Colonial Park Cemetery.

Terror overwhelmed Krystal and she dashed to the gate, leaving Leo as a sacrifice. "It's Rene's ghost! Everyone get out of here!"

Odessa and Mohamed saw the lurking figure dash toward the exit and tried to figure out what was going on.

"Get out! It's Rene! It's Rene!" Krystal repeatedly screamed as her light trailed off into the darkness.

Leo was stricken with fear, but his overwhelming curiosity nailed his feet to the ground. He watched as the shadow moved toward him and the groaning grew louder. Leo followed the outline of the long shadow back to a black figure silhouetted in the mist against the flashing streetlight.

Mohamed and Odessa froze in place, not sure if they should investigate and help Leo, or run for their lives.

The mumbling was nerve wracking and sounded like complete gibberish. "I knew it," Leo said, "this is no ghost; it's a zombie fo'realz!" Leo reached down to take out his large Zombie Apocalypse knife from his Bug-Out Bag, but his hand searched in vain. "Dang, I forgot." He then balled up his fists and leaned into a fighting stance, holding his ground.

The figure finally got close enough that his characteristics could now clearly be seen. A small, old man stumbled into the light and continued talking to himself. The drunken man finally noticed the tall boy and slurred, "Park's closed. Go find your own place to sleep."

Leo couldn't believe his eyes. He relaxed his fists and stared at the homeless man in disbelief.

The intoxicated man grew angry and threw his empty, paper-bag-shrouded bottle toward Leo. "Park's closed!...*mumble, mumble, mumble*...MY PARK! *Mumble, mumble*...MY BENCH!*" he babbled as he staggered back into the darkness.

Leo shook his head and whispered to himself, "Oh I am not telling the others I got fooled again. Forget it. I will just say it really was a zombie, but it got away." He nodded to himself and said, "Yep, this would be a satisfactory story for the others; they would believe it."

ZOMBIES & TOMBSTONES

"**M**ista Hughes? It's Bines," said the fat man into his cell phone. "You neva gonna believe what I'm lookin' at. I just got off at the bus stop and I saw that brat Leo an' those otha three medlin' kids gettin' out of a carriage here at Colonial Park Cemetery. They out there now searchin' all the tombstones for somethin'. Whatchya want me to do?"

"Don't do anything but watch for right now," stated the extremely agitated Hughes. "I'll go get Ms. Gambit. Sneak in there and watch them until we get there."

"But Mista Hughes, I can't get in. The carriage driver be sittin' right at the entrance," Bines protested.

"There is a back entrance at the south end of the cemetery where the homeless people sleep. Go in that way and we'll be there in five."

"Come on, Krystal. Come back in and help. We don't have much time left and I think we are getting close," Odessa pleaded.

"No way! I am stayin' right here ridin' shotgun," she said as she pointed at the carriage.

"Okay, chillun, one more time; what happened in dere exactly?" the Gullah man questioned.

"You heard it right the first time; we saw a zombie. It was so scared of me it ran off," Leo fudged.

"A zombie, ya say? Is it safe now?" the old man pressed.

Leo waved. "Come on, Krystal. It's all good now. The creature is not coming back."

"I know what I saw out there; it was the ghost of Rene. Nope, y'all go on without me. I am stayin' behind. Consider me as useless as a pocket in ladies underwear," the frightened girl said, refusing to leave.

"She is not going guys. Let's go back in and find this gravestone, come on," Mohamed pushed.

The three ran back into the graveyard and split up to cover more ground. After fifteen minutes they came up empty handed. The three met at the Dueler's Monument, a gravestone that honored those who died dueling in Savannah's brutal past.

"I think we are out of luck. Most of these headstones are not old enough and are a hundred years too new. I guess Shamus Red's tombstone is not here anymore," Mohamed said, letting out an annoyed sigh.

Leo protested, "But we are so close! Maybe we should check them all again to be sure."

Odessa's mind cranked up and she smiled. "You know, we forgot about all the mystery tombstones that General Sherman's army vandalized in that war." She pointed into the mist and said, "Don't forget all the broken headstones that are bolted to the brick on the back side of the police station."

Leo grinned. "I forgot that a wall of the police station is part of the boundary of the cemetery. Let's go back and take a look before Jah makes us leave."

The three walked to the east side of the cemetery, surveying the loose and broken grave markers pinned up along the wall and slowly illuminated the vandalized stones. "Some of the artwork on these old stones are amazing," she whispered. "Look, this one has a grim reaper on it. Major creepy!"

The students inspected each one, but eventually came to the last one without any luck. "This stinks. I really thought we would find it on this wall," the Greek girl cried out in an upset tone.

The three hung their heads in defeat, neither wanting to return to face Jah and Krystal. Leo broke the mood and started to laugh. "Wiki, did I tell you how awesome your big brain is today?"

A puzzled look crept onto her face. "*Umm*, nooooooo."

"Most of the stories you tell just kinda go over my head, or I don't listen, but one kinda stuck in there," stated Leo. "Didn't you say many the graves were vandalized by Sherman's troops?"

A gleam of hope flashed in the Greek girl's eyes. "Yes, that's correct. The Union soldiers kicked them over or scratched out and changed their names and dates. See that one? It says he was born in 1726 and died in 11776"

The tall boy flashed a bright white smile. "Come on, I want to show you something."

The treasure hunters jogged down until Leo stopped and shined his light at an inconspicuous tombstone pinned on the wall. The skater started laughing. "See? That's hilarious!" he said. Mohamed and Odessa leaned in to get a better look.

"I don't get it, Leo. What's so funny?" Mohamed asked. "All this stone says in S. Redrum."

"Come on guys! Don't you watch any old movies? Think 1980 horror classic...let me give you a hint." Leo shined the flashlight on his face, contorted it then smiled like a demon. "Heeeere's Johnny!"

Mohamed and Wiki stood uneasily, staring at the strange display.

"You two are so lame. It's from *The Shining*. You know, "redrum" is what the little kid Danny says." Leo mimicked the talking finger from the movie and spoke in a strange, high-pitch voice. "Redrum, Redrum, Redrum!"

Odessa interrupted his performance piece. "I have no idea what you're talking about, but what does a 1980s movie have to do with this headstone?"

Leo confirmed. "Well, you said it had already been vandalized in the War of Northern Aggression."

Vandalized tombstones pinned to the wall

Odessa agreed. "Yes, that's right, but I probably said it was broken in the Civil War, but go on with your train of thought."

His dark hair hung over his left eye as he smiled. "What if it was vandalized a second time in the 1980s? Probably some kids thought it would be cool to spell murder backwards"

"That's what 'redrum' means, it is the word 'murder' spelled backwards!" Mohamed shouted.

This idea clicked with Odessa and she put her face inches away from the name etched in the stone, holding the light at an angle across the chiseled lettering. "I think you're right. The words "S. Red" are chiseled in deep, but the word "rum" looks like it was just scratched in, is very shallow and off center."

"What are we looking for?" the African teen asked. The three stared intently at the archaic rock, scanning for clues. They reached out and palpated the cold stone, probing for a secret message. After five minutes of vigorous inspection, Mohamed spoke up. "Is it possible that whatever the clue was, it has now been washed away with time? I don't see or feel a thing on this headstone."

"We are so close; this has to be it. All I see is the name and the year," Wiki exclaimed with a frustrated grunt.

"Well, I guess we should go search the tunnels under here and give Rene's Playground a good look," Leo concluded.

"No way. I have had enough of exploring Savannah's creepy underground. I guess we will have to call it a night and come back again another day," Odessa said and prepared herself to walk back through the eerie fog.

The defeated three slowly lumbered toward the carriage, walking in silence. As they passed the large monument honoring one of the signers the constitution, Button Gwinnett, Mohamed stopped in his tracks. "We need to go back, we missed something."

"No way, man. Three sets of eyes looked at every inch of that thing. We couldn't have missed anything," Leo countered.

"Not true, my friend. We only looked at half of it. We forgot there is a backside of the headstone against the wall we never looked at." Mohamed's dimples appeared on his cheeks as he spoke.

The students raced back to the tombstone pinned against the wall with iron spikes. Mohamed examined the rusted fasteners. "Look, these two have rusted so much over the years I think I can wiggle this side free so we can peek behind it."

"If we do this, it has to be fast. Remember, the gravestone is attached to the police station wall. On the other side of this is probably some cop's desk," Leo warned.

"Hold on, let me get the rubbing paper ready." Odessa reached into the backpack and removed the tissue paper and charcoal.

"*Ohhhhh*, I feel stupid now! So that's what that paper is for," Leo confessed as he watched Odessa take a rubbing of the front of the stone.

Mohamed pleaded, "I need your help, Leo! This is very heavy and I will never forgive myself if we drop and break this thing. I believe the spikes are long enough that we should be able to slide it off the wall some and not take it off completely."

Leo and Mohamed bent their knees and placed themselves in a weight-baring position. They counted together. "One, two, three!" The sound of a thousand nails on a thousand chalkboards filled the air as the headstone scraped against the rusted spikes. Immediately a large black cloud of crows erupted from the trees around them as the sound of the screeching stone had disrupted their slumber. Wiki covered her face to defend herself from the murder of crows exploding around her. Her screams of fear were barely heard above the deafening sound.

"Wiki! Hurry up and get the rubbing. This thing is so heavy; I don't know how long we can keep it balanced up here!" Leo shouted over the flapping of wings.

The Greek girl composed herself enough to wedge the tissue paper onto the backside of the grave marker. There was just barely room for her to squeeze her hand in and rub. The boys grunted as they wrestled with the weight, but Wiki was meticulous and made sure she got a rubbing of the entire backside. She wanted to be sure she would not miss any part of the surface.

"Everyone hush! Do you hear something? I hear something out there! We are not alone," said Mohamed in a quiet, panicky voice.

As they listened to the silent night, they heard, *"Beep"*. Leo said very quietly "Mo, dude, heck of a time to get a text message."

Mohamed responded, "It wasn't my phone. I haven't charged it in days."

Chills ran up Wiki's spine. She said, "Well, whoever got a text is real close to us right now. We need to get outta here!"

Ms. Gambit and Mr. Hughes walked around in the dark trying to find Mr. Bines when Ms.Gambit said to Hughes, "I'll text him. We could be walking around here in the dark for hours."

Before Mr. Hughes could stop the woman, he heard a beep come from the eastside wall of the cemetery. "You stupid woman!" Hughes shouted quietly at her. "You have given us away. Hurry over to the East wall so we can catch those kids." They both ran through the dark toward the direction of the beep.

Mr. Bines stood fifteen feet away from the kids, looking at the glowing text sent by Ms. Gambit. He cursed her for having given up his position. He felt that for a fat man he had tracked those kids in the dark like a tomcat stalking a rat, but now they knew he was there.

The jig was up. The kids knew they were not alone. They could hear voices coming from everywhere now and a group of people with flashlights could be seen approaching from the North.

"Okay, Wiki, pull your hand out," Leo commanded. "We gotta go now!"

The second she moved, the two boys pushed the stone back onto the rusty metal spikes. The noise the stone made against the metal cut through the quiet, foggy night like a banshee wail.

"Hey you, freeze! Police!" the officer's voice echoed in the graveyard. A powerful police flashlight cut though the sixty yards of mist. It illuminated the grave robbers and now the children saw Mr. Bines standing mere feet away from them.

"Run!" Leo shouted at his friends. Leo took off running in one direction in the fog, while his two companions took off towards the gate. Ms. Gambit continued toward the ensuing mayhem, while Mr. Hughes ran out the back gate.

"I can't be caught with them here. It will ruin me for sure," Hughes thought to himself as he deserted his two minions in the cemetery.

Mr. Bines never did too much thinking for himself anyway and just took off after Leo. If he could only catch one, it was going to be that kid who had cost him his job. He shouted at Leo, "I'm coming to get you kid! I don't care none about the Popo. I'm gonna wring your neck!"

Jumping over tombstones and graves, Leo hollered back over his shoulder, "Only if you can catch me first, fat man!" Leo reached the wrought iron fence and scaled it easily. The huge man tried in vain to get his roly-poly rear over the fence. The police were rapidly approaching, so Mr. Bines abandoned his futile attempt to catch Leo and started heading towards the back exit. He was panting so hard and getting so dizzy that he didn't even notice the approaching officer until he was eating the grass. The officer smashed Mr. Bines' face hard into the ground and shouted at him, "You're under arrest! You have the right to remain silent..."

Ms. Gambit watched from behind a tree as the officer took her partner down and smashed his teeth in the dirt. "Well," she thought, "Hughes is not going to be happy with us at all. I guess I better get out of here before they get me, too."

Mohamed and Odessa practically dove into the carriage and lay down on the floor. Jah saw Leo about a block away, jumping the fence. He started the carriage up to meet him. Leo jumped into the carriage and shouted, "Get out of here, quick!" The old man knew better than to ask questions right then and gave the horse a "giddy-up." The buggy made its escape while the five of them watched beams of light frantically searching the mist.

Once they gained distance enough to declare a safe getaway, Jah asked, "Chillun, ya want ta tell me what dat was all about?"

Leo deflected the question and only answered with one word, "Zombies!"

The other two criminals tried to keep a straight face and nodded in agreement.

Leo changed the subject and pressed Odessa, "Okay, Wiki, pull out the rubbing. Let's see what you found."

The Greek girl looked down in her clenched hand and was thrilled to see the delicate paper had somehow survived the great escape unscathed. She tugged out the wrinkles while Mohamed shined the flashlight on it.

Even Jah stopped what he was doing and leaned in to get a closer look. After a minute of silent study, she gave a vague conclusion. "Well, it looks like it is just a random bunch of holes. Like a group of circles in a strange pattern."

Odessa passed it to Leo for a better look. "Maybe it is a map?"

Krystal leaned in, "Or maybe it is like connect the dots and it becomes a picture or something."

Jah even took a stab. "Perhaps it be like a pictographic secret language, ya know? Like da pharaohs had."

A quiet humming could be heard from Mohamed's seat. The group slowly turned to him as his tune became louder and louder. A grin swallowed the Ugandan boy's face. "Nope. Guys this is no map; it's a song!"

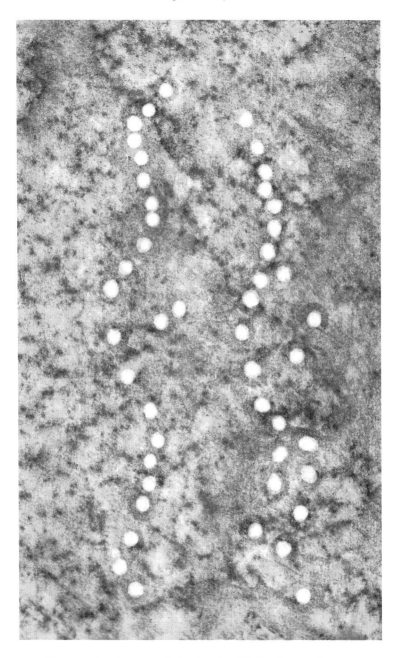

Charcoal rubbing of the back of S. Red's tombstone

27 CHAPTER

THE MUSIC OF THE DEAD

I t was almost midnight by the time the students broke down the carriage and put Harricane out to pasture. Krystal gave Jah a big hug and ran over to join her friends. "I am going to scan this rubbing in the computer before we ruin it and then email it over to Mohamed." Turning to Mohamed she said, "See if you can figure out what it means."

The Porcupines knew music was not their area of expertise and placed their faith in Mohamed's brain. The four spilt up and got ready for bed.

A stressful week had gone by while the group waited for Mohamed to come up with anything pertaining to the rubbing. One morning, Krystal, who had already been up for hours doing barn chores, delightfully gnawed on her traditional breakfast of apple puff pancakes and waited for her treasure-seeking cohorts.

Finally, the other three friends arrived together and joined the girl. Leo Stedman started complaining right away. "Man, that garden is killing me. Ruby is going to be mad if she doesn't see some sprouts soon. I am growing without pesticides, so I can sell the food as organic and get a higher price for them. The only problem with that idea is all the wild things come and eat the seedlings before they are old enough to handle the nibbling. The squirrels and rats keep digging up and eating the seeds. I think I need to borrow a cat for a while."

Krystal joined in. "I hear yuh. Rats keep gettin' into our barrels of feed. I think we should get a few cats to patrol the garden and barn. I will ask Ms. Mendel if we can work it into the budget; I know there are many cats at the Humane Society who would love a home. We could also contact the Milton Project. They help spay and neuter feral cats and I'm sure they can point us in the right direction."

Odessa shook her head. "I don't know how long I can keep stalling. Ms. Mendel wants me to finish my pirate research and hurry up and lay out a tour. Once I start to help Jah as a tour guide, I will never be free to find the treasure."

"Sorry, you guys," Mohamed said, "I am so close. I am trying. I feel I know this tune, but I can't place it. Something is really wrong with it. I will keep trying. I know Mr. Loko needs that money soon. My problem is I have had no time to study it. Ms. Mendel has been all over me making sure I have entertainment set up for the alumni ball," Mohamed explained.

The four continued to share in each other's frustrations that came along with responsibility and managing your own business. When breakfast was finished, Mohamed agreed to keep working on the mystery tune.

Later Leo, Krystal, and Wiki showed up in Mohamed's room just as he was finishing his afternoon prayer. He rolled up his prayer mat and took down the picture of Mecca he was kneeling towards.

"We have been waiting all day. What did you find?" Odessa demanded.

"Let me show you what I figured out, but please never tell anyone you were in here. My dad would freak out if he knew you girls were in my room." Mohamed pulled out a copy of the rubbing from his backpack. He placed the paper on his music stand and the group crowded around. Mohamed then pointed at the copy. "Take a good look, guys. I drew a staff in and figured out the correct meter for this. You will see how it directly lines up on the ledger lines. The pattern is in excellent shape if you look at it. Now have a listen."

Mohamed composes the music notes from S. Red's Tombstone

The musician removed his deep red-colored trumpet from its protective case. He fluttered his fingers over the keys to knock the stiffness out of them. The Porcupines listened as Mohamed started to play a soft ballad. The students were impressed until he played the second measure. Their ears were attacked with a steady rhythm of off pitch notes and an ear-assaulting melody.

"Stop man, please. That is terrible. I think you need to practice a lot more and then come get us when it sounds better," Leo begged.

Mohamed was offended. "I don't need to practice. I am playing it perfectly. The song is just awful; it's not me, man."

"I don't get it. How is this the clue April talked about in her diary?" Odessa inquired.

"It took over a week, but I think I cracked the code. Here, listen to this." Mohamed then pulled out another piece of sheet of music and prepared to play. This tune sounded similar, but was not auditory abuse like the last song. The group listened quietly until Mohamed finished.

Krystal smiled. "That tune was real pretty, Mohamed. It sounded real old."

Leo agreed. "It sounded like an old sea chanty or something I would have heard at the renaissance festival. What is it?"

"I knew I had heard it before, but it took me a week until I remembered where. A few years ago, I had to do a concert playing colonial music and this was our closing song," Mohamed recalled.

"It almost sounds Irish or Scottish. I like it," Krystal complimented.

Mohamed was impressed. "Very good! It is a very old Scottish, Irish, and English tune. All three nationalities try to take credit for it and there are over one hundred versions of it. It is called "Barbara Allen."

Mohamed smiled at the girls and continued. "It is a love ballad about a man named William who dies and professes his secret love to a woman named Barbara Allen on his death bed. She pines for him the rest of her days until she is buried next to him. Two red rose bushes grow on their graves and the flowers climb all the way up the top of a tower. When the branches grew as high as they could, they twisted together on the very top to form a love knot."

"Aweeeee!" The girls let out a collective sigh of romance while Leo rolled his eyes in annoyance.

Mohamed explained more. "It took me a while, but I removed all the off-pitch notes and this tune was what was left."

Wiki scratched her head and searched her memory. "April's last journal talked about how Shamus was leaving a hidden trail so his infant son could follow it and find his treasure later. This is definitely a clue trying to tell his son something, but what?"

The group stared at the sheet music and pondered.

Krystal finally piped up, "What if the clue is not the song at all?"

The other three stared at the tomboy.

She stuck her muddy hands in her overalls. "Look, I know I am not the most educated and am prolly the slowest wit here, but y'all hear me out on this one. I don't know music that well, but what if that pirate was tellin' his son a secret message with the notes removed from the song? Like, what if Shamus put the off-key notes there on purpose so only someone that really knew about music would figure out which notes to remove?"

Odessa grinned and squeezed the dirt-covered girl. "That's genius! Mo, can you write down all the off-pitch notes you removed in the order you took them out?"

Mohamed flashed his dimples. "One minute!" He grabbed his notebook and began transcribing. After three minutes he finished and showed the sheet of notes to the group.

"I don't know what all these circles and dots mean, but don't these notes have corresponding letters? Can you write the names of the notes under them?" Leo requested.

The musician quickly wrote little letters under each note. "How's that?"

Odessa pointed at the transcription. "Whoa! Do you guys see that? It is just the same word over and over."."

28 CHAPTER

GABECAGE

"Look at the pattern. If you lay out all the notes in the order they were removed, it says the same eight-letter phrase over and over." Odessa held the paper up to show her friends. "You see? It says 'gabecage' twice."

Puzzled looks shot across the group. A Ugandan accent cut in. "Anyone know what it means?"

A moment of silence swept over the Porcupines while they searched their memories. Leo took a guess, "Maybe it is a place; let's find a map."

Krystal took a stab. "It sounds like the name of a boat or something."

Odessa started laughing. "A map? Do we live in 1970? Silly boy, we got the Internet. You are such a luddite some times!" Leo shot her a disapproving look while she pulled out her ever-present notebook laptop and began searching. "*Hmmmm*, all I see here is some kid's YouTube channel. We can rule out that gabecage is a town or a boat," the history geek concluded.

The Greek girl's eyes lit up. "What if this was a person named Gabe Cage? I just found a mention of a man named Gabriel Cage. It looks like he lived in Savannah about the right time."

"What else, girl?" Krystal demanded with excitement.

The wind came out of Wiki's sails. "*Hmmmm*, that's it. I can't find anything but that one sentence." She let out an annoyed grunt. "I guess I will be spending some more time at the Georgia Historical Society's library again."

Leo busted out with a sarcastic laugh. "Where's your precious Internet now?"

"Okay, I will tear that place apart and find everything I can about Gabriel Cage. I will get down there as soon as I can," Odessa announced.

"Wait darlin', what about the wrinkled old bat that works there? I bet she is still mad as a frothin' filly chewin' on bumblebees. Yuh know she's watchin' us for that Hughes guy. It ain't safe; we shouldn't let you go alone," Krystal reckoned.

"She is right. We should each take a shift guarding her. We still have to do our jobs here or we will all get kicked out of here," Mohamed warned.

"That's a smart idea. Let's make a schedule so Wiki will never be left alone down there." The four students gathered around the laptop and planned their attack.

Krystal complained to Mohamed over a game of billiards, "I can't believe it has been over a week now and Wiki still ain't found nothin'!"

Mohamed nodded. "I agree. It is getting very hard to keep up progress on my music when a third of my day is spent on watching Odessa work. I tried to help her, but she said I was just in the way and slowing down her research."

"Yep, I couldn't help Wiki out either. I was about as useful to her as a pogo stick in quick sand. Did you see any signs of that wrinkled, old saddlebag, Ms. Gambit?" Krystal probed.

"Yes, I saw her cleaning twice. She was definitely very interested in what Odessa was doing. That creepy lady kept a watchful eye on us the entire time. Although she has never said a word to us, I know she is watching us for Mr. Hughes. They are all just waiting to make a move on us again. She watches

Odessa like Gollum watches Frodo." Mohamed Obunto forewarned.

As Krystal sunk the eight ball in the corner pocket, the pool-playing duo was interrupted by the entrance of Leo and Odessa. They were both grinning from ear to ear.

"When I see yuh that excited, I'm happier than a tornado in a trailer park. Yuh both look like a matching pair of Cheshire Cats. What'd yuh dig up, Wiki?" Krystal asked.

Wiki hugged her friend and beamed. "You will want to sit for this."

They sat back down at the dining hall table and all eyes turned to the young Greek girl.

"I know this took along time, but that is not from a lack of trying. I found this first thing this morning, but that old sea hag was watching us. So, after I got the information I wanted, I stayed all day and pulled out one hundred more books. I acted like I was making notes, too. The nasty woman won't have a clue where to find what I did."

She took a deep breath and continued. "I finally found something, but it is just a little mention of Gabe Cage."

Leo butted in sarcastically. "Wait a second. I want credit and an official apology."

Odessa grimaced. "Leo was right; I found the information on an old map."

Leo chuckled. "The Internet doesn't know everything yet, plus old maps are just really cool."

The irritated, acne-covered girl got back to her story. "Anyway, as I was saying, I found this old map with a description. It says "tween the Isles of Montgomery and Skidaway lies a small island, mostly salt marsh, with a high center and a sandy beach on one side'. Odessa continued, "The locals know it as Pigeon Island these days. It lies situated, well protected, between Moon River and the Skidaway Narrows. Today it's the Intracoastal Waterway. I grew up near there. There's a boat landing and a little, sandy, clay beach there. People have started calling it Butterbean Beach. I used to swim there when I was little."

"Yuh lost me, Wiki. So yuh found an old map? What does this have to do with Gabe Cage?"

"On that map, on what is now Pigeon Island, there is the name 'Gabe's Island' and a drawing of a bird, maybe a pigeon. I wonder if this is why they call it 'Pigeon Island' now. Then there is a drawing of a little house with the words "Gabriel Cage's House." I know it isn't much, but it's the only thing I could find in there with his name on it. Still, I think it is a great find. We need to go out and see what's on that island," Odessa declared with excitement.

Mohamed ruined the moment by stating the obvious, "How are we going to get there? None of us have a boat."

PIGEON ISLAND A.K.A. GABES'S ISLAND

Krystal studied the map harder. "I think I done recognize this place. Yeah, I am sure of it. This be the area where the Gullah people of Pin Point live. They be super famous for their fine horses and one day I'm gonna own one. That place there," she said pointing to a beach-like area on the map, "be where they would take the horses swimmin' in Moon River."

Wiki added to the conversation, "The Gullah slaves also raised horses on Skidaway Island and Tybee Island, too."

Leo summarized saying, "So, this is Gullah horse country? I think we know a certain old man that might be of some help right now. In the morning, let's go tell Jah Loko what we found and see if he knows anything that can help us."

The next morning, all four students were waiting as the man in the sweetgrass hat arrived for work. "Dis is quite a greetin', chillun. What's dis all 'bout?"

Krystal stepped up and hugged her mentor. "I hope yuh find yuh self in good health this mornin'. We might need a small, tiny, wee bit of a favor."

The Gullah man grabbed his wallet and protected it. "Sorry, chillun, I don't gots no money. I be so broke the homeless give me their change."

The group snickered and Krystal kept talking. "We found somethin' really important and we need your help again. Odessa, can yuh show him what we found?"

The Greek girl stepped up and showed Jah a photo of the map she had taken. "We need to find a way to get to this island near Pin Point," she said to the old man.

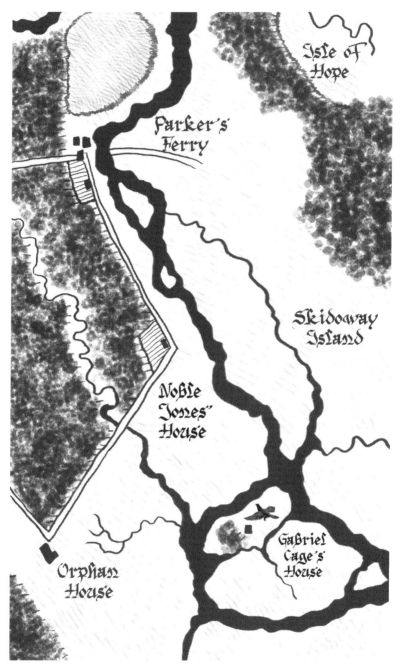

Map of Gabriel Cage's Island.

Jah adjusted the brim of his sweetgrass hat as he thought. "Would dis be sometin' dat I be gettin' into a mess of trouble for?"

Leo down played it, "No, no I don't think..."

Krystal cut him off. "Yes, Mr. Loko, we might be gettin' ourselves into no good. We're lookin' for treasure and we're real close to findin' it."

The Gullah man appreciated the stable hand's honesty. "Well, my health won't let me keep dis job much longer anyway, so I be not afraid of gettin' fired now."

The small girl charged the unexpecting man and hugged him. "Thank yuh so much! I knew yuh would understand. Can yuh help us get there?"

"If we hurry, I tink I can get ya a ride on da *Waving Lady*. If ya be ready now, make ready Harricane. We have ta hurry if we want ta catch da shrimp boats in Thunderbolt before dey leave."

The students snapped into action and helped Krystal get the buggy ready. Leo walked out of the barn holding a small spade. "Jah, can I borrow this for the day?" The old man agreed, so Leo tossed it into the buggy with the rest of the supplies.

The group mounted up and Jah made quick time to Thunderbolt's docks. Mohamed felt very anxious as the shrimp boats grew larger in view. Krystal picked up on the Ugandan boy's discomfort. "What's wrong, hun? Yuh look like yuh just kissed the wrong end of a baby."

His deep brown eyes filled with worry. "I have never been on a boat before. I have a touch of motion sickness on planes. I am worried it will be worse on a shrimp boat."

The girl in the cowboy hat placed a comforting hand on his shoulder. "I don't think it is a long trip; yuh'll be fine."

Jah pulled up at the dock and another large man appeared wearing a worn out baseball hat. "Jah Loko, what on earth are you doing here?"

Jah put his hand on the man's shoulder and both turned their backs to the four teens. The Gullah man whispered to the shrimp boat captain and pointed at the Porcupines. The students watched as the man in charge adamantly shook his head no.

Leo sarcastically whispered to Odessa, "Well this is going real well."

After another few minutes of arguing, both men approached the four treasure hunters. Jah spoke up. "Dis is Cappy Brewer. He has agreed ta take ya where ya need ta go. He has conditions, doh."

Captain Brewer stepped up and spoke. "I am only doing this because I owe Jah a great deal. Takin' you four to an empty island and dumpin' you there is completely against my better judgment. I can only give you two hours to do whatever you are doing. You'll be treated just like any of the other strikers on the *Waving Lady*. Once you step onto my barky, you do what I say. Do you understand?"

Mohamed slowly raised his hand as if he were asking a question in class. Captain Brewer rolled his eyes. "Son, you can just ask; you don't have to do that."

"I don't understand; what's a 'barky'?" Mohamed asked.

Odessa answered for the captain. "A barky is what sailors call the boats they have fond feelings for."

The captain smiled at the Greek girl. "Very true. It be what my great-grandpappy called his boat, too. He was the captain of a merchant sailing vessel in the time before steam and electric engines. I love my barky and while you be on her I expect you four to love her, too. Since none of you has earned your sea legs, I've gotta insist that you wear these life jackets the entire time."

They arranged a pickup time with Jah and thanked him for his help. The greenhorns donned their lifejackets and climbed aboard.

The phone on the prospective school board president's campaign desk rang and he answered it with a pretentious smile. "Hello! Good morning and thank you for calling. Gordon Hughes speaking."

"Sorry to bother you boss, but those kids be up to no good again. They be at the docks here in Thunderbolt right now," said the voice on the other end of the line. "They gettin' on the *Waving Lady*. I got a friend on the *Waving Lady* who tells me they wanna be dropped off over near Buttabean Beach on some little island."

Mr. Hughes' expression fell slightly, but in a room full of reporters, campaign managers, and financial supporters, he quickly regained his composure. He plastered a joker's smile on his face and answered with a false bravado. "Very well! I'll look forward to it. See you soon!" he said and then hung up on the man without further instruction.

Click. Mr. Bines stood there looking at his cell phone. "Hello? Hello? Are you there?" He clicked the cell phone off and thought to himself, "He don't pay me enough to be hangin' up on me."

Mr. Hughes looked around at the room full of people and announced, "Something very important has come up and I must cancel all my appointments for the day. I'll be leaving immediately. Please direct all questions to my manager and I'll be back in the office tomorrow." Walking quickly to his iridescent-pearl-colored Cadillac Escalade, he grabbed his phone and called Ms. Gambit. "I'm coming to get you and we're going on a boat ride."

Within minutes of the children boarding the *Waving Lady*, the vessel cast off and an overpowering smell of fish and diesel filled the air. The three watched Mohamed nervously as the motion of the water overtook his stomach.

"Just watch the horizon and not the boat," Krystal advised. The advice just prolonged the inevitable and Mohamed spewed his breakfast into the water. His friends couldn't help at all, so they backed up and gave the sick boy space to empty his gut. The area around Mohamed was being treated like a crime scene; the three did not and would not cross the imaginary yellow tape.

The trip went as fast as expected and the *Waving Lady* pulled close to a small beach with a clump of trees on it being surrounded by a great deal of marsh. "This is as close as my barky can get. It is shallow enough for y'all to wade to shore." The captain pulled out a ladder and dropped it off the back of the boat.

The students carefully climbed down one by one into the waist-deep ocean. "Keep your life vest on till y'all get to shore. Once I know you're safe I will be on my way. Remember, you only have two hours before I come back," Captain Brewer reminded them.

The four linked hands as they waded to the shore. It was a slow process and Wiki kept getting her feet stuck in the thick mud. They finally made beach-fall and Odessa examined her favorite saddleback shoes. "I really should have planned this better; I think I just ruined my favorite shoes."

The others did their best to knock the mud off and clean up. A quick stroll around the island did not reveal anything but trees and mosquitoes.

"What are we looking for, Odessa? I feel about as useful as a sidesaddle on a pig!" Krystal joked.

"I am not sure. I was hoping there would be some old ruins or an old house. We are looking for anything that would have lasted two hundred years," Wiki explained.

The castaways searched for clues on the tiny island for over an hour and a half, while Mohamed sat on a large rock trying not to throw up anymore. "Wiki, all I can find is some stones from a burned down house. Whatever we had to find is long gone by now," Leo stated in a defeated tone.

Krystal held up a wine bottle. "I found this bottle with a note in it washed up on the shore line."

The four gathered around as Wiki wrestled the cork loose. She turned the bottle upside down and smacked the bottom of it to try to coax the mysterious message out. The excited teen carefully unrolled the parchment and read it. "I don't get it, what kind of message-in-a-bottle is this?" She looked toward her companions to see if they could make something of it. Her fellow treasure hunters were equally dumbfounded until Leo read the note.

"Ha, ha, ha! Oh, that is classic!" he chuckled aloud, reading it to himself again. Leo handed the note to Mohamed who had finally recovered enough to participate. "I don't get it," said Mohamed. "All it says is, 'Be sure to drink your Ovaltine.' What is Ovaltine?"

Leo said exasperatedly, "Really, you guys? Do you never watch old movies? This pays homage to the 1983 flick, *A Christmas Story*. They only show this movie a thousand times in the month of December. Let me refresh. The main character, Ralphie, spends months waiting for his *Little Orphan Annie* decoder ring to come in the mail. He is super psyched about finally being in the secret club and deciphering his first message. When he breaks the code, all it says is 'Be sure to drink your Ovaltine' and he complains that the super secret message was just a commercial. Whoever made this message in a bottle is just having a good bit of fun and is laughing at us right now."

The angry Greek, olive-skinned girl dropped the bottle. "Just great, keep laughing. We are almost out of time and we have not found a thing yet."

Mohamed interrupted, "Oh, Allah, I am going to be sick again."

Leo pointed. "Well, go puke behind that big rock so we don't have to see it again."

The African boy ran to the boulder and kneeled down to upheave one more time.

"We are just so close; it does not make sense. There has to be something we are missing!" Wiki blurted out.

Leo answered her saying, "I don't know what to tell you, Wiki. We have torn this island apart. There is nothing here. I guess we need to go back to the library and look again."

Mohamed's faint voice floated down the beach and tried to cut in. "Hey, guys!"

Krystal agreed with Leo. "Whatever was here is long gone, darlin'. I think we will have to start again."

Mohamed tried to get their attention again and moaned louder. "Hey, guys!"

Odessa's tone turned angry. "I doubt I missed anything at the Historical Society. I spent over a week in there digging through every piece of colonial history they have and I am telling you, there is no other information about Gabe Cage."

Mohamed finally yelled loud enough to end their conversation. "Hey, guys! I think I found what we are looking for!"

This finally registered with the three and they ran over to take a look.

"When I bent over to get sick, I noticed this faint carving on this big rock. Do you guys see what I do?" he said and pointed at a worn etching.

A glimmer of hope sprang back into Odessa's eyes. "Yep, I recognize Admiral April Read's mark. If you look close you will see three circles and a cat."

The group cooed in excitement as they also saw what Odessa was pointing to.

"But look, there the cat is followed by U S 30. What the heck does that mean?" The skater teen barked.

"Okay, everyone calm down. Y'all, we only got a whole half an hour to solve this code. Do yuh think it is the name of a road, like US Route 30?" Krystal took a stab.

Wiki thought for a minute. "No, the highway system didn't appear till last century. Look close at it. The letter "U" is much larger than the "S 30." I think the "S 30" means thirty paces south."

"That sounds like a fine guess. What the heck do yuh reckon the U means?" the tomboy inquired.

A light went off in the Greek girl eyes as she remembered something. "I think I know; follow me." The four cryptographers circled around the boulder when suddenly Odessa started jumping up and down with excitement. She pointed at a section of the rock that was indented. "Do you guys see how it looks like a seat was chiseled in here? Maybe that's what that "U" means. Maybe it's a starting point. You sit in this seat, find south then take thirty paces. I remembered reading about this in a book about Jesse James. He used to hide his gold using the same idea. He must have gotten the idea from pirates."

Leo sat in the dirty groove. "So how do we find dead south? Did anyone think to bring a compass?" The group shook their head with a collective no.

Mohamed offered, "Let's just guess using the sun. I know, generally, where south is. I have a good sense of direction because I have to pray everyday. Oh! My phone!" Mohamed exclaimed, pulling out his smart phone. "Uggghhhh.... It's dead."

Krystal shook her head with disapproval. "What's new? Maybe guessin' about the direction would be okay if we had days to dig, but we only got about twenty-five minutes more to find this. We gotta be a lot more exact."

"Well, unless you can make a compass in the next few minutes, we are out of luck," Leo grunted.

"As a matter of fact, I can. Like most all girls in Savannah, I was a Girl Scout. Do you boys even realize the Girl Scouts was started right here in Savannah?" Krystal challenged.

Leo rolled his eyes. "Of course I know that! I get suckered every year into buying cookies in front of the Gordon Lowe house. The Girl Scout Mafia is strong in this town, so you will buy the cookies if you know what's good for you."

"I think I can make a compass," Krystal said. "First, I need somethin' that holds water; second, I need somethin' that floats. Leo, I'm gonna need your Zombie Awareness Month ribbon and the pin holdin' it on."

Leo responded as he was taking off the ribbon to hand to her, "So you have finally come around, huh? So glad to see that you have accepted that the Zombie Apocalypse is coming."

"No, silly boy," Krystal said as she took the ribbon from him. "You said it was made of silk, right?" Leo nodded in affirmation as he handed her the pin.

Krystal took charge and sent the others to find what else she needed. "Leo, go search the beach for that bottle we found earlier; I need the cork out of it."

She pointed at Mohamed. "Find anything that will hold water. Fill it up and bring it back."

While the boys were off searching, she disassembled Leo's ribbon. She started running the cloth from the eye to the point over and over.

Wiki questioned, "What are you doing? The needle looks clean enough already."

"I am not cleanin' it, darlin'; I am magnetizin' it. It takes a good while. I will have to run the needle though the cloth a good one hundred times to get the magnetic charge strong enough," the country girl explained.

The needle was sufficiently charged when Leo returned with the cork. Mohamed arrived holding a horseshoe crab shell filled with water. "I found a puddle of rain water. I thought it would be better to fill it up than with salt water," he said.

Krystal assembled the compass. She floated the cork on the water and carefully placed the magnetized needle on it. The needle slowly swung back and forth until it steadied out. "Okay, I charged the needle so the sharp end is pointin' south. Leo, you got the longest legs; start pacin'."

The tall boy took a few strides and counted. Krystal then used the compass to confirm he was still on the correct heading. They repeated this process until they reached thirty paces. Leo finished counting, shouting out loud, "...Twenty-eight, twenty-nine, thirty!"

A blood-curdling scream came out of Odessa as she looked down at her feet.

"What's wrong? What is it?" Krystal yelled.

"Oh yuck! It's so gross! Someone move it now!"

Mohamed pointed to a used Band-Aid lying on the dirt. "Are you upset over that little bandage?"

Leo reached down with his shovel he had been carrying and carefully removed it from Odessa's presence. "Mohamed, few things are as terrifying as a bloodied, rogue Band-Aid! Yuck! Now you know what grosses me out!"

The boy with the shovel leaned away from the dirty piece of sick plastic as he carried it away. "This is silly. You guys act like you are removing nuclear toxic waste. Sometimes I just don't understand your culture."

With the offending hazard gone, Leo dug his spade into the soft ground. The excitement grew in proportion to the size of the hole. "Hurry up! Dig faster!" Wiki commanded.

"Here, I need a break," Leo said and handed the Greek girl the shovel.

"Fine, stand out of the way!" She dove into the ditch and started digging. The young girl drove the spade deep and heard it strike a rock. The group dove into the edges of the hole and started digging with their hands. Within five minutes they uncovered the top half of a broken, clay vessel.

"Wiki, I think you broke that container with the shovel." Leo handed her the top half of the broken jar. Leo searched the cracked pottery and unearthed an ivory object. "Look at that, y'all," Krystal pointed.

THE SCRIMSHAW RIDDLE

L eo unearthed the white ivory tusk. He held it up to the light and wiped away the thin layer of dust that somehow permeated through the large fjar. "I don't get it. It looks like it is a horn or something."

Odessa pushed in to examine it closely. "It's Scrimshaw, Leo; the ancient art of engraving into bone or ivory. Look closer and you will see the pictures." The tall boy then noticed the elaborate, faint etchings carved into the powder horn. It appeared to be a picture of a great sea battle, under which was the title *"The Battle of Myrtle Swash."*

"What is The Battle of Myrtle Swash, Wiki?" Leo asked as he hand the tusk to her. "Pirates used to call Myrtle Beach, South Carolina, Myrtle Swash. Judging from the picture I think this is supposed to commemorate a great sea battle involving Admiral April Read's ships. I don't see much of a clue though; we need to study this better."

As if on queue, a blast of the horn of the *Waving Lady* interrupted the four. Leo warned, "We best hide this from the people on the ship. Anyone have any ideas?"

Krystal snatched up the powder horn and removed her large straw cowgirl hat. She used the cover to wrap around the treasure. As long as she clutched her hat around the artifact, it would stay concealed in her hand.

The students waded in the warm, muddy water and made their way to the shrimp boat. With some awkward ladder-climbing, they soon found themselves on the deck, staring at Captain Brewer.

"Did ya greenhorns find what ya were looking for?" the sailor pressed.

Odessa stumbled around and then answered, "It looks like the information we were looking for is long gone. Thanks so much for picking us up."

The suspicious sea captain glared at the group and then shrugged his shoulders. He mumbled as he walked off, "The things I do for that Gullah man."

"Dang!" Ms. Gambit exclaimed. "That's them getting back on the *Waving Lady* right now, Mr. Hughes."

"Well, we'll ride over there anyway and see what they were up to. My boat is much faster than theirs, so we can still probably beat them back to the docks at Thunderbolt," Hughes said to the skinny cigarette-toking dragon-lady as he continued to offload his speedboat at the Butterbean Beach boat ramp. It wasn't but a few minutes later when they pulled up on the beach at Pigeon Island.

"It looks like those kids were all over this little island. I can't tell what direction to start. The footprints are all over the place. You go that way, I'll go this way, and we'll meet up on the other side."

The duo split up and began searching for clues when Ms. Gambit spotted a deep hole in the ground with lots of foot activity around it and broken pottery shards everywhere. She started hollering for Mr. Hughes as loud as she could.

Hughes came running through the woods and tried to quiet the wailing woman. "Gambit!" he shouted at her, "I swear your voice is so loud a deaf man could hear it." It was clear that the kids had indeed found something. The two stared and poked at the hole for a minute then headed back to the boat. "We'll head back to the docks at Thunderbolt now. The *Waving Lady* will have to deliver her catch to the fisheries before she can drop the kids off, and we'll be there waiting for them.

The small group of Porcs tried to hide Krystal from the view of the crew, doing their best to look inconspicuous.

The ruse worked for the most part. Most of the shrimpers were much too busy going about their duties to pay much mind to the teens. One of the crew tried to get all buddy-buddy with them, but Captain Brewer kept the striker on his task of hauling in the nets. After they delivered the catch to the fisheries, the group found themselves back at the docks. There was much activity at the dock. Since they had left in the morning, Tubby's Tank House Restaurant had set up an outside seafood festival and there were people milling about all over the place. Krystal fought hard and resisted the overwhelming urge to examine their booty. She continued to hide it in her hat from all the people wandering about.

The four of them walked up the steep deck ramp towards the top of the bluff where all the people had gathered. They reached the top and started looking around for Jah in the crowd. Suddenly, a loud shout caught their attention. The teens turned to look and saw Mr. Hughes standing behind Ms. Gambit and a very disheveled Mr. Bines.

"Well now children," spoke Hughes, "seems like you have something that belongs to me."

Leo retorted, "SEEMS to ME that hardly anything you 'own' belongs to you, so what makes you think that we have something that belongs to YOU?"

"I know you found something on that island; I saw the hole and the pottery shards. Give it up. You know that anything you found belongs to me, um, I mean the Historical Society. Don't make me have to take it from you because I will!" shouted the angry man.

Krystal clenched the hat tighter around the powder horn and slinked behind Mohamed, trembling, when Leo spoke back to the red-faced man as if he were his equal.

"I'd like to see you try to take anything from us," Leo responded loudly. "Also, don't make me remind you that I have video of you committing crimes against the people you work for. I am sure this close to your election you don't want any of that to get out."

"If I can get my hands on Shamus's treasure, I won't have any need or desire to be school board president or part of the Historical Society or anything like that. Now, GET THEM and search them!" Hughes shouted angrily as he waved Mr. Bines and Ms. Gambit towards the teens.

"Stand still, this won't take long," Mr. Bines laughed as he hurried towards the children. He hadn't gotten to search anyone since Leo got him fired and he was looking forward to it.

Jah had been watching the altercation from down the street and hurriedly rushed the carriage toward them through the crowd of people. Just as Mr. Bines was bearing down on them, Jah pulled up along side of them and shouted, "In da buggy wid ya, chillun!"

All four children turned to see their savior and jumped into the carriage as Mr, Bines grabbed at their heels. Jah gave Harricane a giddy up and they bolted through the crowd, back toward the school.

When they were safely on their way and sure they weren't being followed, they pulled the ancient swag out. The four passed it around while Jah pretended not to look. "I don't get it; is there something I am missing, or is that hidden in the picture?" The African's brow furrowed as he stared intensely at the Scrimshaw art.

His other three friends passed it back and forth and each was just as dumbfounded. The carriage pulled over into and empty parking lot. Jah finally spoke up. "Do ya mind if I take a look-see at it, chillun?"

Krystal handed the horn over and the old man held it up to the sun to inspect it in the bright light. He stared at it silently and traced the fine etchings with his fingers. The man in the sweetgrass hat grunted and nodded his head as he gazed into the intricate design. After what seemed like an eon, he finally spoke to the teens. "Chillun, dis be a very nice powder horn. I likes da art very much."

Odessa impatiently snapped at the man, "But does it mean anything? Do you see a clue?"

"Oh, ya be lookin' for a hidden meanin'. I just was enjoyin' the art."

The group let out a frustrated, collective moan.

"Calm down, chillun. Let me takes another looks-see." Jah started surveying the ivory again. After a minute, he spoke saying, "Miss Krystal, I need sum 'a da black river mud from your boots."

The tiny girl was taken aback by the odd request. "Sorry, Mr. Loko, did yuh say yuh wanted to borrow mud from me?"

The tour guide nodded in affirmation.

"Okay, here yuh go." The tomboy then ran her finger down the side of her foot and handed Jah a clump of black sludge.

The Gullah man took the clump and smeared it into the inside of the hollow horn. He then wiped the dirt out and cleaned it up. A smile cracked on the old man's face. "Now, Miss Krystal, look INSIDE the horn. Dere be a very faint carvin' ya missed until I added some black to it." The tiny girl assayed the inside of the tusk. "Y'all, the mud brought out the writin' in here. It's a message carved on the inside of the powder horn. It says, "The secret lies with Barbara Allen. She carries the answer you are looking for. Shamus Red."

Odessa squealed and jumped up and down, shaking the buggy. "We are so close! This is it! I can't believe it!"

The boys bumped each other's fists together, the girls hugged each other, and Jah grinned ear to ear.

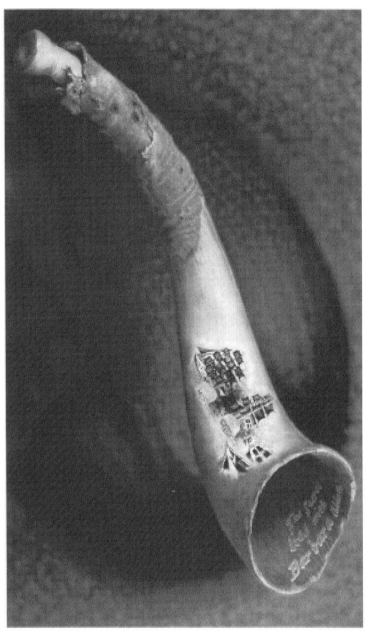

Scrimshaw powder horn with the inscription "The secret lies with Barbara Allen."

THE SEARCH FOR BARBARA ALLEN

Krystal froze in place and stopped celebrating. She asked the obvious question that hung in the air. "Wait a second, who is Barbara Allen?"

"That was the same name of the song on the back of the tombstone. That song had been around a long time before Shamus Red; do you think he actually knew a woman named Barbara Allen?" Mohamed questioned the group.

The three swiveled their heads and focused on Odessa. "What? Why are you looking at me?" She shook her noggin. "Fine! I guess I will go back to the Historical Society and see what I can dig up."

The excited students could barely contain themselves; they knew they were closer than anybody has ever been to Shamus's booty. The journey back to the school was quiet as dreams of gold and silver started filling their minds.

As they arrived at the academy, they scattered, returning to their jobs. It was hard to focus on their tasks, but they knew treasure hunting would have to wait until Barbara Allen revealed herself.

The students returned to their routine of escorting Wiki back to the Historical Society over the next few days while she dug for clues.

One hot morning, Krystal sat down at lunch and expressed her concerns. "Y'all, I just came back from muckin' out the stables, and we got a problem. Jah's health is takin' a fast turn for the worse. He just laid in the barn for over an hour holdin' his belly and groanin' in pain. I begged him to go to the hospital and get help, but he refused. He said there ain't nothin' they can do except that expensive operation."

"I know we got to help him soon," Leo said, concerned. "Odessa is working hard on it and even I am searching the Internet all night long looking for anything about Barbara Allen."

Mohamed interjected, "I am sorry to bring more bad news, but I overheard something the other day. Mr. and Ms. Mendel were arguing about the school's money problems. It sounds like the school is very close to failing and going under. Ms. Mendel said they are only one bill away from bankruptcy. We need to help them, too."

The country girl's voice quivered with fear. "If they go out of business, that means they will sell Harricane and the stables. I love this place. It can't close. For the first time in my life I can be exactly who I am and I don't have to worry about gettin' bullied. I don't care what I have to do; I ain't goin' back to public skoo, no way! I want to go to skoo here from now on."

Her fear was mirrored in the other's faces when they came to the realization they would have to leave the academy if the four didn't try to help.

"I am afraid my parents will force me to go back to the government school. I understand how you feel, Krystal. I don't want to return and face my bullies again either. The only reason my parents even let me come here was because I would be sending them the money I earn here. They see this as a summer job, not really an education. I don't want to go back either," Mohamed empathized.

Leo spewed his frustration. "I don't care what anyone says; I am not going to that police state of a school ever again. It's like flying on a plane every morning. They search me like I am their property. I now know how prisoners feel. I just can't handle all the stupid rules and the way they try and control every little thing I do. I mean, who in the real world raises their hands and begs permission to go to the bathroom? This place is my last hope. If it closes, I will just drop out of school and start a business instead. I am just not getting anything out of going in that oppressive environment."

"This place is the closest thing to home schooling I've ever gotten to experience," Odessa said. "I always wanted to be home schooled. My mother is super smart and I've spent summers learning under her guidance after she got off work. She made learning fun, just like this place does. She knows I hate going to public school and feels guilty she can't keep me home." The Greek girl continued, "Well I only see one solution that solves everyone's problem; we need to find a great deal of treasure. Unfortunately, I can't find anything in the Historical Society's library and that old bat is still there watching everything I do. Not to mention, I have to spring some more bad news on you guys. Ms. Mendel volunteered us all to help out tomorrow at the History Museum. They are hosting a special, one-week colonial exhibit of Savannah. They need to help clean up and break down the exhibits. Normally, I would think this would be super cool, but it is just distracting me from our goal."

Krystal tried to turn the mood positive. "How much gold do yuh think he left his son? Do yuh think we will find the golden leg, or the golden hook, or the diamond eye patch?"

Mohamed's morality interrupted the group. "Shamus Red left all this treasure to his son; don't you think that his ancestors will want anything we find? Since we found the Scrimshawed horn still buried, we can assume his son never found anything. It also makes me wonder what ever happened to his son."

"Well, I can answer that," Wiki said. I found that Shamus had a newborn son the same year as his fake funeral. Then there is no more mention of him. I think Shamus hid all his swag and his son must have died young or something. I tore apart the genealogy of his family and it all stops at his son. I don't think he has any direct descendants left, so we shouldn't be worried that a relative will come claim it," Wiki reassured them.

"Guys, we will have to pick this up a little later. This heat is killing my garden, so I need to go water it again. By the way, Krystal, I do like the new black cat you got out at the barn. He's cool. What did you name him?" Leo asked.

"Yep, the Milton Project and the Humane Society hooked us up with him. I know he only has three legs, but he is still a great mouser. We have already seen a reduction in our horse feed from gettin' eaten. I think we should get him a little peg leg and call him Shamus," the girl with the braids joked.

They all chuckled, said their goodbyes, and returned to their schooling.

The next morning, Odessa gathered everyone and they prepared for their trip to Savannah's History Museum. The group could tell Jah did not feel well. He hunched over holding his stomach and let Krystal take control of the driving. By the time they arrived at their destination, Jah Loko seemed to have recovered. Krystal was still concerned for the old man. "Are yuh sure yuh don't need me to stay with yuh today? I don't mind keepin' on eye on yuh."

The Gullah man wiped the sweat from off his forehead. "No, I will be fine, Miss Krystal. Go help your friends."

The students approached the massive building and took it all in. The parking lot was loaded with buses from some of Savannah's finest tour companies. The museum was a refurbished train station. When they entered they were immediately greeted with a wonderful gift shop jam packed with some of Savannah's coolest stuff. Odessa gave an unsolicited tour. "Upstairs is the information center and another gift shop. Outside is the train museum and the children's round house. There is even some stuff about the revolution and the siege of Savannah out there, too. We won't have time to explore any of that because we are going to be working in the Savannah History Museum all day. Follow me, I will show you."

The four volunteers were given jobs that involved cleaning the areas before the colonial artifacts were brought in and set up. The students found themselves doing the grunt work and were not really allowed to handle any of the ancient pieces.

Odessa grew very excited when she was asked to help in the sailing exhibit. "Check out this super old red coat from the South Carolina Independent Company. They made these heavy

Travois

Li Go Che Indian Chief

Fort Mose Warriors

Drawings at the Savannah History Museum.

wool things for the British before the Revolution. I can't believe they had cloth that lasted that long."

The Greek girl continued, "Oh, wow! Look at this old sexton. It is so hard to believe the sailors were able to cross the entire ocean using this and only a few primitive tools. Oh, wow! Look here! This is a casting mold that colonists used to make their own bullets."

She continued into the afternoon, giving her friends unsolicited information about each area they set up.

Mohamed was in charge of setting up a Yamacraw and Creek exhibit. He thought about how practical the local indigenous peoples were. They even used their dogs as pack mules by attaching large wooden frames behind the animal called a travois. Mohamed spent most of the morning studying a drawing, trying to figure out how to attach a travois to a big, stuffed toy collie dog. He even added some bags of fake alligator meat to the diorama to make it more like the original drawing.

Leo took on the slave exhibit. Much of it was drawings and woodcuttings of slave practices. There was a good bit of information about the Stono River uprising in which a large group of slaves turned on their masters in South Carolina. Those slaves headed down to Georgia and liberated other slaves on their journey. The exhibit also had a section about Fort Mose and its band of free warriors. Based in Florida, which was the first settlement of free black men and woman in colonial times, Leo learned it was also considered the beginning of the Underground Railroad.

Krystal helped out with the early colonial transportation exhibit. There was a beautifully restored buggy and a cart. Next to the cart was a collection of old saddles and tack. They were all recreations of historical saddles, but the tomboy appreciated them anyway. One of the reproductions caught her eye and she did a double take.

The small girl stood slack-jawed and just starred at the horse seat. This odd display caught Odessa's attention and she approached her friend. "Are you okay, Krystal? You look like you just saw a ghost."

The tiny girl was tongue-tied. The only reply she could muster was to just point. As Odessa's eyes followed Krystal's finger, she gasped aloud. "I can't believe it!"

32 CHAPTER

TALKING HORSES

"No way...is that what I think it is on that saddle? Hey, fella's! Come see this!" Odessa yelled to the boys. The group of four treasure hunters stood silently and examined the reproduction. Leo approached the exhibit very closely and extended his digit. "It sure looks the same. I think we need to find out everything we can about this saddle."

Wiki pulled out her digital camera from her purse and took a picture of the three circles and black cat that had been burned into the leather.

"That is April's mark. What on earth is it doing on this saddle? Let me find the curator and ask her all about this. In the meantime, you take pictures of every inch of this saddle," Wiki said then handed Mohamed her camera and went to get answers.

Mohamed was very thorough and took so many pictures that the camera's memory filled up. Odessa was gone for a good twenty minutes while the others examined the set up.

Krystal knew something was odd about this tack. "Y'all, the seat, cantle, and back housing have all been remade. That's to be expected though. Real, old saddles are super rare because the leather always falls apart over time. What's catchin' my eye is some of this tack is original and real old. Look at the bit and the stirrups. Those are old colonial-style and I bet they are original."

The small girl looked around to make sure nobody was watching them and then started fiddling with the stirrups. She untied the tread covers on the bottom of the stirrups and smiled. "Mo, make room on that camera and take some pictures of this."

Mohamed erased some shots of some wild birds Odessa had taken and replaced them with detailed images of the stirrups. When Mohamed finished, Krystal retied the tread covers back onto the stirrups so no evidence was left behind. Wiki returned ten minutes later with the curator.

"This is the saddle I am talking about." Odessa pointed at it. "The seat has been replicated and is fairly new, so where did you guys get it from?"

The woman replied, "Oh, this collection of colonial horse tack has been passed down from museum to museum for over one hundred years. I assume it was donated a very long time ago. It has been here ever since I started working here."

Wiki pressed on. "Where did you get the idea for the markings of the black cat and three circles?"

The museum worker explained, "This particular colonial saddle was in horrible shape when we dug it out of storage. We saved and restored all the pieces of the tack we could, but the seat and all the leather was a complete loss. Luckily we had this woodcutting with it. The image on it is of the original owner and his horse. We recreated the saddle markings from that picture on the wood cutting."

Odessa was practically drooling. "Can I please see the original woodcutting?"

"Stay here and I will bring it out. Please remember; do not touch anything. Most of this stuff is hundreds of years old," the curator warned.

Mohamed and Krystal exchanged suspicious looks and giggled. "Oops. I guess she was a little late tellin' us that since I already done messed with them stirrups," the country girl confessed.

The worker returned with a small, airtight, plastic tub and a folder. She carefully opened the plastic container. "Take a look, but please don't touch." The four crowded together and examined the ancient woodcarving. The students could not see much; the etching was so faint it was lost in the grain of the wood. A wave of disappointment overtook them.

"Don't look so sad, y'all. Woodcuttings are tough to see. Let me show you something." The woman from the museum opened a folder see was carrying. "Here is a rubbing we made of it. You can see the image much better."

The rubbing revealed an old, man, in a tricorn hat holding the reigns of his horse. Careful examination of the drawing showed the black cat and three circles on the fender of the saddle.

Woodcutting of Gabe Cage and his horse Barbara Allen.

Odessa squealed. "Do you guys see that! Mo, get a picture of it!" The group honed in on what Wiki was so excited about and joined her in her revelry. Mohamed took a photo of the rubbing. "Be sure to get a good picture of the title of the picture!" Odessa commanded.

Mohamed zoomed in to get a clear shot of the phrase "Gabe Cage and his horse, Barbara Allen."

MAD MAGAZINE

The four sat at the dining room table at the academy studying the digital pictures that Mohamed had taken. "So this whole time I was thinking we were looking for a woman named Barbara Allen, but Shamus was talking about his horse?" Leo vented.

Krystal snapped, "Don't knock it! If I could afford it, I'd have paintin's of all my horses, too. That don't seem a bit odd to me at all. I love my Ruane Manning horse clock with twelve different horse paintin's. It plays the real sound of approachin' hooves and gives gentle neighs at the top of each hour," she said, holding up her wrist for the others to see. "It came with a matchin' wrist watch, too."

"Anyway, I agree that was some dumb luck the way we found the saddle tack," said Krystal, getting back to the point. "I just keep thinkin' there be higher forces at work here helpin' us. I been prayin' extra hard about this, and I think I got through."

Mohamed smiled at the small girl. "I was praying extra hard, too. Maybe Allah listened because we are working together."

Leo shook his head. "You all believe what you want, but I will at least agree with you; that find was some serious dumb luck."

Krystal and Mohamed reassured each other that asking for help from above only helped. Leo dismissed the two's religious bonding moment and went on saying, "The point I am trying to get across is, how many more clues did Shamus leave? I am getting the feeling this guy is a practical joker. It'll be like Pee Wee's bike in the basement of the Alamo."

The three stared at Leo like they were deer in the headlights of a car. Leo waved his hands in the air. "Really, you guys? Not one of you gets my joke?"

Odessa spoke with a sarcastic tone, "Is this some weird joke again about some '80s TV show or movie that none of us will understand?"

Leo's feelings became hurt at Odessa's snide comment. He mumbled quietly, "Well there was no basement in the Alamo is all I was going to say"

Wiki felt bad she crushed her friend's feelings. "Fine, go on. Finish your story."

The agonized boy blurted, "No! You ruined it now. We can go back to trying to solve this clue."

Odessa shot Leo a look that he was being overdramatic and then carried on. "Shamus said on the powder horn that '...your inheritance awaits with Barbara Allen.' I am going to go all Sherlock Holmes on you and use deductive reasoning. Logic tells me he could not have hidden a golden peg leg or a bunch of gold and silver on a horse. So the booty is either in the horse's grave, or he left a clue on that saddle. Why else would he go through all the trouble of burning April's symbol into the leather?"

"Well, before we tread all over Savannah looking for a horse's grave, let's really take a good look at this saddle," Mohamed encouraged.

"I have looked at all these pictures over and over all night long and I still don't see anything," Wiki said, smacking her notebook.

Krystal spoke up. "I can cut that search time way down for ya darlin'. I would focus on the bit or the stirrups. I know my tack and all that stuff was new 'cept those two pieces of gear."

"Alright, Krystal. I will have to say you would know a heck of a lot more about horses than any of us. I am going to take your advice and start with the bit," Wiki conceded.

The group examined the full screen shots of the bit. "Look right there. I can't believe we missed it," Odessa emoted. "There are two letters stamped into the metal, a B and an A. I assume that stands for Barbara Allen. Why would Shamus have marked the horses bit?"

"Oh darlin, horses are very particular about their bits. Once yuh find one that fits their mouth well, yuh stick with it. When yuh own more than one horse, it can get confusin', so folks mark the bits to match them with the right horses. I guess he stamped it into the bit so other folks knew to use it with Barbara Allen," Krystal said, educating the group.

"So, we definitely know we have the correct horse now. Let's take a look at the stirrups." Odessa zoomed in on the pictures. "Nothing stands out until you look at the bottom here. These stirrups have some lines, circles, and half circles. It doesn't really make any sense."

"That is because you are only looking at half the clue," Leo Stedman grinned. "I should always remember that when in doubt, think of *Mad Magazine*."

The Greek Girl became furious that she could not follow the teen's comments. "*Mad Magazine?* What on Earth does *Mad* have to do with this clue?"

Leo calmly explained, "At the end of every *Mad Magazine* issue, there is a joke that you can only see if you fold the paper down the middle, so that the edges line up. I think if you put those two stirrups side by side it will make a new image."

She responded by quickly cropping the images so they were reading the bottom of the stirrups side by side. "Now flip the whole image over," Leo suggested, "and...THERE!" A new, complete image could be seen.

"It's three circles and...is that a lighthouse?" asked Odessa.

Bottom of stirrups with engraving.

34 CHAPTER

THE TRIP TO TYBEE

"Ah, very good; all four of you are in one place," Ms. Mendel said, interrupting their treasure research. "I have been trying to catch y'all for days. I need a progress report. It has been a significant amount of time and I hope y'all got some results to show me. Miss Bennett, you fill me in first."

"Well, ma'am, I believe I am fully trained to hitch the horse to the carriage proper. I can do routine maintenance and minor repairs to the buggy. Harricane is happy and in good health and great spirits. He gets a great deal of attention and groomin' from me. Left to my own devices, I feel confident I could drive the carriage without Jah if I had to. Gettin' a cat also helped cut down on feed loss and contamination which has saved the school a little money."

Ruby ran her hand through her long blonde hair. "I am impressed. You have made a great deal of progress this summer. Mr. Stedman, how is the garden?"

"Well, I would say we are about a week or two away from our first harvest. This heat is frying everything, so I finally went on the Internet and learned how to make a drip irrigation system out of some old hoses. It seems to be much more efficient than blasting them with water two times a day. I am also experimenting with fertilizing the crop with worm castings tea."

Ruby raised an eyebrow. "Worm castings?"

"That's right, worm poop. It lets me fertilize without chemicals. I have grown these completely chemical free. When I go to the farmers market next month, I should get a much higher profit."

The skinny woman nodded her head. "Very good. Keep me updated and let me know when they are ready to eat. Mr. Obuntu, how is the alumni banquet coming?"

"We are almost all set with music. I have talked to some of the other students and they each have agreed to play an original piece they composed. We are also practicing some big band music as well. I have also been working on another theme as a back up. I thought it might be fun to have a colonial-themed event, too. We could dress up and play very old music. I will put together and present both packages to you and you can pick which one you like better."

Ruby applauded. "Wow! I get a choice of themes! Very good, Mr. Obuntu. Now, to Miss Skouras; what do you have for me?"

The Greek girl floundered. "Well, um, I almost have my presentation ready. I just need a little more time."

Ms. Mendel grew impatient with Odessa's excuses. "I have been asking you for weeks to show me your progress, yet you always have a reason you can't. You are all out of time, Miss Skouras. I want to see something now."

Wiki pulled out her best puppy dog eyes and tried to look sad. "Ms. Mendel, I promise what I have will knock your socks off. It is just not ready yet and I need a little time to find this last piece I am missing. You are going to love it, but I want it to be perfect when I show it to you."

Ruby twirled her long hair while she processed this request. "Okay, I am giving you one more day to find what you need. Tomorrow night you will sit in front of my desk and show me something."

"Yes ma'am," Odessa said and bobbed her head.

Ms. Mendel slowly walked off and prepared to interrogate the next table.

Wiki grew dead serious. "Okay, you heard her; we have got just one day to solve this clue and present it to her. Let's look at everything again. First, it has April's mark of the three circles. We have found it on every clue so far, so I think it is safe to assume April and Shamus set all this up. We just need to keep looking for this mark and it will lead us to the treasure."

She moved her black curls out of her face. "The next piece that is easy to solve is the light house. There are only two lighthouses in Savannah; The Cockspur and the Tybee Island lighthouse. The Cockspur Island lighthouse would be the wrong period. It wasn't built until around the War of Southern Independence."

Krystal interrupted. "Jah would be so proud of yuh right now for not callin' it the Civil War."

Odessa shot her an annoyed look. "Anyway, that only leaves the Tybee lighthouse. We need to get down there and figure out the rest of the clue. Any idea how we can get there tomorrow morning?"

The country girl offered, "I can talk to Jah one more time and maybe we can hitch a ride on the shrimp boat again."

Odessa took charge. "See if you can set that up; I am going to go dig up every scrap of research I can find on Tybee lighthouse. Come on boys; this is going to be a late night of Internet research."

The four were up and ready before dawn. Leo had packed a makeshift Zombie Bug-Out Bag out of Mohamed's designer backpack. Mohamed had taken some motion sickness pills and was wearing some acupressure wristbands that Leo said would help. Krystal had talked Jah into coming extra early so they could be up and out the at the Thunderbolt docks before morning. Odessa arrived with a folder of stuff printed from the Internet and a bag full of food and water.

The students met up with Krystal and Jah who had already hitched up Harricane to the carriage. The old man moaned in pain. "Tis bad for me tis early, Miss Krystal; ya have ta drive." She placed a sympathetic hand on his shoulder and then took the reins. With a soft snap, the massive equine pulled the students towards Thunderbolt.

The Gullah man rolled back and forth, moaning in pain as the students tried to comfort him. The Porcupines felt helpless and realized there was nothing they could do for him. The sky was turning a brilliant shade of orange as the sun started to rise. The outline of the shrimp boats at the dock could barely be made out in the distance. Although still very early, the port was already full of activity.

The carriage pulled up to the *Waving Lady* and the teens dismounted. "Jah, I really don't want to leave yuh in this condition," the stable hand pleaded.

"Miss Krystal, I be fine in about twenty minutes. I just goin' ta sit here and watch da sunrise wid Harricane. Go now; ya must not miss ya boat."

"We will be back at sundown! Please don't forget us!" the tiny girl said as she hugged the sick man.

Captain Brewer met the group of treasure hunters on the dock. A group of brawny shrimpers were loading the ship while the captain spoke. "I can't believe I am doing this again; haven't any of y'all ever heard of a taxi? Jah tells me you want a ride to the lighthouse. Well, I can get you close, but it will be a long walk. We will pick you up about an hour before sunset. Don't be late or we will leave without you, understood?"

The gang gave a collective nod.

"Fine, get your life jackets on and climb aboard," the salty shrimper barked.

The four strapped on their protective vests, climbed on, and tried to stay out of the way. Large men were still loading equipment in the dark.

The captain belted out, "Listen up crew! We are taking a short detour this morning. We need to drop these kids off at Lazaretto Creek. I want to drop them off at the fishery and will need to pick them up there right before the sun sets. Hurry up and finish loading so we can get an early start."

The crew of the *Waving Lady* finished their duties and in a short time the shrimp vessel was on the river. A fat dockworker watched as the ship pulled away. The silence of the morning had set in so all that could be heard was his heavy mouth breathing. The dockhand pulled out his cell phone and dialed. "You will never guess what I just saw." He paused. "Yep, all four of those brats are together and they look like they are definitely on to something. Get up and come pick me up; I overheard where they are going."

The sun was up as they arrived at the fish processing dock. The *Waving Lady* dropped the four off and headed out to work the morning catch.

Mohamed muttered, "This place stinks; what is this place?"

Odessa explained, "This is a holding dock for fish, crabs, and shrimp. Crews hold their catches here and sell them to local restaurants."

The students worked their way past large rectangle holds that were cut into the docks. Mohamed pointed at one and asked, "Wiki, what are those?"

"Those holes contain big cages lined with nets full of live crab, shrimp, and bait fish. They are much bigger than they look and are at least 8 feet deep. Do you see how they also have smooth safety walls around it so landlubbers like you don't fall in?"

The Ugandan boy commented, "Those walls are only like two feet high; that does not look real safe."

"Well, the fishermen have to be able to pull the nets of fish out, so they can't be all that high," Wiki responded.

Mohamed grinned. "Wow, Wiki, you really do know something about everything. I have to say I'm impressed."

The Greek girl blushed at the compliment. "Come on, enough lessons about fisheries; we have a clue to solve."

Odessa took inventory before their long journey. "What supplies did you pack, Leo?"

Leo spun Mohamed around and unzipped his backpack. "Well, I got a flashlight with a full charge this time and a bunch of water for us. I also got this cool, old army trench shovel." He held up the compact spade for everyone to see. "Check it out; it folds up on itself. I also got these old binoculars. They are kinda beat up, but still work."

Odessa came back saying, "That is a great find, Leo; well done." She reached into her pocket and pulled out some folded paper. "I printed up all these aerial maps of the lighthouse from the Internet; these might come in handy. This is a long walk; my guess is it's close to four miles. The good news is that after we cross the highway, we will have a secluded trail that leads us right to the backside of the Tybee lighthouse. The trail used to be an old railroad track and now it is a path for folks to walk down and enjoy the water."

Wiki pushed on. "Let's go; it is going to get real hot in a few hours and I would like to be there before the heat arrives."

The four students left the docks and carefully crossed Highway 80. They found the Tybee Railroad's Rails-to-Trail and started heading towards the distant lighthouse on the horizon. The path was lined with palms and palmetto trees, as well as a good bit of marsh scrub.

The shade the trees provided was a pleasant defense against the rising sun's brutal assault. Odessa took the opportunity to study the shore birds. She pointed out the brown pelicans and the blue herons that were starting their morning feeding routines. The other three had a hard time focusing on anything but treasure, but they pretended to listen to Odessa's ornithology lesson.

Ideas of pirates' guns, piles of gems, gold doubloons, and a peg leg made of solid gold danced in their heads as the Greek girl jabbered on about water fowl. Predatory mosquitoes and angry horse flies were constantly interrupting their daydreams.

They stopped for some water at a historical marker called Battery Row. Odessa gave another unsolicited history lesson as they guzzled down the first round of bottled water. "We are sitting in a very important historical spot. This is where the Union soldiers laid siege to Fort Pulaski in the Civil War."

The other three shot her a look of disapproval while they drank some water.

Wiki conceded, "Okay fine; I mean the War for Southern Independence. On this very spot, Union troops used the new technology of rifled cannons. What I mean is they cut grooves in the barrel so when the ball flew out it had a steady spin and was much more accurate. This allowed the Union to hammer the same spot repeatedly until a wall of the fort collapsed and they could get a direct shot at the Confederate powder magazine."

Leo took interest in her story for once. "So you're saying Savannah fell to the North because they had better cannon technology?"

"Yep, that is the gist of it. Look through those trees there. You can see the high walls of the fort and Savannah's other lighthouse on Cockspur Island."

"Wow, Wiki," Leo responded, "you really do know a little bit about a lot of everything. So, tell me," Leo joked, "what's another name for thesaurus?"

Odessa shot Leo a look of disdain while Mohamed and Krystal laughed.

"Hey, Wiki, Krystal keeps telling me to 'Git along lil' doggie.' Do you think she is telling me I need to get a dachshund?" said Mohamed, giggling hard as he put on his best Krystal impression.

Leo and Mohamed continued poking fun at Wiki. "What is a 'free' gift? Aren't all 'gifts' free?" said Leo. Before Odessa could even respond, Mohamed chimed in, "What if there were no hypothetical questions?"

Odessa was completely befuddled by the barrage of questions that she couldn't answer. She could only stare and sort of snort as the other three were engulfed in raging laughter. As she was trying to come up with a retort, Leo said through tears of laughter, "HEY! Wiki! You're Catholic right? I heard protons have mass. Is that true?"

Odessa stammered and finally blurted out, "THAT is not even a logical question!"

Krystal responded immediately, "If the world was a logical place, it'd be men that rode horses side saddle!"

They all paused a moment to think about what she meant by that then broke out in hysterical laughter again. They were all in a good mood as they finished up their short rest.

Mohamed chugged the rest of his bottle of water and threw the plastic container into the scrub brush. Krystal walked over and retrieved the litter. "What are you doing, Mo?

We take our trash with us; we don't just throw it out for others to clean up."

"Oh, sorry; in my country we do. I am still not used to that custom. Besides, look how much trash is already here. Apparently, not everyone in your culture agrees with you and throws their trash wherever they want." He pointed at the debris strewn across the scrub brush. The country girl followed his digit as he pointed to a tire, miscellaneous Styrofoam cups, plates, and random trash.

"Sometimes I really hate the human race. Look at all this junk people so rudely left behind." She picked up a large picnic blanket out of the grass. "Just look at this. Someone was in such a hurry they forgot their blanket. This is too nice to leave behind to get ruined; I am takin' this. One man's trash is MY treasure, y'all." Krystal started folding up the blanket and got ready to move on.

"Let's get moving, guys, before the heat overtakes us." Odessa prodded the others to move on. The thrill of the hunt encrgized the teens as they made great time. As they closed in on the lighthouse, Krystal stopped the group. "Wait y'all; look at all this great stuff!" She charged into the dumped mounds of trash buried in the marsh grass.

Mohamed shook his head. "You have fun with that. I need to take a few minutes and pray while you search for trash treasure." The Muslim boy excused himself and went down to the water to pray.

"Since we gotta wait on Mo anyway, I am gonna look and see if can find any good stuff over yonder." In just five minutes, Krystal had salvaged a boogie board, some bungee cords, a *Dukes of Hazard* lunch box, and a cooler with a top that would not shut.

"What are you planning on doing with all that stuff, Krystal?" Leo inquired.

Odessa added, "And how on Earth are you going to carry all of it?"

"Well, I ain't sure what I am gonna do with it yet, but I am sure somethin' will come up. Besides, I have not showed y'all

the best thing I found yet! Stay right here; I will go haul it up."
The tomboy ran back into the bug-infested mud patties and
reappeared towing a filthy shopping cart. She grinned so much
that the corners of her mouth touched the brim of her hat.
"Take a gander at this push cart I found. It rolls good and
everything."

Odessa could not hide the look of disgust on her face. "All
this stuff is so gross, look how dirty it is. Just put this garbage
back where you found it."

"Come on now, y'all. Just got to hose the marsh sludge out
of the cooler lunch pail and push cart and they will done work
just fine. Y'all seem so wasteful; I can use this pushcart to haul
hay in and store drinks in the barn with this cooler. Y'all gots
no vision sometimes," the tiny girl in the muddy overalls
complained as she loaded her new swag into the shopping cart.

Mohamed finally resurfaced and broke into a laugh. "Did
you go shopping when I was gone? Where do you think we can
check out with all your stuff?"

The three chuckled as Krystal defended her thriftiness.
"Y'all laugh all yuh want; this stuff is gonna be great."

The students walked ahead as Krystal proudly pushed the
shopping cart through the gravel and dirt. They arrived
midmorning and the trail dropped them out in a neighborhood
right next to the lighthouse. The lighthouse was preserved and
was surrounded by some historically reproduced outbuildings.
A large field that doubled as a parking lot surrounded the
tower. House communities surrounded the lighthouse and
pushed new construction as close as they could get to the
historic site. A line of palm trees ran across the parking lot and
through the large adjacent grass field.

"Why don't you park your shopping cart behind those
trees so nobody sees them? People will think we are freaks if
you go hauling that mess-on-wheels through the lighthouse
grounds," said Odessa. The girl in the cowboy hat shot back a
dirty look, but then followed the advice and parked the cart out
of sight.

Tybee Island Lighthouse

"Why don't you park your shopping cart behind those trees so nobody sees them? People will think we are freaks if you go hauling that mess-on-wheels through the lighthouse grounds," said Odessa. The girl in the cowboy hat shot back a dirty look, but then followed the advice and parked the cart out of sight.

"Hey, you guys, let's go look around and see if we can find anything with three circles or black cats," suggested Odessa.

The group approached a ticket booth that had been shaped and painted black and white to match the real lighthouse. "We are in luck; it looks like it just opened," Leo said as he jetted for the counter. He greeted the booth attendant. "The four of us would like to take the tour."

The worker was still in the process of getting her workstation in order. "Y'all are our first visitors...and aren't you early? It's a good thing I came in; nobody else is even here yet. That will be six dollars for each of you."

Leo turned to Odessa. "Okay, pay the woman so we can get started."

Wiki looked confused. "I didn't bring any money; I assumed you did."

"I did not. I didn't know they charged an entrance fee to see this place." The tall boy confessed. They looked at the rest of the group. "Did either of you two bring any money?"

Mohamed shook his head no. "I don't even get to handle my own money. Every time I make over twenty dollars, Ms. Mendel ships it to my parents. I don't have anything on me, sorry."

All eyes turned to Krystal. The tiny girl grew uneasy. "Well y'all, I have been savin' some silver dimes to send to my momma, but that is all I got."

Leo extended his palm. "Let me see what I can do with them." The country girl unbuttoned her chest pocket on her overalls and dropped a small velvet bag in his hand. "Now Leo, I always carry my money on me because I still don't trust folks. It took me a mighty long time to save all dem dimes and I skipped a lot of meals to save that money to help my momma."

"Don't worry, we will all pitch in and pay you back." He dug eight silver dimes out and handed them to the worker. "Here that should cover it."

An annoyed look shot over the ticket lady's face. "Sorry, sir; you still owe me twenty-three dollars and twenty cents."

Leo leaned in and turned up his charm. "Ma'am those are pre-1964 silver dimes. Each one is worth about three bucks at today's silver price. So eight dimes should cover our twenty-four dollar fee."

The ticket-taker held the ten-cent round up and studied it. "Look, honey, my drawer has to balance at the end of the shift or I will get in big trouble. I don't care if they are made of gold; my register has to show six dollars for every ticket. So to me, those are only worth eighty cents."

Leo let out an irritated grunt. "Fine. Let me see if I can sell a few of these to some other folks who understand the value of real silver money."

The tall boy spun around and studied their situation. "It seems we arc the only ones here because it is so early. So we got two choices; we can either pay the lady with the dimes, or wait around all day and hope someone buys some of them. What should we do?"

"I worked hard to save all that silver. I have sixty-eight dimes saved up. That is only enough to pay for one person," Krystal calculated.

Mohamed counted on his fingers. "Not to mention that six dollars of silver dimes equal about one hundred and eighty dollars right now. So, because none of us thought to bring your American greenbacks, we are going to pay a one hundred and seventy-four dollar mark up."

"I know it hurts, but we only have a few hours to find something. We are going to have to buck up and just pay it. Since I have the most knowledge of this place and I have the maps, I think we should send me in," Wiki volunteered.

"I don't think that is real fair; it is my money," Krystal argued.

Leo chimed in. "I am in the best condition and can search the area faster than anyone else. I should go."

Three sets of eyes all turned towards Mohamed. "What? You want me to decide? Um, you are all good choices; I can't decide between my friends."

The punk teen demanded, "Dude you got to pick someone! Just do it."

The African boy nervously fiddled with his hat. "I hate choosing, but I guess I pick Wiki. I think knowledge beats out speed on this. Although Krystal should be the one to go, too; it's her silver we are spending."

The girl wearing the cowboy hat cut in. "Mo is probably right. Wiki, yer our best chance; yuh should go. I want y'all to know I expect y'all to pay me back for this."

The Greek girl hugged Krystal and snatched the bag of dimes out of Leo's hand. "You guys look around the outside for clues. See if you can find something on the grounds. Don't forget, this was nothing but a lighthouse and horse land back then. Well, technically, the tower did not have a light back then, so this would have been more of a day marker. Also, there were two other Tybee lighthouses that blew away and fell into the river before this one was built. We are real lucky Shamus faked his funeral when he did. If he had done it a few years earlier, the treasure would probably be underwater."

Leo interrupted, "Um, Wiki? You think you might want to save the history lesson and go look for clues?"

She snapped her focus back to the task at hand. "Oh, right; I am going. One of you guys hang out at the fence line in case I need you." The curly-haired girl walked back up to the lighthouse-shaped booth and poured the dimes out of the little bag with the Porcupine logo. The attendant counted up the silver and handed her a ticket. "Enjoy your day. Don't forget to stop by the gift shop when you're done."

"Finally time to turn over every inch of this place." The Greek girl pushed through the gate and entered the tour grounds.

35 CHAPTER

RUNNING IN CIRCLES

Tybee Island Lighthouse was in a large field surrounded by a white picket fence. There were a few small houses like the historic day kitchen scattered through the grounds. Odessa started her search with the outbuildings.

After examining a few of them she remembered what her research on the Internet said about them. She slapped herself on the head. "I'm so stupid sometimes! The only original structure was the lighthouse. All the rest of the buildings would not have existed back then. I got to focus better or I will waste all our time" She turned her attention to the imposing black and white tower. "I guess it's time to start the long climb up those stairs. Man I wish I was in shape," she vented aloud.

"So who wants to stay on the fence line incase Odessa needs something?" Leo asked.

"I'll stay, y'all. Yuh boys look around. I am goin' back to clean up some of the stuff I found. There's a hose over there; I doubt anyone would mind if we use a little water. After all, we did just pay them one hundred and eighty dollars for a ticket," the tiny girl justified.

"That is fine with us. Go clean up your stuff and we will go check out where the original lighthouses fell into the water. Maybe there is some rubble left on the beach or something," Mohamed explained.

The boys left her alone and walked toward the adjacent fort. Next to the lighthouse was an old Civil War bunker called Fort Screven. "Dude, check out these cool gun pits at that fort! I totally want to stop and check them out," Leo said as he pointed.

Mohamed burst his bubble. "It looks like someone bought this fort and made it into apartments. Look, there is a realty sign and everything."

Leo grew excited. "Oh man, how cool would it be to live in one of those things? You know they got to be totally haunted. I bet the people that live there hear ghost cannon fire and shouting. That's what I will do with my portion of the loot; I want to buy an apartment here."

"Well, it does look like it would be a perfect place to fight off a zombie hoard; it appears to be very defensible," Mohamed said, playing into Leo's fears.

"That is an excellent point, dude. Just for that, I might let you come take shelter here when the zombie apocalypse comes." He slapped Mohamed on the back and smiled.

"You are such a good friend to me, thank you," Mohamed said in a sarcastic tone.

Krystal had returned with her cart and started spraying all the mud from her marsh booty. The cooler was particularly hard to get clean, but the *Dukes of Hazard* lunch box cleaned up nicely, considering its age. The cleaning took much longer than expected and the tiny girl guessed that an hour had passed by the time she was done. She looked around and realized the boys were still missing, and there was no sign of Odessa either. The tiny girl did notice a carload of tourists drive in and an idea came to her.

The country girl put on her best, friendly smile and approached the family unloading out of their car. She approached a woman she assumed was the mother. "Excuse me, ma'am. I am in a might bit of a pinch. My friends and I didn't realize it costs money to get in here, so I was wonderin' if I could talk any of yuh into buyin' this." The frugal girl held up the vintage *Dukes of Hazard* lunch box that had a picture of The General Lee leaping over a police car.

The mother took pity on the cute little girl. "How much is it dear?"

"Well, I reckon twelve dollars would be fine."

The father came over and inspected the lunch pail. "Little girl," he said, "twelve dollars would be unfair."

A disappointed look came over her face. "Oh, alright. What are yuh offerin'?"

"This looks like a classic box. Heck, it has to be at least thirty years old. I would also say you should get double your asking price. Does twenty four dollars sound fair to you?"

The surprised girl giggled and swatted her cowboy hat on her hip. "Yes sir! That would be wonderful, thank yuh!" They made the exchange and the tiny girl excused herself. "Thank yuh so much. I have to go take care of somethin' now."

Krystal immediately handed a twenty-dollar bill to the ticket lady in the booth. "Ma'am, I would like yuh to make some change; I need all the dimes yuh got, please." The clever girl smiled as she reclaimed all her silver dimes.

Meanwhile, Odessa slowly examined the bricks and each step of the tower. It was a slow process and, so far, had not bared any clues. She had been at it almost two hours and was only about halfway up.

To her surprise and delight, she heard a familiar voice. "Yuh need some help, darlin'?" Wiki spun around to see her three companions in the circular stairwell. "I would love some help! How did you guys get in here?"

Leo grinned at the girl in the oversized straw hat. "It appears Krystal has a heck of a head for business. She sold that *Dukes of Hazard* lunch box and had enough profit to pay for all of us and get all her silver back."

Odessa processed the information. "Wow that is amazing! I guess I will never again make fun of you for picking up trash."

The tiny girl tipped her hat. "Thank yuh, darlin', for the nice fine words." Wiki shifted gears. "Okay guys, we are running low on time. I have searched every inch of the base on this lighthouse and found nothing. The top half was burned in the Civil War, so I don't think any clues would have survived that. You guys have any ideas?"

"I guess we should look anyway, just in case. With the four of us looking, we can move pretty fast," Mohamed answered.

"Here we go! Off like a herd of turtles," Krystal joked.

The Porcs meticulously scanned the walls step by step. They slowly climbed for twenty more minutes before reaching the top. They were greeted with the intense midmorning heat as they took in the amazing view of Tybee Island. "Well, I don't see a point to searching the lens much up here. Not much in this top part is original," Odessa surmised, but the four did a final search anyway, not wanting to give up.

"I guess the lighthouse doesn't hold the clue we are looking for. I say we all go back down and check out the grounds some more. Maybe something will show up," Mohamed suggested.

The group admitted defeat and headed back down to ground level. Krystal threw in a cup-half-full remark. "At least it was a done fine view, y'all. The ocean breeze was sure fine, too."

The grounds started filling up with tourists as the morning became the afternoon. The unschoolers took a break for a few minutes and split some granola bars Odessa had brought along. She reached into Mohamed's backpack and handed them out. A woman wearing a lighthouse polo shirt approached the four and introduced herself. "Hi! I am the Tybee Lighthouse historian. I can answer any questions you might have about this area."

Leo shook his head. "You might be real sorry you made that offer, ma'am."

Odessa started up. "Yes, I have some questions." The girl pulled out a large list of questions from her dress pocket. "This is a list of everything I could not find answers for on the Internet." The Greek girl started to fire off obscure question after obscure question and put the historian through her paces. The other three students giggled as they watched Wiki drill the helpful worker.

After twenty minutes of back and forth questioning and answering, Wiki finally came to her last question. "What was here around 1770-1780?"

"Well, the third lighthouse was completely constructed a little before that and not really much else. Because the soil was poor for planting and mosquitoes caused so many diseases, no one wanted to live out here and run the lighthouse. There were only slaves and horses out here. The only things left here after that time period were the tower and mounds of ballast rocks the pirates and horse traders had dumped all over the place when they came to pick up their horses."

The wheels started spinning in the young girls head. "You have been so helpful. Thanks for answering all my questions."

"Well, I am really impressed that you know so much about this lighthouse. When you get a little older, you should think about getting a job here," the worker offered as Odessa made a fast exit.

Wiki jumped to her feet. "Well, you guys heard her! What are you waiting for? Come on!" The pudgy girl moved with surprising agility and took off toward the tall, black and white cylinder.

The other three followed and exchanged confused looks. "Did I miss somethin', or are the rest of y'all just as confused as me right now?" Krystal asked.

"No, we are lost, too, but I say follow her. Look how excited she is; she must have figured out something," Mohamed coaxed.

The teens made their way to the top of the lighthouse in record time. Leo spoke with a winded tone. "Wiki, what is all this about?"

The out-of-shape girl could barely speak and gasped for breath. She held up a finger to signify she needed another minute to catch her breath. Leo impatiently tapped his foot as he waited. The color returned to her face and she started to explain. "Do you guys remember when we toured River Street? Do you remember we talked about how the cobblestone streets came to into existence? Ships needed weight when they made sea voyages so they would fill the hold with rocks called ballast stones. When they reached their destination, the ship would dump all the stones out and replace it with cargo. After a while, ports found themselves overrun with stones."

"So what do rocks have to do with anything?" Mohamed inquired.

"When I was reading the first journal we found in the library, I was really only focusing on the map of the secret passage. The beginning of the journal was all April's shipping records. I didn't put it together until just now. She mentions dropping off loads of ballast stones and picking up horses over and over. Admiral Read had plenty of time and lots of stones to help Shamus hide his treasure."

Leo cut to the chase. "So what you're saying is we need to be looking for some mounds of rocks?"

"Well, it was over two hundred years ago, so it would more likely be mounds of dirt now covered with grass and trees and stuff," Odessa assumed.

The group used the aerial view to scout the land for a good five minutes. "I don't see any mounds, Wiki," Mohamed informed.

"Me neither," Leo Stedman added.

Odessa refused to give up. "It has got to be here; look harder."

Krystal offered, "I think I might have somethin', y'all. When I was pushin' my shoppin' cart to the water spigot, I kept goin' over big ol' grooves. Look over in that direction."

They focused their attention in the direction Krystal was pointing and finally, Odessa saw it. She bounced up and down and squealed. "There it is! Look!"

"What? What do you see? I don't see it!" Mohamed barked.

The Greek girl calmed down and caught her breath. "Okay, stop looking for small mounds and look at the big picture. Do you see Krystal's shopping cart? Well look to the right of it and you will see a long, semi-circle ridge of dirt. Now keep following it and you will see that the ridge is the side of a giant ring mound."

Mohamed's eyes lit up as he finally started to see what she did.

"Leo, can I see your binoculars, please?" The tall boy handed Odessa the beat up pair. She peered through them and grew even more excited. "Guys, look! There is a part of a second circle that converges with the first. It's not a full circle anymore because of the tree line and the parking lot, but enough of it is still there to trace it out."

"And look there, y'all. I see a third circle criss-crossin' the other two. These look just like April's mark we found before. I think I see the three circles, but where is the black cat that is always in the design?" Krystal wondered.

"I am not real sure, but I'm going to draw on this map what I see." Odessa then reached into her dress pocket and pulled out an aerial map that she had printed out. She took her time and tried to trace exactly what she saw. "Okay guys, I drew the circles in where I think they were originally. We should go back down and search this area where all circles cross and share a common space." Wiki motioned they should go back down as they heard the sounds of tourists approaching from below.

Map printout of Tybee Lighthouse with circles.

"I am not real sure, but I'm going to draw on this map what I see." Odessa then reached into her dress pocket and pulled out an aerial map that she had printed out. She took her time and tried to trace exactly what she saw. "Okay guys, I drew the circles in where I think they were originally. We should go back down and search this area where all circles cross and share a common space." Wiki motioned they should go back down as they heard the sounds of tourists approaching from below.

ESCAPE FROM TYBEE

Odessa checked the circles on the map and compared it to where they stood. "The ridges are real faint now that we are at ground level, but it looks like the circles all share that patch of grass behind those trees. Let's dig in that depressed area between the circles."

Leo pulled out his compact trench shovel and unfolded it. He took his best guess at where dead center was and started digging. Krystal looked around. "These trees will hide what we are doin' a little bit from this one side, but I gots an idea, y'all." The tomboy ran off to retrieve her beloved shopping cart.

Mohamed watched the spade pierce the ground over and over as a small hole in the earth opened up. Leo dug rapidly as the rush of treasure hunting overtook him. By the time Krystal returned, the hole had grown into a wide trench. The zombie-obsessed boy was already drenched with sweat; even his gray ribbon was wet. "Here. You take a turn; I need some water," he said as he handed Mohamed the shovel.

The Ugandan teen climbed into the shallow, dusty hole wearing his expensive leather shoes and new khakis. He continued Leo's feverish pace for a good ten minutes until the sound of metal striking stone rang through the air. Mohamed dug around the large rock to free it from the sandy dirt. Odessa was so excited she jumped into the small pit and cleaned off the rock using some water and the edge of her dress. "Everyone, look! This rock has a silhouette of a cat carved in it! I was wondering why there wasn't a cat made of stones on the ground. I guess we found the final piece of April's mark. Looks like the cat marks the spot," she said, giggling at her own joke.

Krystal ruined the moment, "Everyone, get up here! Hurry!"

Odessa fumbled around. "But we are so close! This is the last piece."

"NOW!" Krystal replied in a demanding tone.

The two teens climbed out of the shallow pit. "What's so important that we have to stop?" Wiki griped.

The tiny girl pointed at some tourists wandering over. "Quick, help me with this picnic blanket I found. Use it to cover the hole and then we all gotta sit on the corners to hold it up." The four stretched the fabric over their dig site and pretended to be casually having lunch. Krystal even pulled out the broken cooler and set it next to their blanket.

A family of tourists walked up to them and one asked, "Is there something interesting to see over here?"

"No, ma'am. We are just takin' a break and usin' these trees for some shade. We're about to enjoy ourselves a good ol' fashion picnic." She pointed at the prop ice chest. "There is absolutely nuthin' interestin' over here at all," the country girl said and flashed a nervous smile.

The tourist continued, "Oh, we just thought this area was part of the exhibit. Enjoy your lunch." The family slowly walked off, arguing about where they could buy the best ice cream on Tybee.

Leo shined a grin at the quick thinking Krystal. "You are one smart girl. That was epic, dude."

"I have to admit, I am also a might impressed with myself right now! Let's find out what is under this rock." Krystal Bennett pulled the blanket off the hole. The four worked together to slide the rock over and started digging under where it used to sit. A half hour passed and the hole had grown over three feet deep. The four took shifts shoveling. They worked as hard as they could until they felt close to exhaustion and then passed the spade off to another. Using this technique, the hole grew very quickly.

Screech! The sound of the shovel scratching something from below rang out of the pit. The four dove in and dug carefully in the sandy dirt until they uncovered a green, rectangular box. The friends jumped up and down with joy laughing and hugging.

The metal chest reminded Leo a little bit of a footlocker. It was almost three feet long and had handles on each narrow end. Wiki was overwhelmed with excitement and started ordering the others around. "Okay guys; let's pull this thing out of the hole." The other three were too distracted to even care about Odessa's bossy tone. Everyone surrounded the box and lifted. Their efforts were futile. They could barely even budge the green-patinaed chest.

"Holy cow that thing is heavy! I think we're gonna have to grab the same end and drag it up a little at a time. I think I might have somethin' that will help." In a flash, Krystal retrieved the broken boogie board from the shopping cart. "The board is smooth; let's put it under the chest and slide it out of the hole."

The students worked as a team as they wedged the small surfboard under one side of the box. Then they used their collective force to pull the heavy crate a few inches. The Porcs repeated this process over and over until the chest was finally out of the hole. The exhausted and dirty group gathered around the copper box. "Let's open it together." Odessa suggested. The others nodded in approval and laid their hands on the lid. They counted in unison. "One...two...THREE!"

The four teens pulled with all their might, but the top resisted. "Wait, guys! I think it is locked. Look at the big, old hinges. Back then they used to try to hide the lock and disguise it as a hinge. Mo, please tell me you brought that key with you we found in the tunnels." Odessa pleaded.

Mohamed hung his head. "I am sorry; I forgot it."

The others let out a collective cry of frustration. "I guess we will have to wait till we get back to the school before we can find out what's in there. One thing's for sure; it is really heavy for such a small chest," Leo stated.

"Well, y'all, I hate to point this out, but how the heck are we gonna get this heavy thing back to the school?" Krystal pondered.

Mohamed perked up. "I got an idea! Krystal, do you mind if I borrow your grocery cart?" She nodded and he rolled the cart into the pit. "I was thinking; without a system of pulleys and levers, I don't think we would be able to lift this into the shopping cart on our own. So let's put the cart in this hole and just slide the chest into the cart."

Odessa nodded. "That is genius. Never let anyone tease you for being a Mathlete again."

The four carefully lined up the cart and the copper box so they could just slide it in. With a mighty crash and a jingle, the chest sat in the cart perfectly. The four worked as a team pushing and pulling the reinforced plastic grocery buggy out of the pit. The team celebrated and lavished Mohamed with praise for his brilliant idea.

A new group of tourists pulled up in their car and started unloading in the parking lot. Leo looked at all the new activity happening around them. "Dudes, let's hide this thing and clean this place up so nobody knows we were here. There are too many eyes around and I think it is time to go."

The girls covered the chest with the blanket and used the bungee cords to tie it down tight. They then stacked the broken cooler and boogie board in to hide the chest even more. Meanwhile, the boys filled the hole back in the best they could. When they felt like that they had done a satisfactory job, the group moved on and started back toward the boat. Covering their tracks took much longer than expected, and the sun was starting to drop in the sky. It was a slow journey as the wobbly wheels on the cart kept getting stuck on the gravel and dirt path. Besides the occasional biker that passed by, it was a quiet trip back to the dock.

Their imagination ran wild as they all took guesses about what treasure awaited them in the mystery chest. By the time they arrived at the dock, the last few rays of the sun sparkled on the river. Most of the ships were already tied up and the area was deserted. The four took great care as they pushed their buggy of treasure down the boardwalk and around the large live bait cages.

"Well, I guess we are a smidge early still. Might as well enjoy the sunset," Krystal said and took off her boots, dangling her feet into the river water. "I don't get to play in the water too much; I am going take advantage of it, y'all." The other three shrugged their shoulders and sat down next to her.

The friends were so busy exchanging silly stories and jokes while they waited that they did not notice the two figures approaching them on the docks. It wasn't until the obese man's foot made a plank bend and creak that their approach was noticed. Mohamed's head spun around and he alerted the others. The three scrambled to their feet while Krystal tried locating her boots.

A guttural voice stated, "You four have been very busy this month." Ms. Gambit flashed her tobacco-stained teeth. She surveyed the shopping cart. "Now, it is still way too hot for a picnic at the beach, so what do you really have strapped down under that blanket?"

Leo stepped in between the predators and his treasure. "I've had all I am going to take from you two. What is your problem? Why have you two had it out for me since day one?"

Mr. Bines snorted. "I hate all ya spoiled, snotty kids. You always think you're so much better than us. I see how y'all look down on us just because we work a dead end job."

Ms. Gambit waved her boney, yellow hand and cut her partner off. "I have a feeling that is all about to change. All we want is what you found today and we won't have troubles."

Leo became enraged when he noticed Ms. Gambit had the audacity to `be wearing his Zombie Bug-Out Bag she had stolen from him. "Are you enjoying my bag, you thief?" he shouted at her.

She snared her brown teeth at him. "I have been enjoying it. Look, I even sewed the strap back up and fixed it." She taunted him by pushing her hips forward and showing it off like a fashion model. "Although it really doesn't match anything I own, I figured it would be good to carry back anything we find on y'all."

Leo took the bait and started shaking with anger until a hand touched his shoulder. Odessa held him back as she stepped up next to him. "Shouldn't you be checking in with your handler? Did that crooked Mr. Hughes finally let you guys off his dog leash?"

Leo joined in. "He is too busy forcing his student-slaves to dig up valuables for him than to waste his time talking to these two morons."

Mr. Bines snorted like a bull at the insult and looked to Ms. Gambit for permission to attack. She raised her palm and told him to stay as if she was ordering her dog to do a trick. "This is your last chance. Just give us the cart or I let him loose on you."

Mohamed stepped up and stood shoulder to shoulder with Odessa and Leo. "Tell Mr. Hughes, I am sick of bullies. This stops here."

"Oh, dear boy, we didn't tell Hughes anything about this. We're keeping this one for ourselves. He's been kinda nasty to us, too and I see no reason why he even has to know about this. If we get the treasure then we'll be the rich ones and we can boss him around. Now, I tried to be civil, but you decided to be defiant brats. GET THEM!" Ms. Gambit shouted and lowered her hand, releasing the fat Kracken on them.

Mr. Bines stomped his feet and exhaled out of his nose like an angry rhino. The three friends linked arms and held strong. Like a deranged game of Red Rover, the massive man charged the human chain. The bull burst through the line and Mohamed took the force of the blow. The attack sent the African boy flying into the water. Leo swung his fist, but it just bounced off his thick shoulders. The angry brute swung back and landed a blow to Leo's chest.

The forceful strike knocked the skate rat backwards and he flew into the marsh. Odessa stood in place shaking, paralyzed with fear. The attacker tucked the Greek girls head into his sweaty armpit and dragged her to the edge of the dock. Wiki did the only thing she could think of and bit down hard into his blubbery arm. The Goliath screamed with pain and tossed Odessa into the creek.

Just then the small girl's cowboy boot flew threw the air, end over end, and struck the aggressor right in the nose. Mr. Bines bent over and let out a string of curse words. Krystal summoned superhuman strength from the major adrenaline rush and charged the heavy shopping cart towards the fat man and his companion. She screamed at them, "Yuh want this cart so bad? Here, take it!"

She lined up Mr. Bines like she was shooting a game of pool and rammed the fat man with the full force of the cart. Still bent over holding his nose, his elephant legs stumbled backwards into Ms. Gambit. Krystal continued the momentum and rammed the two of them again with the buggy. Both the thieves fell backwards and tipped over the safety wall of the live bait hold. Krystal moved as fast as a cougar and made a grab for Leo's bag. Mr. Bines fell into the large crab hold with a giant splash, but Ms. Gambit continued to teeter on the edge, supported only by the strap of the Bug-Out Bag being held by Krystal. She and Gambit exchanged eye contact as a loud ripping sound came from the shoddily repaired strap.

The skeletal woman tumbled backwards as her poor stitching job came back to haunt her. Krystal laughed as she watched the woman fall into the bait hold onto her accomplice. "Learn to sew!" she shouted triumphantly.

The three waterlogged students had climbed back on the dock and ran over to check on Krystal. They hugged her and could not believe she had bested both of them. The scrappy little girl stood over the pit and was enjoying the show. Screams of pain were coming from the crab pit as the crustaceans repeatedly pinched the two bullies.

The students started to chuckle loudly as the thieves got what was coming to them. Odessa gave more unsolicited advice. "Try not to move or you will just upset them even more."

Mr. Bines and Ms. Gambit in the live crab hold.

"Get us out of here!" Ms. Gambit pleaded.

Leo shook his head. "No way! You earned this!" Mr. Bines coughed up water as he tried to stay a float. "Please, we'll drown!"

Mohamed's morality tugged at him. "Krystal, you know our God would not be real happy if they died. I think we have to do something."

She shook her head. "Yes, Jesus wouldn't like it none. Hold on." The tiny girl took the cooler and the small surfboard over to the hole. She threw them in. "Here, both of these'll float. Just hold on until the dockworkers show up in the morning."

"Let's go to a different dock so when Cappy Brewer picks us up, he doesn't ask any awkward questions," Leo advised.

"Yep, that's a bright idea, but we are not going anywhere until we find my boot I threw. By the way, I got something for you." Krystal handed Leo his beloved Zombie Bug-Out Bag.

A tear welled up in the usually stoic boy's eye. "Krystal, when the apocalypse finally comes, I promise I won't let zombies eat your brains first." He hugged the tiny girl, thanking her.

After finding the aerobatic footwear, they moved to the furthest dock away from the live bait hold that now held a pair of criminals. The *Waving Lady* pulled up an hour later and Captain Brewer jumped down to the dock to talk to them. "Lads, why do you have a grocery cart?"

Odessa stepped up to the salty shrimper. "I know this seems odd, but all I can tell you is this; we have something that can probably save Jah's life. Please, just trust us and don't ask questions."

The grizzly man scratched his beard. "Fair enough. Let me lower the gangplank and we will roll it on. We are running a little late, so let's hurry it up."

The shrimpers helped the students roll the buggy onto the deck and they were quickly off to Thunderbolt.

THE REPORT

J ah Loko greeted the teens as they rolled the cart down to the waiting horse and buggy. "Finally. I thought da shrimp done ate ya. What's ya chillun got dere in dat push cart?"

Krystal hugged the sick man. "We ain't sure yet, but it is real heavy. I think we will have to just tow it behind the carriage."

"I tink I got a leather horse strap strong enough to do it. Let's hook it up and gets ya chillun home."

Within a few minutes, the shopping cart was tied to the carriage and they headed toward the academy.

It was now nightfall as they pulled into the barn and unhooked the treasure chest. All eyes turned to Mohamed. "I will be right back with the key as fast as I can," the Ugandan boy said and dashed off, disappearing into the main building.

Jah hunched over and held his belly in discomfort. "Miss Krystal, ya goin' ta have ta stable Harricane for me."

She put her small hand on the Gullah man's shoulder. "Yuh just relax; I got this Mr. Loko."

The three students helped break down the touring carriage and took care of the draft horse while they waited for Mohamed to return.

The African teen burst into the barn. "I got it!" He handed the copper patinaed key off to Odessa.

Copper key with April's mark.

"What makes you think this key will open this chest?" Leo pressed.

"Because they are both copper and copper was fairly rare back then. Do you see how the key is the same shade of green as the chest? And it has April's mark on it. We are lucky Shamus used copper because if it were a wooden box or any other kind of metal, it would have rotted away. Once it oxidizes and turns green, copper can last hundreds of years."

Leo grew impatient. "Dude, enough with the history lessons; open it already"

Odessa laughed at herself. "Oops, you're right. Let me see if I can figure this out."

She searched the hinges and spied a large hole in one of them. Odessa carefully slid the ancient key into the socket and softly turned it. *Click, click, click.* A series of tumblers could be heard moving. As if on queue, Krystal's three-legged black cat jumped and sat on top of the box, preventing them from opening it. The children all groaned that they were again being denied access. Krystal reached out and pet the cat then gently shooed it off. When the cat jumped off the box, the lid cracked open and an ancient, musty smell escaped. The four Porcs grabbed the top of the chest and threw the lid back.

The barn light was not the best, but there it was. Finally, after all that, a golden pirate peg leg shimmered in the night, illuminating the children's smiling faces. The teens celebrated and screamed so loud it made Jah almost fall out of the carriage. Leo dug the flashlight out of Mohamed's backpack and shined it in the chest. Gold and silver doubloons surrounded the leg. On closer inspection, the chest looked like it had been custom made specifically to carry around Shamus's leg; the pirate had then poured as many extra coins in it as would fit. The leg itself was covered in ornate relief. It depicted a God-like man riding a sea horse kind of creature and also had a pattern of three swirls around the top and swimming dolphins. It was in perfect condition.

"It is the most beautiful thing I've ever seen!" exclaimed Odessa.

Everyone was grinning from ear to ear when Krystal presented the group with two empty feed buckets. "Let's count these coins." The four dove in and started dropping the rounds into the plastic bucket. They counted in unison as each coin struck the bottom. "One, two, three...one hundred and forty-one, one hundred and forty-two gold coins and one hundred sixty-seven silver."

"Look at all that gold and silver!" Leo cracked himself up. "TREASURE BATH!!!" He hollered in his best Caesarian accent. "I think we have enough to take one."

His three friends cut their eyes at him. *"Ugghhh!!!"* Leo responded. "It's from the classic Mel Brooks movie *History of the World.* Mo, remind me to explain that one to you later when we are alone."

Jah let out a hardy laugh as he watched. "I can't believe ya chillun found Savannah's missin' pirate treasure. I be glad I lived long enough ta see it."

The teens exchanged looks and all nodded their head in agreement. "Funny yuh should say that, Mr. Loko." Krystal walked over to the man with the heavy bucket of gold coins and dropped it in his lap. "We all want yuh to take this gold and get yuhself fixed up. Just don't tell nobody where yuh got them from, okay?"

Shamus's golden peg leg.

The teens exchanged looks and all nodded their head in agreement. "Funny yuh should say that, Mr. Loko." Krystal walked over to the man with the heavy bucket of gold coins and dropped it in his lap. "We all want yuh to take this gold and get yuhself fixed up. Just don't tell nobody where yuh got them from, okay?"

The old man was shocked by this act of generosity. "No, chillun, I can't take all dis."

Odessa smiled. "Look, operations are very expensive. Use whatever you need and if anything is left, you can buy us something we need."

Tears welled up in the old man's eyes. "Okay, I knows how ta be grateful. Thank ya's so much. I will go set up da doctor in da morning. Now come give dis old man a hug."

The five took a minute to enjoy the moment and felt good about themselves. Odessa finally interrupted. "Oh, man! I forgot! I have to give my report to Ms. Mendel tonight. I bet she has never seen a business report update as great as this."

"Hey, before we do that, what about the silver coins?" Leo asked the other three. "Maybe it would be fun to keep something for us in the future, just in case this doesn't work out for the school like we want it to. You know that some government zombie will try to take this stuff away from us when they find out we have it."

"I agree!" Krystal said. "All this other treasure should be enough right now to help save Jah and the Mendel Academy. Let's hide it and come back for it when we need it. Mo, come help me. I got the best hidin' place right here in the barn."

"This better be good. It's already late and I don't care for doing business at this hour," Ruby Mendel lectured the four.

Odessa took a step forward. "I am sorry about that, ma'am, but this can't wait.   First off, let me apologize for our appearance. We have not had time to clean ourselves up yet."

"Okay, you definitely have my attention, but why are the other three of you here? This is Odessa's report," the blonde woman inquired.

"Well, ma'am, this kinda involves us all." Wiki stood up straight and went into her professional presentation mode. "I believe we have the best tour Savannah has ever seen and we have a whole lot more than that. We are going to show you some stuff that is hard to believe and some stuff that might make you a little mad, but I ask that you let us show you everything before you say something."

Ruby yelled for Scott in the other room to join her. As he walked in, Ms. Mendel pointed at the four, dirt-encrusted children. "Join us; I have a feeling you are really going to want to see this."

Odessa turned to Mohamed. "Go ahead and get the stuff." The African teen disappeared and Wiki continued. "It all started with Tomochichi's rock. I am giving that old chief props for getting this ball rolling. I had a dream about a book in the Historical Society that led me to the lost journal of Admiral April Read."

Her story was interrupted as Mohamed pushed in the plastic shopping cart. Its contents were being covered by the dirty picnic blanket. Scott and Ruby exchanged inquisitive looks.

Odessa went on to recount the entire summer's adventure. Every time she finished a section of the story, she legitimized it by producing the relevant artifact. The Mendel's' eyes shot out of their heads as the students produced the original jack of the *Vendetta*, April's legendary axe-pistol, an original pirate journal, a Scrimshawed powder horn, and the copper key.

The four students smiled at each other for the big reveal. Odessa threw off the blanket to reveal the copper treasure chest. The administrators' jaws dropped as they showed them the golden pirate peg leg. "That, Ms. Mendel, concludes our presentation," Wiki laughed.

Ruby and Scott stood silently in shock. After she snapped back into reality, Ruby slowly gasped. "I can't believe what I am looking at, y'all! This is the most amazing story I have ever heard. You're right, I am pretty darn mad that you kids did all this without telling me, but I am having a hard time staying mad when I see all this unbelievable stuff you found. What are y'all going to do with all this?"

Odessa answered the stunned woman, saying, "Well, we have a proposal for you. We know the school is having money problems."

Ruby shot a nasty look at Scott. "Don't look at me! I never said anything to any of them."

Wiki cut in. "Scott did not tell us, ma'am. We overheard you guys fighting. Anyway, we want to help you. We know when the government and our parent's find out about it, they will all try to take it from us. So we thought you could say all this stuff was anonymously donated to the school or something. We know if our parents found out we discovered all this stuff, they will each demand a cut and it will become a huge mess. Sometimes, still being a minor really sucks."

The blonde woman with obscenely big hair cocked an eyebrow. "So what's your proposal?"

"You take everything we found and create a pirate exhibit. You include it at the end of the new pirate tour I designed. In return, we get to go to this school as long as we want and we expect a significant raise in pay for our jobs around here."

Ruby lost her composure and started crying. Tears rolled down her sun-damaged cheeks and wrecked her mascara. "You children are a blessing. We accept your business proposal." The raccoon-eyed woman threw her arms around the group and crushed them together.

Leo let her have her moment and then spoke up. "There is one thing you need to know, Ruby." Ms. Mendel threw the boy a disapproving look for calling her by her first name. The cocky boy continued. "Mr. Hughes and his henchmen are still out there, and I don't think he is going to just let this go."

"We will stay vigilant, Mr. Stedman. You let me worry about them," the woman with the smeared make-up reassured him. "Now y'all give me one more hug."

Old world music filled the ballroom. The place was jam packed with guests dressed in colonial and Victorian attire.

Odessa and Krystal, escorted by Leo, made their formal entrance into the ball. Each young woman clung to the arm of the tall boy and tried not to trip over Odessa's elaborate colonial dress. Leo was wearing a colonial pirate costume complete with a fake peg leg and a hook. Krystal adjusted her stuffed toy parrot that kept sliding down her pirate outfit. She continued to stumble into chairs and tables as she adjusted to wearing an eye patch.

"This was such a fun idea Mo had. I am glad he went with a colonial-themed dance instead of a swing dance party. Where is he anyway?" Odessa questioned.

Krystal pointed at the stage. "He is up there conducting the band. See? He is the one dressed like a sailor."

"It looks like our parents are enjoying all of this. I think even Mo's dad is smiling." Leo pointed at the Ugandan man watching his son.

The tune "Barbara Allen" concluded and Ms. Mendel stepped onto the stage. She was dressed in an amazing Victorian dress complete with a parasol. Her hair was exceptionally large tonight. "We have the most amazing stuff to present to you this evening. We are gonna let y'all get the first sneak peek at the artifacts on our new Pirates of Savannah tour. Please remember, we need your help to bring this tour together, so if you like what you see, please donate and help make this happen. Okay, Scott. Bring in the first antique piece."

A man dressed as a red coat wheeled in the *Vendetta's* jack displayed in a protective case. The crowd oohed and aahed as Scott revealed the ancient pirate flag. Ruby gave a detailed description of the piece while her brother rolled it around for everyone to see. They repeated this process over and over with each artifact until they finally unveiled Shamus's golden peg leg to the audience. Audible gasps echoed across the chamber and the patrons started opening their checkbooks to support the school and its new pirate exhibit.

After the excitement died down, Ms. Mendel came over to the four. "I can't thank you enough. We got enough donations tonight to completely get this school out of debt." She hugged the group again. "There is something I think y'all need to know. When my brother was cleaning that leg he found something on the backside of it. I guess y'all never took it out of the case because it was so heavy."

Odessa's eyes lit up. "What was it?"

"We are not sure; there is some writing. I think it is a poem or a song. We want you guys to take a look at it later," the woman with the monstrous blonde hairdo told them.

"Yes ma'am, we would be happy to check it out tomorrow," Wiki grinned.

Mohamed spoke up. "I can't believe this summer is already over. I am not looking forward to going back to school and my old life."

"I don't wanna think about it, y'all. I can't imagine leavin' this place," Krystal added.

Odessa reminded the group, "We have so many things left undone. We have to figure out what to do with the silver and there is still a diamond-encrusted eye patch, a golden hook, and Sam Scurvy's silver sword out there somewhere. They are begging for us to find them."

"I know we got some issues to still figure out, but lets just take a breath and enjoy the moment. Dudes, this is our night, so let's go and celebrate it." Leo offered his arm to his friends. "In the words of the immortal '80s singer, David Bowie, 'LET'S DANCE!'"

End of the Summer group photo in front of the Mendel Academy

AFTERWORD

I hope you really enjoyed the read. I know I left a few things dangling, but if there is enough demand from the readers I might be talked into doing a sequel. At the end of my historical fiction books, I like to share with the reader what parts of my books were real. I will break everything down for you in this section. Please remember to check out all of my books at www.Lupolit.com

1 CHAPTER

The pirate and smuggler tunnels under the Pirates' House Restaurant and the Trustee's Garden are real. Much debate and speculation has occurred about when these were built. Since they were used as illegal smuggling and Shanghai tunnels, no records of them exist. Official records from Oglethorpe's letters to England do state he commissioned other underground passages all over Savannah. The corridors under the city were later used to move cargo, and for military movement.

Tarrin seems to think from some misguided history tour he was on that women used these passages to walk through in the heat of the summer. Ruby vehemently disagrees that any Southern Belle would find herself in the dank underground wearing her Sunday best. Since neither of us can find actual proof that this did or did not happen, I will say, I am right and this never happened. -Ruby wrote this.

2 CHAPTER

The month of May is Zombie Awareness month, and it is signified by wearing a gray ribbon.

Black Flag really was a popular punk band in the 1980s. Henry Rollins was the singer, but later took on movie and TV roles.

The anarchy sign was also very popular in the 1980s movement, although today its meaning has toned down and has returned to its classical roots. Today the word "anarchy" does not mean a violent revolution, but simply means to live without rulers.

The idea for the crooked security guards confiscating kid's personal effects and selling them for a profit was based on a real story I saw on the net.

3 CHAPTER

Tomboys, or I should maybe say tomgirls, are all over the Georgia countryside.

4 CHAPTER

Pirates really existed all up and down the Lowcountry coastline. Although most of the very famous pirates were all hunted down by the time Savannah was founded, smugglers and rumrunners were very active in the Lowcountry. Odessa's report about the "Golden Age of Pirates" was accurate in the fact that governments accidentally created the scourge of the sea. Blackbeard, Gentleman Stead Bonnet, Calico Jack Rackum, Anne Bonny, and Mary Read were all very famous pirates.

5 CHAPTER

Although there are many Muslims all over Africa, they are not the majority in Uganda.

The trumpet is a difficult instrument to get good at; I can testify to this personally.

Everyone knows *Star Trek II: The Wrath of Khan* was the best of the *Star Trek* movies.

Because of its unique position, Savannah is usually ten degrees hotter than the towns around it. If you visit Savannah in the summer, be sure to bring a hat and plenty of water.

6 CHAPTER

The Santa Cruz Jason Jessee Sungod was one of the first designer skate boards made in the 1980s. It is a highly desirable collector's item. Even today it is not unusual to see them going for $2000 on eBay.

The description of Sago palm propagation is accurate.

Hidden pen cameras can be bought for less the $50 these days and record images and sounds that are as good as cell phones.

7 CHAPTER

Horsin' Around is a real horse charity in Savannah and they have an excellent reputation for helping kids with special needs and equines.

Some horses really do puff out their chests so their tack will be loose enough to dump their riders. Horses are much smarter than some people give them credit for.

8 CHAPTER

Odessa and Stacy's relationship and the events surrounding the party were based on a real experience that happened to me in fifth grade. I hope you never do this to someone for your birthday party, they'll remember it forever! Thanks for the memory Emily.

9 CHAPTER

In most sects of the Muslim religion it is forbidden to eat any products made from a pig.

10 CHAPTER

Ernest Hancock is real and is a libertarian talk show host. He is famous for asking this phrase; "There are two kinds of people in this world, those who just want to be left alone and those who just won't leave them alone; which one are you?"

Unschooling is a real method of educating children and is quickly gaining ground in America. It involves letting a child learn everything about what they are interested in, when they are interested in it. It promotes a higher level of learning as it caters to the individual and not the group.

The celebrity Paula Deen is really from Savannah and she really does love butter.

Although they speak a combination of languages in Uganda, Kitara is one of the most popular.

Obuntu is a Kitara word referring to generosity toward fellow humans. Another variation of the word Obuntu is Ubuntu, which is also the name of a very popular programming platform on Linux.

11 CHAPTER

The Dodge Dart was famous for is reversed concave back windshield. The odd-shaped windshields are very expensive to replace, so be careful never to break it.

Esprit, Le Sac, Jordache and Sportsac were all considered designer luggage in the 1980s, but mainly make folks giggle when they talk about them today.

Bug-Out Bags are real and many people have these emergency bags always packed and ready in the house. It is an excellent idea to have one ready in case of natural disasters, forced evacuations, or the Zombie Apocalypse. A quick search on the Internet will help you make a basic Bug-Out Bag.

Although accounts of real zombie attacks are all over the last 2000 years of history, none in modern times has yet to be caught on film. However, the Haitian voodoo doctors who use drugs to mimic death and bury their victims alive are real and there are many real documented cases in the last fifty years about that.

12 CHAPTER

There really are unschooling academy's that quietly exist all over America. You can find one close to you with a quick search on the Internet.

Increasingly young folks are making their own media as technology gets easier to use. You will find all kinds of young adult podcasts, blogs and vlogs if you just look for them.

Odessa's story about Purple Martins needing man-made housing is also based on reality. There is a large movement in this country to help the birds by providing them with Martin boxes to nest in. They are fascinating birds to watch and I encourage you to look into owning a Martin box.

13 CHAPTER

When Jah Loko and Ruby Mendel have their first exchange, Jah is really speaking examples of Gulluh.

Odessa's description of the Gullah people's plight and settling of the Lowcountry are accurate. The Gullah people are still thriving on the coast and are famous for their intricate sweetgrass basket weaving.

Savannah does have some excellent horse-drawn tours of the city.

Odessa and Jah Loko's discussion about the history of "riding shotgun" is based on reality, as well as Jah's tale of the history of the shotgun.

Many southerners refuse to call the event the Civil War and will refer to it as the War of Northern Aggression, the War of Succession, or the War for Southern Independence. Try to avoid using the term "Civil War" in the Southeast because it is deemed offensive to some people.

It is true that the modern day is much more violent than the Wild West. According to a recent study, a person has thirty-six times the chance of being murdered in Baltimore, Maryland, than the most murdering town during the Wild West time period. The danger and violence of living without law has been greatly exaggerated by Hollywood.

The narration where Jah Loko tells the history of Wright Square, William Washington Gordon, the Central Railroad, Nellie Kinzie Gordon, Tomochichi, and his gravesite is factual.

14 CHAPTER

Forsyth Park has been host to the Savannah Shamrock's world famous rugby tournament for almost thirty years. The enormous tournament takes place during Savannah's legendary weeklong St. Patrick's Day celebration.

There is a real underground morgue and tunnels underground at the Warren A. Candler Hospital. It is believed by most local historians that there are more tunnels running from the Warren A. Candler Hospital to Mary Telfair Hospital under Forsyth Park and that they were used to bury yellow fever victims and soldiers. Some of the contaminated persons were rumored to be buried alive in those tunnels. Jah's recounted stories of the yellow fever outbreaks are also historical record.

The Pirates' House is a real restaurant containing the oldest house in Georgia. All history recounted by Jah and Odessa are accurate, including the Shanghai closet, the rum cellar with secret smuggling tunnels, and the Trustee's Garden. It is also famous because a good part of *Treasure Island* was written there while the author dined. It has some awesome food and a really cool gift shop hidden in the attic, but beware of the pirates who roam around the grounds.

People were really Shanghaied and pressed to serve aboard vessels in Savannah. Savannah was rumored to be a very colorful place back in the day.

15 CHAPTER

The tour of Colonial Park Cemetery is all true. Even though it has only 600 gravestones, ground-penetrating radar has shown over 9,000 bodies.

River Street and the history of the *Waving Girl* statue are real. Florence Martus, as a child, started waving at ships from the docks on the river and later moved to Cockspur Island with her brother who tended the Cockspur Island lighthouse. She was said to have waved at every ship that passed with a sheet during the day and a lantern at night. Her collie dog always accompanied her. Savannah's Zombie Crawl meets once a year under the statue to stagger down River Street and search for brains.

The tradition of running backwards around Tomochichi's rock and asking him a question is a local custom. On any given day, one can see kids of all ages and particularly Girl Scouts yelling his name while running around it.

Always check your change and keep any dimes and quarters that are older than 1964 because they are made of real silver.

16 CHAPTER

The apple pancake from "The Original Pancake House" in Savannah is possibly the best food on the planet. The wait staff is super nice and Sherri, on a good day, can use her psychic abilities to predict your order.

The Georgia Historical society is located adjunct to Forsyth Park and has an amazing library.

Pterypelgia: or the Art of Shooting Flying is a real book and was very popular in the early 1700s. It is considered the first manual on how to use a shotgun and introduces birding parties to the masses.

17 CHAPTER

Martin does really have the best *Call of Duty* videos on the Internet, just search for "MCnDaHouse" on YouTube. Also, it is lame to use airdrops and care packages as kill streaks, I am just saying.

18 CHAPTER

Oglethorpe outlawed hard spirits during the founding of Savannah. In response, a profitable rum running black market sprang up to work around the prohibition.

19 CHAPTER

Many people get stuck in a gray area where their health issues are chronic and will lead to a painful slow demise, but their treatment is deemed not medically necessary by the government or their health insurance. I based Jah's illness on a real patient's plight who I knew back when I used to practice.

20 CHAPTER & 21 CHAPTER

One can see one of the exits to the pirate's tunnel at the edge of the Trustee's Garden, but it is fenced off to keep intruders out.

22 CHAPTER

Sherlock Holmes used deductive reasoning to solve most of his mysteries. If you have never used it, try it; it is very powerful.

Most experts agree that to rekill a zombie, one must land a blow to the brainstem. Decapitation and blows to the midbrains are usually sufficient in bringing one down.

23 CHAPTER

The 1703 Swedish boarding axe-pistol is an extremely rare firelock. As far as I know, none of the original guns exist. William, at King's Forge Armory, has been the only one to make a reproduction of this weapon. You can find him on the Internet pretty easy if you who want to commission him to make you one.

24 CHAPTER

Most Muslims do five short ritual prayers a day.

25 CHAPTER

The story of Rene's Ghost is a real legend tied to Colonial Park Cemetery. Reports of seeing his ghost in the cemetery and the catacombs have been going on for over two hundred years.

Pentecostalism places a strong emphasis on the literal interpretation of the book of Acts from the Bible. Spiritual gifts, miracle healings, the laying of hands, and speaking in tongues are commonplace in most sects. In some very rare Pentecostal churches, handling serpents as a test of faith is still practiced.

The Greek Orthodox Catholic Church considers itself to be the One, Holy, Catholic and Apostolic Church established by Jesus Christ and his Apostles almost 2,000 years ago.

Orthodoxy is the second largest Christian community in the world with approximately 300 million followers.

Muslim is the Arabic term for the "one who submits to God." Islam is a monotheistic, Abrahamic religion based on the Qur'an, which Muslims consider the verbatim word of God, or Allah, as revealed to Prophet Muhammad.

Atheism is the absence of a belief in any deities.

26 CHAPTER

Sherman's troops really did vandalize Colonial Park Cemetery when they camped there during his march to the sea. The loose grave markers are pinned to the wall of the police station.

27 CHAPTER

The Milton Project is a private organization to help feral cats in Savannah. Find them on the web and throw them a few bucks to help out.

"Barbara Allen" is a Scotch-Irish-English song that is hundreds of years old. The lyrics are rather morbid.

28 CHAPTER & 29 CHAPTER

Pin Point, Georgia, is a real town founded by freed slaves. Most of them are descendants of West African peoples and identify themselves with the culture of Gullah. They are historically known for breeding and raising horses, and for having a crab cleaning facility on the famous Moon River.

Pigeon Island is a real island near the Gullah town of Pin Point.

Butterbean Beach and boat landing is a real place. You can go there and get your feet wet in the brackish waters of the Skidaway Narrows.

30 CHAPTER

The art of Scrimshawing or carving scenes into bone and ivory was very popular in the 1700s.

Myrtle Beach was originally known as Myrtle Swash because of the numerous Myrtle trees.

31 CHAPTER

The Savannah History Museum is huge and has a ton of great stuff to look at. The staff is extremely nice and helpful.

The history revolving around the exhibits the students set up are all factual.

32 CHAPTER

Very few paintings or drawings survived from the 1700s. Much of the recovered art is either woodcuttings or engravings.

The Ruane Manning horse clock and watch are real. They are uber awesome and all your friends will envy you if you are ever lucky enough to ever own them.

33 CHAPTER

Mad Magazine really has a fold-in joke on their last page. Even after all these years, Mad is still funny. This shameless plug better win me a year subscription!

Sadly, there is no basement in the Alamo.

34 CHAPTER

There have been four Tybee Island lighthouses and numerous remodels.

There really is a Rails-to-Trails path from Lazaretto docks to Tybee Lighthouse.

35 CHAPTER & 36 CHAPTER

Tybee Island is rumored to have been a real hangout for pirates at one time.

Ballast stones where often made into cobblestone streets.

The original *Dukes of Hazard* lunch boxes are very collectable.

37 CHAPTER

Solid gold is extremely heavy. A leg-sized bar would be very difficult to pick up and would most likely be wheeled from place to place.

Pirates *Aaaarrrrr* awesome...but you knew this already!

ABOUT THE AUTHORS

Tarrin P. Lupo is a full time author and liberty activist. Some of his other books include the *Pirates of Savannah: Birth of Freedom in the Lowcountry* trilogy, *Stash Your Swag,* and *Catch that Collie.* He enjoys rugby, chess and cuddling with his cats and dogs.

Ruby Nicole Hilliard is a full time artist, illustrator and author. She enjoys painting, cooking and researching history and genealogy. Ruby spends her days defending herself from being chewed on by sharp puppy teeth.

10076645R0016

Made in the USA
Charleston, SC
05 November 2011